REASSESSING FOUCAULT

STUDIES IN THE SOCIAL HISTORY
OF MEDICINE
Series Editors: Jonathan Barry and Bernard Harris

In recent years, the social history of medicine has become recognized as a major field of historical inquiry. Aspects of health, disease, and medical care now attract the attention not only of social historians but also of researchers in a broad spectrum of historical and social science disciplines. The Society for the Social History of Medicine, founded in 1969, is an interdisciplinary body, based in Great Britain but international in membership. It exists to forward a wide-ranging view of the history of medicine, concerned equally with biological aspects of normal life, experience of and attitudes to illness, medical thought and treatment, and systems of medical care. Although frequently bearing on current issues, this interpretation of the subject makes primary reference to historical context and contemporary priorities. The intention is not to promote a sub-specialism but to conduct research according to the standards and intelligibility required of history in general. The Society publishes a journal, *Social History of Medicine*, and holds at least three conferences a year. Its series, Studies in the Social History of Medicine, does not represent publication of its proceedings, but comprises volumes on selected themes, often arising out of conferences but subsequently developed by the editors.

REASSESSING FOUCAULT

Power, medicine and the body

*Edited by Colin Jones and
Roy Porter*

London and New York

First published 1994
by Routledge
11 New Fetter Lane, London EC4P 4EE

Simultaneously published in the USA and Canada
by Routledge
29 West 35th Street, New York, NY 10001

Reprinted 1995

First published in paperback 1998

© 1994 Selection and editorial matter, Colin Jones
and Roy Porter; individual chapters, the contributors.

Typeset in Baskerville by
Pat and Anne Murphy, Highcliffe-on-Sea, Dorset
Printed and bound in Great Britain by
T.J. International Ltd, Padstow, Cornwall

British Library Cataloguing in Publication Data
A catalogue record for this book is available from
the British Library

Library of Congress Cataloging in Publication Data
A catalogue record for this book is available from
the Library of Congress

ISBN 0–415–07542–4 (hbk)
ISBN 0–415–18341–3 (pbk)

CONTENTS

CONTRIBUTORS

David Armstrong is Reader in Sociology as Applied to Medicine at the United Medical and Dental Schools at Guy's Hospital, London University. He is the author of *Political Anatomy of the Body: Medical Knowledge in Britain in the Twentieth Century* (1983) as well as of a number of papers applying the ideas of Michel Foucault to modern medicine.

Martin Dinges works as researcher and archivist at the Institute of the History of Medicine of the Robert Bosch Foundation, Stuttgart. His research interests lie in early modern social and medical history and in historical anthropology. His books include *Stadtarmut in Bordeaux, 1525–1675* (1988), *Der Maurermeister und der Finanzrichter: Ehre, Geld und soziale Kontrolle im Paris des 18. Jahrhunderts* (1994), (co-edited with Thomas Schlich) *Neue Wege in der Seuchengeschichte* (1995), *Homöopathie. Patienten, Heilkundige und Institutionen. Von den Anfängen bis heute* (1996), *Weltgeschichte der Homöopathie, Länder – Schulen – Heilkundige* (1996), *Medizinkritische Bewegungen im Deutschen Reich (c. 1870–c. 1933)* (1996) and *Hausväter, Priester, Kastraten. Zur Konstruktion von Männlichkeit in Spätmittelalter und Früher Neuzeit* (1998).

Felix Driver is Reader in Geography at Royal Holloway, University of London. His research interests lie in the cultural history of exploration and he is currently completing a book, *Cultures of Exploration: Geographical Knowledge in an Age of Empire* (1998). He is the author of *Power and Pauperism: The Workhouse System, 1834–84* (1993) and (co-edited with Gillian Rose) *Nature and Science* (1992).

Dieter Freundlieb is Senior Lecturer in the School of Humanities, Faculty of Arts, at Griffith University, Brisbane, Australia. His publications include *Zur Wissenschaftstheorie der Literaturwissenschaft: Eine Kritik der transzendentalen Hermeneutik* (1978) and (co-edited with Wayne Hudson) *Reason and Its Other: The Problem of Rationality in Modern German Philosophy and Culture* (1993) as well as numerous essays on literary theory, contemporary continental and analytic philosophy, and aesthetics. He is currently working on a study of the German philosopher Dieter Henrich.

Colin Jones is Professor of History at the University of Warwick. His books include *The Charitable Imperative: Hospitals and Nursing in Ancien Régime and Revolutionary France* (1989), *The Cambridge Illustrated History of France* (1994) and (with Laurence Brockliss) *The Medical World of Early Modern France* (1997).

Randall McGowen is Associate Professor of History at the University of Oregon. He has written articles on prisons and the reform of criminal law in eighteenth- and nineteenth-century England including, most recently, 'Civilizing punishment: the end of the public execution in England', *Journal of British Studies*, 1994. He is co-author with Donna Andrew of *A Case of Faces: The Trials of the Perreaus and Mrs Rudd* (forthcoming) and is currently at work on a book on forgery in eighteenth-century England.

Sarah Nettleton is a Lecturer in Social Policy at the University of York. She is the author of *Power, Pain and Dentistry* (1992) and articles in journals including *Sociology of Health and Illness* and *Social Science and Medicine*.

Thomas Osborne is a lecturer in the Department of Sociology at the University of Bristol. He is co-editor (with Andrew Barry and Nikolas Rose) of *Foucault and Political Reason: Liberalism, Neo-liberalism and Rationalities of Government* (1996) and author of *Aspects of Enlightenment: Re-configuring the Terrain of Social Theory* (1998).

Roy Porter is Professor of the Social History of Medicine at the Wellcome Institute for the History of Medicine. He is currently working on the history of hysteria. Recent books include *Mind Forg'd Manacles: Madness in England from the Restoration to the Regency* (1987), *A Social History of Madness* (1987), *In Sickness and in Health: The British Experience, 1650–1850* (1988), *Patient's Progress* (1989) (these last two co-authored with Dorothy Porter), and *Health for Sale: Quackery in England, 1660–1850* (1989).

Nikolas Rose is Professor of Sociology at Goldsmiths College, University of London. He is the author of *The Psychological Complex* (1985), *Governing the Soul* (1989) and *Inventing Ourselves* (1996) and co-editor of *The Power of Psychiatry* (1986) and *Foucault and Political Reason* (1996). He is currently researching the history of empirical social thought and writing a history of twentieth-century psychiatry.

Stephen Watson has written a Ph.D. thesis on moral imbecility, a category of mental illness introduced in the 1913 Mental Deficiency Act. He has taught the history of medicine and the history of ideas at Sheffield Hallam University and Teesside University.

ACKNOWLEDGEMENTS

Earlier versions of the papers by David Armstrong and Sarah Nettleton were given at a day conference organized by Colin Jones under the auspices of the Society for the Social History of Medicine, at the Institute of Historical Research, University of London, on 5 May 1990 on 'Michel Foucault and the History of Medicine'. Other papers were by Dorinda Outram, Olivier Faure, and Roy Porter. Discussion at the conference suggested that a volume on these lines would be welcome. We thank the successive General Editors of the *Studies in the Social History of Medicine* series, Margaret Pelling and Jonathan Barry, for their encouragement in the production of this volume. Our thanks are due to the latter, and to Barry Barnes and Josephine McDonagh, for help with the Introduction.

Colin Jones
Roy Porter

1

INTRODUCTION

Colin Jones and Roy Porter

Has any intellectual been more influential since the 1970s than Michel Foucault? His vision and temper perfectly suited that moment in American and English intellectual affairs when the upsurge of liberationist optimism characteristic of the 1960s imploded under the weight of its own contradictions. The 1970s sank into a soberer recognition that walls did not come tumbling down at the first sound of the trumpet, whether the latter was played by Herbert Marcuse, R. D. Laing, Che Guevara or whoever. Foucault gave substance to the new realism (or pessimism) through his own brand of intellectual radicalism, whose challenge to existing political, institutional and cultural structures was grounded upon the most profound appreciation of their extraordinary tenacity.[1]

In all his mature writings, Foucault called into question the liberal vision of the autonomous individual, past or present, able by personal choice to make his or her own way in the world. He constantly pointed to the priority over the free, thinking individual, the Cartesian *cogito*, of what were widely called 'structures' of thought and practice[2] – the 'epistemes' or overriding, holistic mental paradigms of *The Order of Things*, the 'discourses' of much of his later *œuvre*.[3] He mocked as shallow and self-serving all manner of Whig or progressive views that purported to show the rise in the West of that humane, emancipatory reason blueprinted by the Enlightenment and constructed by bourgeois liberalism. In a manner which seemed to carry echoes of Nietzsche, Weber and the Frankfurt School,[4] Foucault argued – notably in *Madness and Civilization* (1967) and *Discipline and Punish* (1979) – that the rise of rationality should be read as the legitimizing of power rather than as a challenge to it. This collusion of knowledge and power (*savoir/pouvoir*) created institutions, of disciplination – schools, prisons, reformatories, psychiatric facilities

1

– which, though often promoted in the name of 'improvement', in reality consolidated administrative authority, bureaucratic regulation and what a quite different sociological tradition called 'hegemonic social control'.[5] Force was power no doubt; but whether in the Catholic confessional or the court of law, so was the inquisition of truth.

Somewhat comparable in its robust overturning of conventional judgements, Foucault's *History of Sexuality* – originally planned as a six-volumed enterprise, though only three volumes appeared before the death of the author in 1985 – portrayed the development of sexology in the nineteenth century up to and including Freud not (as it liked to represent itself) as humankind's delivery from sexual ignorance and regression, but as the forging of newly enveloping systems, with underpinning labels, identities and rules. From the eighteenth-century emergence of the Cameralist polity to the modern welfare or therapeutic state, the new technologies of control, Foucault seemed to be suggesting, could thus entail not less but more subjection, a more exhaustive, protracted and panoptic[6] disciplining of the person. The mailed fist, the hangman's noose, had given way to the velvet glove, operating in recent times through such 'enlightened' innovations as the juvenile officer, the psychiatric social worker, probation officer, parole worker and, more peripherally, the doctor, marriage guidance counsellor, psychotherapist and other voluntary agencies.[7] It was clearly with good reason that Foucault cast a disenchanted eye over today's pieties. Are the modern 'caring professions' really, as we sanctimoniously hope, less physically intrusive than their predecessors? 'Pindown', the system of retraining youths used in Staffordshire child-care centres until 1991, when it became the subject of public exposure, was shown to be as brutal as anything experienced in the Dickensian workhouse.[8] Foucault thus drew attention to the shifting profiles of social power and resisted easy moral judgements upon them. In the administration of justice or the upholding of public order, a long-term curbing of brute force – or at least its discreet muffling – may have occurred; but has not this been accompanied, perhaps outweighed, by a creeping growth in subtler control mechanisms?

Aiming to write what he called 'histories of the present', Foucault undoubtedly created a sombre and largely persuasive vision of the expanding and tightening mesh of power. But was what he said about the past genuinely historical? Foucault could be as scathing about conventional history-writing as about some of his fellow philosophers.

He chided the latter for slavish adherence to a limited canon – he himself ranged as an outsider on the margins of the philosophical enterprise, gave special attention to what he saw as 'limiting' cases, and immersed himself in the little-known works of little-known technical authors. (His *œuvre* is, among other things, a tribute to the range of holdings of obscure printed works in the *Bibliothèque Nationale*.) He saw the conventional historical enterprise as riven with trifling and time-serving prejudice: academic historians wore particular blinkers; they assumed the status quo was somehow natural; they took for granted slow, fore-ordained, evolutionary change; and they aimed to plot 'influences'. Where academic historians saw the interconnectedness of events in the past, Foucault by contrast depicted startling 'ruptures'; where they charted change over time, he emphasized synchronic strands of continuity. His rejection of liberal humanism in fields – psychiatry, medicine, penal reform – traditionally dominated by *bien-pensant* gradualism cost him dear amongst historians, as did his iconoclastic calls for the 'death of [the category of] man' and his demolition of the notion of the author. The conviction that class and class struggle were the motors of history – that creed of Left-Bank Marxists – Foucault dismissed as the opium of the intellectuals; Marxism itself needed to be understood as an expression of the nineteenth-century project to create an overarching 'anthropology' of that discursive subject, 'man'. Foucault even devised a new terminology to distance himself, his critics have held, from routine academic enquiry: 'history' was to be rejected in favour of 'genealogies' or 'archaeologies'.

Partly perhaps for these reasons, there has been a conspicuous distrust among many Anglo-American historians towards Foucault's renderings of the past, as Randall McGowen in this volume suggests. 'Indifference, scepticism and downright hostility' is Felix Driver's summing-up of the views of the Anglo-American academy. Foucault's French *confrères* have been cautious, too, in according him his *titres de noblesse* as a historian, while the reception of his work in Germany, as Martin Dinges documents, has included a wide spectrum of hostile or uncomprehending views.[9] Foucault has been widely accused of wilfully and provocatively turning his back on the events which compose the customary warp and woof of the past, and of extrapolating back from a priori theoretical positions, thus inventing a fantasy past, a reversed image of Whig history, characterized not by the ever onward and upward march of progress, but rather by the sad chronicle of ever more powerful control mechanisms. For some, his approach has faults widely assumed to be directly connected to the sin of being French: he is accused of playing fast and loose with the facts – and getting away with it, thanks to the deceitful opacity of his jargon! On occasions, it is suggested, Foucault seemed to espouse the post-structuralist position that texts and language, as it were, 'wrote them-selves' and that, in some sense, all history was 'scripted' by, or inscribed within, discourse – a position held to bear at least super-ficial similarity to the Hegelian, idealist position that all history is the history of *Geist* (spirit).[10] Thus, for example, in his account of the development of concepts of sexuality in the nineteenth century, while systematically denying the validity of the obsolete commonsensical language of agency, he contended that 'we must not look for who has the power in the order of sexuality (men, adults, parents, doctors) and who is deprived of it (women, adolescents, children, patients); nor for who has the right to know and who is forced to remain ignorant'.[11] Foucault's seeming refusal to relate his analyses of knowledge/power to class, to gender, to professional interests and to the state – most blatantly exemplified in his aloof indifference to mere 'events' such as the French Revolution – have been seen by many as threatening to squander the most valuable conceptual gains made by social history over the last generation.

The exceptional range and thoroughness of his reading, and his immersion in topics which, before he wrote, most mainstream his-torians left to antiquarians and specialists, are sometimes forgotten in the rush to condemn him for the undoubted shakiness of some of the empirical foundations of his work.[12] A number of scholars – most notably perhaps Erik Midelfort and Andrew Scull – have endeavoured to show that *Madness and Civilization* is beset by fundamental empirical flaws, or at least by hasty universalization from the exceptional case of France. Foucault was mistaken, Midelfort argues, to give promin-ence to such doubtful or fictitious entities as the 'ship of fools' or to construe the early modern madman as a symbolic successor to the medieval leper. Roy Porter has contended that, while the notion of a 'great confinement' as adduced by Foucault may make sense of the French way of handling the insane between the 1650s and the close of the eighteenth century, it is not helpful for describing what was happening at that time in other regions of Europe, including Britain, where state policy and interference in the affairs of the mad were less powerful and systematic. Colin Jones has further queried some of the uses to which the term 'great confinement' has been put by Foucault and his acolytes even in the French case.

4

Yet one may still acknowledge that Foucault has had an often highly beneficial impact on the study of the past without necessarily authorizing his exact interpretations or exhibiting wilful blindness to his empirical errors. Foucault's analyses of the histories of madness, of the hospital (*Birth of the Clinic*), of criminal law and the penitentiary, (*Discipline and Punish*) have attracted enormous attention and respect. Historians have particularly appreciated Foucault for his rejection of the common supposition that the objects of history are somehow 'given' or 'natural'. Foucault's aim was to defamiliarize, to expose seemingly natural categories as constructs, articulated by words and discourse, and thus to underline the radical contingency of what superficially seems normal. Nothing in history could be taken for granted; all history was culturally fabricated; everything had therefore to be questioned. No one should approach Foucault in the expectation that his work contained, potentially at least, an interpretation, a solution, of every historical problem, or even a methodology or a tool-kit. He himself was sometimes disarmingly frank about his shortcomings as a historian. Nor must it be forgotten that his viewpoint shifted radically from *The Order of Things*, through *The Archaeology of Knowledge* to *Discipline and Punish* – indeed even between the first and second volumes of *The History of Sexuality*. His reputation does not rest on a set of holy texts. No tablets of granite inscribed with Foucauldian commandments are likely to be unearthed.

In a curious way, the gadfly brilliance and timeliness of his wide-ranging intelligence, which have radically challenged entrenched orthodoxies, provoked debate and shaped research agendas, recall the impact of the controversial writings of E. P. Thompson – a figure very far from Foucault in most respects, and indeed a heavy-handed critic of 'theory', but one similarly located on the margins of the academy and similarly excoriating of 'professional' pieties.[13] Just as the enormous amount of research on English social history in the early modern period is inflected by Thompson's writings, so most current work on the history of insanity and psychiatry, on jails, on the administration of poverty and the Poor Law, on schools of social welfare and rehabilitation and on the wider emergence of the 'disciplines' now has to grapple with the profound issues raised by Foucault. Indeed, research in all these fields which neglects his work does so at the risk of tumbling into unreflected antiquarianism. Foucault's influence has in many cases been determinate in bringing these topics out of the byways of specialism into the mainstream of historical preoccupations. Those who spring to attack him have been quick to forget some of the dismal catalogue of 'filiations', 'influences' and 'precursors' which characterized much of the history of ideas at the time his earliest works appeared. A succession of fine scholarship has, moreover, substantially endorsed Foucauldian positions, as for instance Michael Ignatieff's *A Just Measure of Pain: The Penitentiary in the Industrial Revolution* (1978), a study of the rise of the modern prison in England, and two studies of nineteenth-century French psychiatry, Robert Castel's *The Regulation of Madness* ([1976] 1988) and, in a more modulated way, Jan Goldstein's *Console and Classify* (1987).[14]

Despite much of the sound and fury accompanying the polemics, bridges can be – and indeed have been – built between the Foucauldian and the orthodox historical enterprises. That scope exists for lessening some of these gaps lay behind the organization in 1990 of a conference, under the auspices of the Society for the Social History of Medicine, on 'Michel Foucault and the History of Medicine', from which the present volume has sprung. At that conference it was apparent – as it is clear in this volume – that no consensus exists, or indeed is likely, because of the nature of the stakes at issue, to exist for the forseeable future, between Foucauldians and more classically trained social historians. It would indeed be unnerving to find the tenors from each side singing in unison. There was agreement, however, that there was an urgent need to seek convergences, even if this only resulted in making explicit areas of difference and disagreement. The notions of power, medicine and the body seemed, moreover, among the most promising areas in which this work of clarification and convergence might take place.

One important area of disagreement continues to be the problem of continuity and discontinuity in the past. Throughout his career, but chiefly perhaps in *The Order of Things* and *The Archaeology of Knowledge*, Foucault rejected the notion of piecemeal change and advanced a vision of grand structures of thought and practices, fissured by temporal discontinuities. But is there, many historians have asked, good reason to plump in principle for this catastrophic view of historical transformation? Might not such a belief in discontinuities be in part a consequence of ignorance of the little links in the chain and a rather Olympian posture? Criticisms of Foucauldian 'ruptures' have tended to come especially from the quarter of social historians who have invested in process and continuity, who have not hesitated to call into question Foucault's acquaintance with the historical record.

Foucault tended to distance himself from the academic historian:

his comment that he constructed 'philosophical fragments in his-torical building sites'[15] highlights his self-ascribed role as a kind of interdisciplinary *métis*. He had a sense of how unsatisfactory his intellectual projects would appear to both philosophers (who hope to achieve more than fragments) and to historians (who feel hurt at having their architectural achievements compared to building sites). It is, however, a sad but pertinent comment on the blinkeredness and parochialism of putatively 'professional' historians, most notably in North America and Britain, that they have not even been aware of the very considerable influence evident in Foucault's work of two major, if very different, strands of historical thinking in France. The first of these is represented in the work of Jean Cavaillès, Gaston Bachelard and, especially, Georges Canguilhem, names perhaps less well-known to mainstream social or political historians than to historians of medicine and science, who will be familiar with, for example, Bachelard's *The New Scientific Spirit* or Canguilhem's *On the Normal and the Pathological* and his *Ideology and Rationality in the History of the Life Sciences*.[16] Bachelard and Canguilhem developed the idea of scientific change through 'ruptures' and 'epistemological breaks', a language that was taken up and given a Marxist twist by the influen-tial philosopher – and teacher of Foucault's – Louis Althusser.[17] Canguilhem's emphasis, derived from his analysis of the biological and medical sciences, on the non-linearity of scientific development opened up the idea of temporal differentiality in the history of science – a view that has strong echoes in Foucault's work, which is not altogether surprising, as Canguilhem supervised Foucault's doctoral dissertation, *Histoire de la folie*. Foucault was fascinated by moments when structures break and transform, in ways and along channels which are difficult to foresee. In some senses his work is an attempt to apply to the structures of power and truth (*pouvoir/savoir*) the kinds of analysis which Canguilhem and Bachelard applied to the sciences.[18]

The idea of differential time in Canguilhem's work also appears – in a form better known within the historical academy – in the work of the *Annales* School, which comprises another influence on Foucault's writings.[19] Foucault highlighted radical discontinuities and sudden ruptures; but he was also fascinated with the existence and precon-ditions of long-enduring historical forms. In his account of how the image of the leper was transposed onto the madman in the classical age, are there not some echoes of the long-enduring mental forms, or *mentalités*, which Marc Bloch highlighted in *The Royal Touch* and which Fernand Braudel, arguably the most influential French historian in the twentieth century, dubbed *prisons de longue durée*?[20] Braudel's *longue durée* and his exposition of different temporal rhythms in the past form an essential backdrop to the idea of sudden shifts and discontinuities in Foucault's work.[21] The *Annales* group – Braudel certainly, but also his mentors Lucien Febvre and Marc Bloch – shared Foucault's disdain for the limitations of traditional history.[22] Braudel's cherished belief in the *longue durée* was accompanied by his launching some of his deadliest barbs against what he called 'event history', *histoire événementielle*, mere surface froth on the formative tides of history. This has led to accusations of his flying in the face of the commonsensical historical conviction that the subject of history is *quidquid homines agunt* – whatever people do. Braudel eloquently described the moment when, in writing his account of the Mediterranean in the age of Philip II of Spain, he realised that Philip was 'more acted upon than actor' – that the monarch's policy was less the consequence of his intentions than of transcendent historical forces way beyond his control.[23] Such a view nods, of course, towards the more classically Marxist view that people make their history, but not under circumstances of their own choosing. Foucault's historicization of topics usually enfolded in the ahistorical fabric of the progress of philanthropy such as penal and mental reform also recalls the *Annales* school's relentless quest to extend the boundaries of the domain of history – even down to the minutiae of human diet or eye-colour.[24]

The *Annales* are a broad church but, clearly, Foucault was no Braudellian! In their exploration of the historical cogency of seemingly impersonal suprasocial forces, Braudel's generation of *Annales* historians retained largely humanist perspectives inimical to Foucault's *œuvre*. Foucault, in contrast, foregrounded power in a way strikingly different from the *Annalistes* and had an eye for the transformative value of the event which is strikingly lacking in many (though not all) of them.[25] Yet Foucault's aggressive denial of personal agency as a historical force was thus certainly far more than an idiosyncratic whim. It echoed one of the strongest tendencies prevalent within the postwar French historiographic tradition. In interviews in the late 1960s and 1970s in particular he, moreover, firmly rebutted the charge of some critics that he proposed an anti-history: such critics, he counter-attacked, knew nothing of the historiographical transformation of recent decades, citing besides Braudel the work of *Annalistes* Denis Richet, Emmanuel Le Roy Ladurie and François Furet. The great historian of childhood, Philippe Ariès – another aficionado of the *longue durée* – was also one of his early historiographical referents.[26] His intellectual debts to the *Annales* – and to studies in the history of science area – highlight the extent to which his projects tend to have sometimes unperceived links with the intellectual dilemmas and scholarly endeavours of historians.

The philosophical orientation and often provocatively phrased, polemical flavour of his writings and those of his acolytes (who often tend to be even more Foucauldian than Foucault) has undoubtedly helped to alienate many historians. It has fostered a failure of connection all the more regrettable in that one of Foucault's major themes – the question of power – has been in recent years one of the especial concerns of a renovated social history which has distanced itself from its time-honoured characterization as 'history with the politics left out'. In a way, Foucault – often misleadingly characterized as the historian of the poor, the insane, the imprisoned and the marginal – might have been thought to have been particularly vulnerable to that accusation himself. Yet ironically it is not Foucault, but rather some of the more simplistic and earnest of the English and American school of social history – including some followers of E. P. Thompson – who have bathed luxuriously in the well of a 'popular culture' resistant to élite cultural penetration, and who have maintained a conception of power as something both 'out there' and 'up there' that seems increasingly implausible.[27] Foucault in contrast is concerned with the processes by which the poor and other marginal groups were marginalized. We may legitimately worry that Foucault overrates the density of power's saturation of the wider society, and that – as Felix Driver points out below – the exact articulation and interconnection of different disciplinary modes is often left hanging in his work. But in his emphasis on the omnipresence of power within society, even amongst the ranks of the apparently powerless, his angle of vision dovetails with the current research hypotheses of political scientists and sociologists.[28]

Historians too, in recent years, have rejected accounts of the past which leave scant room for the delineation of the structures of authority and power, and have shown increasing concern with exploring the manifold local instances of social power. Thus the finest recent work in the field stresses the importance of examining the dynamics of professional authority, of parent–child relations, the tensions of family and household, masters and servants, workplace and shopfloor; it probes the complexities of struggle and collusion, duplicity and complicity, hegemony and subversion, control and resistance, individuation and stereotyping, sex roles, socialization and difference.[29] The shift has thus been towards an exploration of the realm of interpersonal cultural politics, and historians working within these fields have unfortunately found Foucault's concerns rather remote from their own: his 'archaeologies' and 'genealogies' sometimes seem curiously above conflict, opposition or resistance – indeed without even the *possibility* of resistance, as in his insistence, in his *History of Sexuality*, that 'we must not imagine a world of discourse divided between accepted discourse and excluded discourse, or between the dominant discourse and the dominated one'. In particular, he assures us, 'there is not on the one side a discourse of power and opposite it another discourse that runs counter to it'.[30] Foucault's preoccupation with deep structures of discourse and his apparent rejection of the view that discourse is essentially *ideology*, that is an expression of the interests of particular groups, has seemed to historians to beg more questions than it solves. The suspicion is occasionally voiced that such an outlook may be more easily recuperated by the Right, that such approaches may end up serving rather reactionary ends through their masking of the historical exercise of power.[31] In his essay in this volume, Dieter Freundlib offers a very critical reading of *The Archaeology of Knowledge*, and the problems which Foucault encounters by wishing to conjure away a theory of agency and relying on a concept of discursive formations which, Freundlib argues, requires further philosophical elucidation. Using the well-known example of John Snow and the causation of cholera, Freundlib suggests it is not sufficient for scholars to restrict their interest to the conditions of medical discourse: they must also pay attention to how physicians reasoned.[32]

It would be sad indeed, however, if historians threw out the Foucauldian baby with the philosophical bathwater. The identification of important areas of divergence is an insufficient basis for total rejection, and does not preclude the exploration of areas of convergence. A model for the harmonious development of good relations between Foucauldians and other scholars is provided by the case of feminist history. At face value, it would appear that women did not exist for Foucault: they are spectacularly absent from almost every dimension of his work. Yet, Irene Diamond and Lee Quinby suggest, a number of convergences between the Foucauldian and the feminist historical projects offer a basis for dialogue: both approaches 'bring to the fore the crucial role of discourse in its capacity to produce and sustain hegemonic power'; both 'criticize the ways in which Western humanism has privileged the experience of the Western masculine elite as it proclaims universals about truth, freedom and human nature'; both approaches 'identify the body as the site of power'; and both 'point to the local and intimate operations of power rather than focussing exclusively on the supreme power of the state'.[33]

If links are both desirable and possible between Foucauldian and feminist scholars working in the historical domain, the history of medicine, broadly defined, constitutes a particularly opportune terrain on which to seek a similar *rapprochement*. As with feminist approaches, the exercise of power and its impact on the body are domains in which the history of medicine could not fail to be interested. A doctor's son, Foucault readily saw in the structures and practices of medicine many of the features of the discursive realm he typically chose to highlight. He was fascinated by the conventions of the medical 'gaze' for eliciting truth; the production of symptoms and signs within determinate frameworks of signification: the vital role of technologies of power and specific institutional settings (diagnostic tests, hospitals, asylums); and not least the capacity of medical power to be – or appear to be – positive and benign rather than oppressive, and to create 'subjects' in both senses of the term: clients subjected to protocols of power, but also specific individuals (everyone has, for example, his or her own unique medical history or fingerprint).

Two scholars in particular – David Armstrong and Nikolas Rose, both of whom are represented in this volume – have in recent years displayed the vast potential of Foucauldian strategies for understanding the modern medical enterprise, indeed the medicalization of life, in terms of power and the body. Nikolas Rose has examined, most recently in his *Governing the Soul* (1990), the constitution of the person or subject by the 'psy-professions' in various practical contexts (for instance, occupational or industrial psychology). In a similar way, David Armstrong has shown in *The Political Anatomy of the Body* (1983) how the project of twentieth-century medicine was to transcend the secure, panoptic institutional space of the asylum or clinic and to survey and discipline society at large.[34] In his chapter in this volume, he situates the 'Foucault moment' in the context of changing conceptions of the body and the patient in medical sociology and history. Focusing on the move to explore from the patient's point of view a relationship traditionally seen through the eyes of the physician, Foucault's impact was to problematize the clinician's gaze and the body of his 'patient' and to link them to the emergence of broader technologies of social disciplination. The moment of the new modes of disciplinary investiture of the body occurred in Paris in the 1790s in the so-called 'birth of the clinic' – the creation of hospital-based teaching and research, and institutional reforms which concentrated the sick under medical control within hospital walls – which is the subject of Thomas Osborne's essay here.

As Osborne underlines, *Birth of the Clinic* has always been one of the most neglected of Foucault's works; yet its account of the interface between politics and medicine in the revolutionary decade of the 1790s is indeed unsurpassed, and Osborne, by tracking against it some of the arguments of contemporary 'anti-medicine' situates it in the broader Foucauldian strategy of writing 'histories of the present'. In a similar vein, Nikolas Rose, in his essay in this volume, also goes beyond considering the impact Foucault has made to essay a sketch of what Foucauldian analyses might yet achieve. He provides a programmatic approach to how one might unravel the contradictions within the present-day 'medical complex', highlighting four domains – medicine as 'social' science, the technologies of medical truths, the apparatuses of health and medicine, and the sufferings of the healthy – each of them with its own distinctive temporality, the interconnection of which provides the matrix for a fuller understanding of both past and present. His approach underlines the essentially prospective mode of much of Foucault's work.

Several of the studies follow Rose along these lines. Taking what Armstrong characterizes as a 'strong social constructivist' position, Sarah Nettleton argues in impeccably Foucauldian manner that 'the mouth with teeth is not a pre-existent entity but an object that has been realized through the discourse of dentistry'. Her account provides an exemplar of what a Foucauldian account of the history of dentistry – a subject Foucault never got his teeth into – might look like. Randell McGowen adopts a similar approach with the topic of abolitionism, a subject much strewn with clichéd pieties, but in which, McGowen shows, crucial questions of power relations are involved which a Foucauldian stance can help to uncover. The lacerations of the body of the slave could only stir compassion in a middle-class audience already groomed for philanthropic benevolence by other domains of humanitarian concern – not least, care of lunatics, prisoners and the sick. On a parallel track, Felix Driver takes as a case-study Foucault's account of disciplinary power in the case of the juvenile delinquent home at Mettray, established in 1844; while Stephen Watson explores the rise of medicine in the British prison service in the nineteenth century. Taken together, these essays show that, even after the biological death of this particular author, those

who work within his shadow prefer to use his writings as a spring-
board to empirically based and conceptually sophisticated research,
rather than fall back on pious repetition and incantation. With their
insistent concern with the inscription of power in the humanitarian
and medical enterprises onto the body, they underline the vitality of
Foucault's legacy, and posit a challenge to the ways we think about
writing history in general – and medical history in particular.

NOTES

1 The intellectual flavour is captured in D. Eribon, *Michel Foucault*
   (1926–84), Flammarion, Paris, 1989; English translation, London,
   Faber, 1992 – the best account of Foucault's life. We are aware that any
   argument which briefly and in condensed form outlines a thought as
   complex, controversial and much contested as Michel Foucault's can
   only end up complex, controversial and much contested! Summaries of
   Foucault's position are made doubly hazardous by the fact that there is a
   strong likelihood that several of his presently unpublished works – most
   notably the fourth volume of his *History of Sexuality* and many of the
   lectures he delivered in his thirteen years at the Collège de France – will
   appear in print over the next decade. For a still unsurpassed exposition of
   basic Foucauldian positions, see A. Sheridan, *Michel Foucault: The Will to*
   Truth, London, Routledge, 1990. See below, pp. 214–16 for a select
   bibliography of work on Foucault.
2 Foucault's own disdain for those who summed him up as a 'structuralist'
   is, however, well-known. See, for example, his responses to interview
   questions in S. Lotringer (ed.), *Foucault Live (Interviews 1966–84)*, New
   York, Semiotext(e) Foreign Agent Series, 1989.
3 See pp. 213–14 for a select bibliography of Foucault's major writings.
4 A. Megill, *Prophets of Extremity: Nietzsche, Heidegger, Foucault, Derrida*,
   Berkeley, Calif., University of California Press, 1985.
5 See for example S. Cohen and A. Scull (eds), *Social Control and the Modern*
   State: Historical and Comparative Essays, Oxford, Blackwell, 1981.
6 The panopticon was the viewing device imagined by Jeremy Bentham as
   a means of surveillance within a model prison. The mechanism is much
   insisted on by Foucault as a blueprint for strategies of disciplination from
   the early nineteenth century onwards. The topic is widely discussed in M.
   Foucault, *Discipline and Punish: The Birth of the Prison*, Harmondsworth,
   Penguin, 1979 (a translation of *Surveiller et punir: Naissance de la prison*,
   Paris, Gallimard, 1975). See also the comments of D. Armstrong and F.
   Driver below.
7 Cf. D. Garland, *Punishment and Welfare: The History of Penal Strategies*,
   Aldershot, Gower, 1985.
8 The crude method of 'pindown', which utilized behaviourist techniques
   involving abuses of basic human rights in order to induce good behaviour
   in children's homes, developed by Staffordshire County Council, is
   graphically outlined in A. Levy and B. Kahan, *The Pindown Experience and*
   the Protection of Children: Report of the Staffordshire Child Care Inquiry, Staffordshire Libraries Publications, 1991.

9 See pp. 113–31 and pp. 181–212 below. For French historians, see the views and exchanges in M. Perrot (ed.), *L'impossible prison: Recherches sur le système pénitentiaire au XIXe siècle*, Paris, Seuil, 1980. Cf. also P. O'Brien, 'Michel Foucault's history of culture' in L. Hunt (ed.), *The New Cultural History*, Berkeley, Calif., University of California Press, 1989.

10 J. Culler, *On Deconstruction*, London, Routledge & Kegan Paul, 1983.

11 *The History of Sexuality 1: An Introduction*, London, Allen Lane, 1979, p. 99.

12 An excellent introduction to debates on empirical substance in Foucault's writings, especially his work on insanity, is provided in *History of the Human Sciences*, 3, 1990. These contributions have now been reedited as A. Still and I. Velody (eds), *Rewriting the History of Madness: Studies in Foucault's 'Histoire de la folie'*, London, Routledge, 1992. See also C. Jones, *The Charitable Imperative: Hospitals and Nursing in Ancien Régime and Revolutionary France*, London, Routledge, 1989; and R. Porter, *Mind Forg'd Manacles: A History of Madness in England from the Restoration to the Regency*, London, Athlone Press, 1989. Cf. also the introduction to S. Loriga, *Soldati: L'instituzione militare nel Piemonte del Settecento*, Venice, Marsilio, 1992. In Foucault's defence, Colin Gordon has pointed out that the charge of assorted Anglo-American scholars that Foucault's speculative theories exceed the warrant of his facts, may be poorly grounded, since Foucault's critics may have read only the abridged English translation: *Madness and Civilization* (1967) is not so much a translation as an abbreviated version of Foucault's original French text, *Folie et déraison: Histoire de la folie à l'âge classique* (1961); see C. Gordon, '*Histoire de la folie*: an unknown book by Michel Foucault' in Still and Velody, *Rewriting the History of Madness*, pp. 19–45.

13 See E. P. Thompson's essays in *Customs in Common*, London, Merlin, 1991; *The Making of the English Working Class*, London, Gollancz, 1963; 'The crime of anonymity' in D. Hay et al. (eds), *Albion's Fatal Tree: Crime and Society in Eighteenth-Century England*, London, Penguin, 1975, pp. 255–308; *Whigs and Hunters: The Origins of the Black Act*, London, Penguin, 1975; and, for his anti-theoreticism, *The Poverty of Theory and Other Essays*, London, Merlin, 1978. Cf. H. Kaye and K. McClelland, *E. P. Thompson: Critical Perspectives*, Cambridge, Polity, 1990.

14 M. Ignatieff, *A Just Measure of Pain: The Penitentiary in the Industrial Revolution, 1750–1850*, New York, Pantheon, 1978; R. Castel, *The Regulation of Madness: The Origins of Incarceration in France*, Cambridge, Polity, 1988 (translation of a text which appeared in French in 1976); J. Goldstein, *Console and Classify: The French Psychiatric Profession in the Nineteenth Century*, Cambridge, Cambridge University Press, 1987. For an extended review of the latter two works in the context of recent historiography of French medicine, see C. Jones, 'Medicine, madness and mayhem from the *Roi Soleil* to the golden age of hysteria (17th–19th centuries)', *French History*, 4, 1990, esp. pp. 378–88. See also J. Goldstein, 'Foucault among the sociologists: the disciplines and the history of the professions', *History and Theory*, 23, 1984, pp. 170–92.

15 Perrot, *L'impossible prison*, p. 41.

16 G. Bachelard, *The New Scientific Spirit*, Boston, Mass., Beacon Press, 1984; G. Bachelard, *L'activité rationaliste de la physique contemporaine*, Paris,

PUF, 1951; G. Canguilhem, *La formation du concept de réflexe aux XVIIe et XVIIIe siècles*, Paris, PUF, 1955; G. Canguilhem, *The Normal and the Pathological*, New York, Zone, 1989; G. Canguilhem, *Ideology and Rationality in the History of the Life Sciences*, Cambridge, Mass., MIT Press, 1988. See also J. Cavaillès, *Sur la logique et la théorie de la science*, 4th edn, Paris, Vrin, 1987. There is a good discussion of this influence on Foucault's work in M. Kusch, *Foucault's Strata and Fields: An Investigation into Archaeological and Genealogical Science Studies*, Dordrecht, Kluwer, 1991.

17 See esp. L. Althusser, *For Marx*, London, New Left Books, 1977.

18 M. Cousins and A. Hussein have remarked on the need for more work on the relationship between Foucault and the French history-of-science tradition: M. Cousins and A. Hussein, *Michel Foucault*, London, Macmillan, 1984, p. 257. See also D. Lecourt, *Marxism and Epistemology: Bachelard, Canguilhem and Foucault*, London, New Left Books, 1975; and Kusch, *Foucault's Strata and Fields*, esp. pp. 24–35.

19 A basic introduction to the work of the *Annales* School, with a particularly useful bibliography, is P. Burke, *The French Historical Revolution: The Annales School*, Cambridge, Polity, 1990. See also T. Stoianovich, *French Historical Method: The Annales Paradigm*, Ithaca, N.Y., Cornell University Press, 1976; and P. Burke, 'History of events and the revival of narrative' in P. Burke (ed.), *New Perspectives on Historical Writing*, Cambridge, Cambridge University Press, 1991, pp. 233–48.

20 The *prisons* comment is made in F. Braudel, *Ecrits sur l'histoire*, Paris, Flammarion, 1969. p. 51. This collection of essays forms a marvellous primer in Braudellian thinking on the place of history among the social and human sciences, including discussion on the plurality of social time. Compare M. Bloch, *The Royal Touch: Sacred Monarchy and Scrofula in England and France*, London, Routledge & Kegan Paul, 1973.

21 For Braudel, see J. H. Hexter, 'Fernand Braudel and the *Monde braudellien*', *Journal of Modern History*, 42, 1972, pp. 480–539 – an amusingly affectionate pastiche of the *Annales* approach.

22 Bloch and Febvre were the two founding editors of the *Annales* in 1929. See Burke, *French Historical Revolution*, Chapter 1. Cf. L. Febvre, *Combats pour l'histoire*, Paris, Armand Colin, 1953, a revealing collection of some of Febvre's most passionate essays.

23 F. Braudel, *The Mediterranean and the Mediterranean World in the Age of Philip II*, 2 vols., London, Fontana, 1972, vol. 1, p. 19.

24 For eye-colour, see articles by J. Bernard and J. Ruffié, and P. A. Gloor and J. Houdaille in *Annales: Economies, Sociétés, Civilisations*, 31, 1976; for diet, see esp. the special number of *Annales*, 30, 1975 devoted to 'Histoire de le consommation'.

25 The *Annales* group are usually accused of indifference to the event: see Burke, *French Historical Revolution*, pp. 85ff. The work of Emmanuel Le Roy Ladurie, one of Braudel's most brilliant successors, suggests otherwise: see esp. his accounts of popular revolt in *Carnival: A People's Rising in Romans, 1579–80*, London, Scolar, 1980; and his article 'The "event" and the "long term" in social history: the case of the Chouan rising', available in English in his *The Territory of the Historian*, Brighton, Harvester, 1979, pp. 111–31.

26 For the interviews, see Lotringer, *Foucault Live*. Furet and Richet were regular contributors to the *Annales*. Their best-known book is F. Furet and D. Richet, *The French Revolution*, London, Weidenfeld & Nicolson, 1970. Le Roy Ladurie became co-editor of the *Annales* in 1969. See also P. Ariès, *Centuries of Childhood*, London, Jonathan Cape, 1962; *The Hour of Our Death*, London, Allen Lane, 1981; and his autobiographical *Un historien de dimanche*, Paris, Seuil, 1980.

27 Cf. the pertinent analyses of T. Judt, 'A clown in regal purple: social history and the historians', *History Workshop*, 7, 1979, pp. 66–94.

28 For example, B. Barnes, *The Nature of Power*, Cambridge, Polity, 1988. For critical discussions of Foucault's analysis of power, see esp. Kusch, *Foucault's Strata and Fields*, pp. 117ff.; M. Donnelly, 'On Foucault's uses of the notion "biopower" ' in *Michel Foucault Philosopher*, tr. T. J. Armstrong, London, Harvester Wheatsheaf, 1992, pp. 199–203.

29 See, for example, D. La Capra and S. L. Kaplan (eds), *Modern European Intellectual History: Reappraisals and New Perspectives*, Ithaca, N.Y., Cornell University Press, 1982; P. Burke (ed.), *New Perspectives on Historical Writing*, Cambridge, Cambridge University Press, 1991, especially the chapters by J. Sharpe, 'History from below', pp. 24–41; by J. Scott, 'Women's history', pp. 42–66; and by P. Burke, 'History of events', pp. 1–23.

30 *History of Sexuality 1: An Introduction*, pp. 100–1.

31 These problems are sensitively evaluated in a fine discussion in Dorinda Outram's *The Body and the French Revolution: Sex, Class and Political Culture*, New Haven, Conn., Yale University Press, 1989. For another and rather more sympathetic assessment, see B. S. Turner, *The Body and Society: Explorations in Social Theory*, Oxford, 1984; B. S. Turner, 'The practices of rationality: Michel Foucault, medical history and sociological theory' in R. Fardon (ed.), *Power and Knowledge: Anthropological and Sociological Approaches*, Edinburgh, Athlone, 1985; and B. S. Turner, *Medical Power and Social Knowledge*, London, Sage, 1987.

32 See below, pp. 152–80.

33 I. Diamond and L. Quinby, 'Introduction' in I. Diamond and L. Quinby (eds), *Feminism and Foucault: Reflections on Resistance*, Boston, Mass., Northeastern University Press, 1988, p. x. Cf. J. Sawicki, *Disciplining Foucault: Feminism, Power and the Body*, London, Routledge, 1991; and T. de Lauretis, *Technologies of Gender*, London, Macmillan, 1989.

34 N. Rose, *Governing the Soul: The Shaping of the Private Self*, London, Routledge, 1990; D. Armstrong, *The Political Anatomy of the Body*, Cambridge, Cambridge University Press, 1983; see also N. Rose, *The Psychological Complex: Psychology, Politics and Society in England, 1869–1939*, London, Routledge & Kegan Paul, 1985; and N. Rose and P. Miller (eds), *The Power of Psychiatry*, Cambridge, Polity, 1986.

2

BODIES OF KNOWLEDGE/
KNOWLEDGE OF BODIES

David Armstrong

The special significance of Foucault's investigations of the body and
the construction of medical knowledge springs from his keen recognition of the biomedical roots of modern ways of thinking in the social
sciences. Without the medical transformations of the eighteenth and
nineteenth centuries we would not now possess the sociologies of
knowledge that enable us to analyse those changes, and consequently
to view them, not as unalloyed scientific advances but as temporary
expressions of knowledge/power.

Recognizing this, David Armstrong follows a double strategy in this
paper, which builds upon certain arguments contained in his *Political
Anatomy of the Body: Medical Knowledge in Britain in the Twentieth Century*
(1983). On the one hand, he contextualizes Foucault's contributions to
the understanding of medicine and the disciplines of the body against
the backdrop of comparable sociological frames of investigation
emerging in the 1960s and 1970s. In so doing, he demonstrates that
analyses like that advanced by the sociologist Nicholas Jewson stressed,
in a manner analogous to Foucault, that purely cognitive factors (the
so-called rise of scientific medicine) were inadequate to account for the
rise of such new biomedical disciplines as pathological anatomy. The
'disappearance of the sick man' and the emergence of the patient owed
much to new institutional structures, therapeutic technologies, and the
new doctor–client relations they embodied.

On the other hand, Armstrong maintains that Foucault's formations
offer us the most comprehensive and powerful account of the successive
creation and re-creation of the body, and the 'invention' of diseases, as
a result of the shifting gaze of medical science and the reorientation of
medical power. Works like *The Order of Things* and *The Birth of the Clinic*
concentrate on particular conjunctures but they also provide analytical
paradigms of wider applicability to other centuries and situations. It
would be instructive to go on from here to examine Foucault's analysis
in the context of the related work in the field by Norbert Elias and
Bryan Turner.

Until the publication of Thomas Kuhn's *The Structure of Scientific Revolutions*[1] in 1962 the sociology of science had relied on an explanatory framework advanced by Merton,[2] which assumed that while social factors might either impede or facilitate the emergence of discovery, they could not affect the content of knowledge. In effect, the sociologist was restricted to the contextual events surrounding the discovery and use of knowledge, but could have no interest in the knowledge itself. The novel Kuhnian position offered important insights into these same social processes, but, crucially, it also showed that the internal cognitive structure of science could be an object of social enquiry. Thereafter, the sociology of science was able to explore the nature of scientific knowledge in its own right.

Despite these important developments in the sociology of science, medical sociology remained relatively immune from any cross-fertilization. At least in part this may have reflected important structural differences between medicine and science, in particular the applied nature of the former, which meant that developments in the study of science did not necessarily have direct applicability to the world of clinical medicine. Thus, those medical sociologists intent on dissecting how medical knowledge was constructed turned to medical history as a starting point rather than the sociology of science, despite the apparent relevance of models of scientific development for the structure of medical knowledge.

THE DOCTOR–PATIENT RELATIONSHIP

In 1973 Waddington's analysis of the development of modern medicine[3] took as its starting point the historical study of Parisian hospitals by Ackerknecht.[4] Ackerknecht had identified the hospital, together with the techniques which went with it – physical examination, autopsy, and statistics – as the basis for the new form of medicine (Hospital Medicine) which swept across Europe in the late eighteenth and early nineteenth centuries. Waddington accepted this broad analysis of the importance of the hospital in the development of modern medicine, but, as a sociologist, came to the same events with questions about the nature of the relationship between doctor and patient. It was apparent that the advent of the hospital provided the opportunity for the traditional dominance of the upper class patient over the doctor to be reversed in that the new public hospitals recruited patients from lowly backgrounds and invited relatively high status physicians to treat them. Waddington identified this shift as a movement of medicine from client control to medical dominance – a configuration which has remained in place for the last two centuries and one which has significantly informed subsequent sociological studies of professions and professionalization.[5]

Despite the contemporary growing interest in the internal cognitive structure of knowledge within the sociology of science, Waddington simply accepted the medical discoveries of the period and was only concerned to see their effects on social relationships. But, writing three years later, Waddington's colleague Jewson offered a more powerful analysis of the link between medical knowledge and the extant form of social relationships:[6] instead of examining the effect of the new hospital-based knowledge on the doctor–patient relationship, as Waddington had done, Jewson inverted the association.

Still employing Ackerknecht's periodization of a pre-hospital Bedside Medicine followed by Hospital Medicine, Jewson examined the effect of the hospital on medical knowledge. Thus, as for Waddington, the hospital provided a locus for a new relationship between the doctor and the patient, but it was this relationship that was instrumental in establishing the new biomedical model of medicine. During Bedside Medicine the patient was in a position to dictate (and define) the nature of illness: hence the existence of a symptom-based medicine. After the advent of the hospital the doctor's dominant role ensured the emergence of a medicine based on pathological lesions which were inaccessible to the patient without medical interpretation. Moreover, this correlation between the doctor–patient relationship and the form of medical knowledge was not only important in the genesis of the latter, it also functioned to maintain that particular relationship. Thus, for the next two centuries the deployment of a medicine based on pathology celebrated and reinforced a relationship between doctor and patient dominated by the former.

The major impact of Jewson's work was to undermine the assumption that medical knowledge was *discovered*. The notion of discovery, in which hidden truths wait to be revealed, allowed social factors to affect only when that truth was revealed, since the truth itself pre-existed the act of discovery. The alternative model was to challenge the notion that truth awaited revelation and to argue that 'discovered' truth was as much a social product as the search which laid it bare. Thus the emergence of pathological medicine, in which disease was reduced to a skin-encapsulated lesion, was not discovery but creation.

Jewson's analysis owed much to a Marxist framework. In a sense it is the social relations of production (the doctor–patient relationship) which produce a form of social order and concomitant knowledges. Moreover, the Marxist notion of alienation is clearly recognizable in Jewson's thesis that the move to Hospital Medicine marked 'the disappearance of the sick man from hospital cosmologies'. The eighteenth-century medicine based on patient dominance, which accordingly recognized the primacy of a patient-defined agenda, was usurped by a medicine which treated patients as objects and ignored their words in the search for the underlying pathological basis of illness. In consequence the autonomous identity of the patient was alienated by the new mechanistic forms of clinical practice.

Jewson's paper of 1976 was very significant in opening up to sociological analysis the citadel of medicine, namely its esoteric knowledge. However, a few years earlier Foucault's *The Birth of the Clinic* had been translated into English, followed later by his *Discipline and Punish: The Birth of the Prison*,[7] and these were to offer an alternative, and in many ways more fruitful, framework for understanding the origins and nature of clinical practice. According to Foucault, changes in medicine were simply one facet of a wider cognitive revolution: certainly diseases were 'fabricated' by medicine, but so were the bodies that contained the diseases; and this production of bodies was common to a range of techniques deployed through schools, prisons, workshops, barracks and hospitals.

TECHNIQUES OF THE BODY

Fundamental to these new techniques of the body was a reconfiguration in the 'power mechanisms' operating in society. The old regime was characterized by sovereign power, in which the body of the king symbolized the concentration of a centralized power: procedures were carried out on the bodies of the king's subjects in the name of the king. Foucault argued that this system of sovereign power was joined by a more pervasive system of disciplinary power in which the supreme body did not belong to the king but to 'everybody'. Sovereign power did not disappear but has continued, at least in symbolic form, to the present day: in Foucault's oft-quoted words 'We still have not cut off the head of the king'.[8] Disciplinary power, however, has grown ever more extensive and pervasive.

Foucault used Bentham's design for an ideal prison, the Panopticon, as the main exemplar of this new power mechanism. Whereas previously criminals had been incarcerated in dungeons or publicly

punished, the Panopticon introduced the new principle of surveillance as a corrective for deviant bodies. Instead of the king's power
being used to brutalize the body of the offender, the new power
sought to appraise and transform the body in its charge. In the prison
and the hospital, bodies were observed and analysed with the purpose
of effecting a passive and malleable body, but at the same time establishing those selfsame bodies as individual and discrete. The effect
was the creation of individuality – not in a form that might be recognized today, but in a mould that was novel for the period: 'ordinary
individuality – the ordinary individuality of everybody'[9] – emerged
from below the threshold of description. The new knowledges of
human anatomy and pathological medicine mark the techniques
through which medicine could know bodies and at the same time
construct them in its own image.

There are a number of parallels between Jewson's and Foucault's
formulations of the nature of medical knowledge, but also significant
differences. Both seem agreed on the broad form of pre-hospital
eighteenth-century medicine: yes, there were individual bodies,
though for Jewson these were the upper classes who commanded the
necessary resources to enlist the help of medical attendants, while in
Foucault's work the individuality of these people was established not
by their class position but by their relationship to the sovereign.
There also seems broad agreement on the role of the newly emergent
hospital which, by contrast, tended to work on the bodies of ordinary
people, subjecting them to a new form of objectification through the
clinical techniques of pathological medicine. But this process of
objectification is where the analyses part.

For the last two centuries there has been in Western culture a
fundamental belief in the ethical autonomy of the individual: this
belief is manifest in the humanist values and civil and political rights
which pervade Western culture. This means that these values can
morally be peddled to, imposed on, or used to judge, non-Western
cultures, and, more significantly for the present argument, be used to
interpret the past. Within such a framework, which dominates liberal
and Marxist thinking alike, individual ethical inviolability is a
universal feature of the human condition: this means that the process
of objectification is a fundamental assault on this state of grace. Thus,
when Jewson referred to the 'disappearance of the sick man' with the
new techniques of hospital medicine, which treated bodies as objects,
he had in mind the loss of the essential individuality of the person who
was treated as an identity-less object. But what if, following Foucault,

there was no ordinary individuality, no autonomy, no discrete body, prior to the advent of the hospital and its clinical techniques (and the associated procedures found in prisons, schools, workshops, and barracks)? Then, the process of corporal objectification becomes not a destructive assault on human individuality but the very practice through which that individuality is given a literally solid foundation and manifestation.

There are a number of studies which have pointed to the historical-cultural specificity of the idea of individuality or individualism. These range from identification of the origins of the concept with the increased division of labour[10] or with industrialization[11] in the late eighteenth and early nineteenth centuries – indeed the origins of the very words can be located in the early nineteenth century[12] – to studies of non-Western cultures that demonstrate the complete lack or poor development of a concept of self.[13] Foucault's major contribution to this line of thought is the insight that individuality was not simply an idea but its concrete realization in the facticity of the body. New knowledges (pathological medicine) serve new social practices (those of clinical medicine), which produce real objects (the body).

SOCIAL CONSTRUCTIVISM

Over the last decade there has been increasing interest in 'social constructivism', which posits that social objects are 'constructed' through perception. Of course, at one level this is a rather trivial observation as it is only through perception that the world is apprehended, but constructivism is not a solipsistic position because its core tenet is that these perceptions are patterned by and through social forms.

Social constructivism is a loose alliance of perspectives which claim different roots. Certainly the 'social problem' framework goes back to aspects of interwar sociology which argued that certain activities become 'problems' simply because of the labels that are applied to them by the social majority. For example, the belief in the extensiveness and the fear of mugging far exceed its actual empirical incidence because it has been manufactured as a major problem of urban living, particularly by 'media amplification'. But this is a 'weak programme' of social constructivism as what is to count as a problem at any time clearly does depend on social consensus rather than any apparent absolute standard against which 'problemness' can be measured.

The strong programme of social constructivism, on the other hand, takes phenomena which have a more concrete reality in that there is universal acceptance that they exist in everyday life, particularly as physical objects. The body is one such object that exists as a totally taken-for-granted phenomenon. It is therefore a radical step – and one that has been challenged[14] – to argue that the body is created, or fabricated, or invented. And yet one has only to look to other systems of medicine, such as the humoral, to see parallels: could the skilled physician of the past identify humours which are currently beyond our perception, or was it a delusion, an error? Of course, from the perspective of the present, with great arrogance, it is all too easy to believe that only the most recent reveals the truth and that the past was marked by error, charlatanism and self-deception. In similar fashion, belief in the integrity and nature of the body is so dominated by consensus that it is difficult to consider even the possibility that the body has only relatively recently been fabricated (though the recent growth of alternative medicines such as acupuncture, herbalism, homoeopathy and osteopathy shows that the hegemony of human anatomy is under challenge). But what would a picture of a constructed body imply for a history of the body?

KNOWLEDGE OF BODIES

The liberal-Marxist notion of power is something that represses, blocks and conceals. Within this formulation it is possible to liberate people and give them back their true identities, which have been removed through the process of alienation, by removing power entirely. This is the essence of sovereign power. Disciplinary power, on the other hand, is concerned not with repressing but with creating. It is disciplinary power, through the surveillance and subsequent objectification of the body, which actually serves to fabricate the body in the first place. If the liberal-Marxist scenario of a body removed from the field of power were to come about then, rather than being liberated, the body would disappear. In short, it is only the power mechanisms which surround the body which constitute and maintain it.

In this way the various clinical techniques which doctors have used to study the body as an object are not merely the symbols of a repressive force but are components in the productive assembly line through which reality is created. The humble stethoscope, invented by Laennec in the early nineteenth century is simply made up from rubber tubing, ear pieces, and a bell, but it functions as a complex piece of machinery in constructing bodies. Every time the stethoscope was (and is) applied to a patient, it reinforced the fact that the patient possessed an analysable body with discrete organs and tissues which might harbour a pathological lesion. Thus, in the history of medicine it is not the doctors who have dominated, subjugated and objectified the patient; rather it is the stethoscope coupled to an anonymous gaze which has had a major impact in celebrating and sustaining the physical nature of the body during the nineteenth and twentieth centuries.

Sociologists who have pursued this approach have tended to start from the objectified and fabricated body that Foucault described. In the main they have gone on to explore what has happened to that body during the twentieth century, in particular the psychological and social attributes which have become attached to it. However, one line of enquiry has been to study the invention of a body that began much later than the body of everybody, namely that of the infant. The actuality of the infant's body – with a beginning and an end – has been traced through the Registrar General's mortality statistics, looking in particular at the changing framework through which the infant's life and death were analysed and thereby given meaning and existence.[15] Thus the replacement of physical analytic parameters for the study of mortality statistics such as season, sanitation and sex by social ones such as social class and legitimacy early in the twentieth century points to the vision of the infant as a social object as well as a biological one. Equally, the first appearance of the foetus as a separate person in obstetric textbooks of the 1940s marks the extension of the body's life to an even earlier period and form.[16]

At the other extreme, the problem of the body's death can be recast as a construction: the movement from the post-mortem room as the temple of truth, a construct which has dominated the medical production of the truth about bodies, to the confessions of the dying patient from the 1960s onwards marks a shift in the nature of death.[17] Indeed, while in the past there was only a brief moment between life and death, the two have now become conflated: there is no longer certainty of when the body moves from the state of life to that of death.

But perhaps the major contribution by sociologists to an understanding of the relationship between knowledge and the body has been to map the various transformations which have been made to the objectified body during the twentieth century. These changes have as their common root the extension of medical surveillance from the detail of the corporeal body to the mind of everyone. The very formalization and institutionalization of knowledges of psychological and social spaces (particularly psychology and sociology) around the turn of the century is evidence enough of the emergence of new techniques for making the body legible.

The task has been to identify the new knowledges of the body and their accompanying practices which sought to transform (fabricate) a new object. For example, there are the various regimes of mental hygiene, which identified the neuroses as endemic in the population (unlike the old insanity which was restricted to the unfortunate few) and then used this knowledge to justify further surveillance of the population's mental functioning;[18] there are the theories and practices surrounding pain control in childbirth[19] and dentistry,[20] which marked out a sentient rather than passive biological patient; there are the analytic techniques which transformed the 'teenage pregnancy' from a moral framework of condemnation to a surveillance machinery of betterment;[21] there are the new analytic techniques, from contact tracing to surveys, which relocate illness from the lesion amongst the tissues, organs, and cells of the human body to the psychosocial spaces of the community;[22] there are the humanizing approaches of medicine which, while offering patients liberation through the confession of their thoughts and feelings, have succeeded in fashioning subjectivity itself.[23]

REFLEXIVE KNOWLEDGES

The form of analysis that Foucault offers is a reflexive one. Analysis – in which can be included bodies of knowledge and their accompanying techniques and practices – is the process through which the reality of the body is created. A body analysed for humours contains humours; a body analysed for organs and tissues is constituted by organs and tissues; a body analysed for psychosocial functioning is a psychosocial object. But surely, the studies – analyses in themselves – which describe these historical processes can be said to be constructing a reality in the same way?

When Jewson bemoaned the loss of identity through medical objectification at the turn of the eighteenth century he was also constituting a reality for 1976, the year his paper was published. This latter period, as subsequent studies have argued, was itself a time when identity was being constructed by a variety of different techniques – from the GP enquiring after patients' feelings to social surveys mapping attitudes to illness: surely then, Jewson's study is less about the late eighteenth century and more about the recent possibility of speaking about and analysing identity? Is there any difference between interrogating a patient, a community, or historiographic texts in analysis of discourses on the self?

Historical studies have long recognized the dangers of a 'Whig' approach in which modern notions of progress are used to interpret events. But is contemporary medical history any less Whiggish for discovering in recent years the importance of the lay view on illness? Does the emphasis on social history not betray an analytic framework which is frighteningly modern in its focus? Above all, does medical history reveal or conceal the recent origins of the human body: is the body a construction, or should we speak of the truth about bodies being discovered or liberated and assume that against the relative contingencies of medical practice the body is an immutable reference point?

It seems clear that medical history, like clinical medicine, medical sociology, and all the other humanist bodies of knowledge that play on the body of the patient, is another of the mechanisms through which the patient's body becomes in itself an arcane body of knowledge, whether of biology, or, more recently, of experience. Of course, the analyses by Foucault and those who have used his approach are themselves facets of this great interrogation of bodies and must similarly have constitutive effects. Foucault observed rather cryptically, that Man, by which he meant this modern notion of discrete body and identity, would one day disappear 'like a face drawn in sand by the edge of the sea'.[24] Whether an analysis which attempts to deconstruct the origins of bodies signifies the beginning of an end for those bodies or indicates further relativity and reflexivity for those bodies must be the work of later analysts.

NOTES

1 T. S. Kuhn, *The Structure of Scientific Revolutions*, Chicago, Chicago University Press, 1962.
2 R. K. Merton, *Social Theory and Social Structure*, New York, Free Press, 1957.
3 I. Waddington, 'The role of the hospital in the development of modern medicine: a sociological analysis', *Sociology*, 7, 1973, pp. 211–24.
4 E. Ackerknecht, *Medicine at the Paris Hospital, 1794–1848*, Baltimore, Johns Hopkins University Press, 1967.
5 See, for example, E. Freidson, *Profession of Medicine*, New York, Dodds Meads, 1970; T. J. Johnson, *Professions and Power*, London, Macmillan,

1972; P. Starr, *The Social Transformation of American Medicine*, New York, Basic Books, 1982.

6 N. Jewson, 'The disappearance of the sick man from medical cosmologies: 1770–1870', *Sociology*, 10, 1976, pp. 225–44.

7 M. Foucault, *The Birth of the Clinic: An Archaeology of Medical Perception*, London, Tavistock, 1973; M. Foucault, *Discipline and Punish: The Birth of the Prison*, London, Allen Lane, 1977.

8 M. Foucault, *The History of Sexuality 1: An Introduction*, London, Allen Lane, 1979, pp. 88–9.

9 Foucault, *Discipline and Punish*, p. 191.

10 E. Durkheim, *The Division of Labour in Society*, New York, Macmillan, 1933.

11 S. Lukes, *Individualism*, Oxford, Blackwell, 1973.

12 R. Williams, *Keywords*, London, Fontana, 1976.

13 M. Carrithers, S. Collins and S. Lukes (eds), *The Category of the Person*, Cambridge, Cambridge University Press, 1985.

14 M. Bury, 'Social constructionism and the development of medical sociology', *Sociology of Health and Illness*, 8, 1986, pp. 137–69.

15 D. Armstrong, 'The invention of infant mortality', *Sociology of Health and Illness*, 8, 1986, pp. 211–32.

16 W. R. Arney, *Power and the Profession of Obstetrics*, Chicago, University of Chicago Press, 1982.

17 D. Armstrong, 'Silence and truth in death and dying', *Social Science and Medicine*, 24, 1987, pp. 651–7; W. R. Arney and B. J. Bergen, *Medicine and the Management of Living*, Chicago, Chicago University Press, 1984.

18 N. Rose, *Governing the Soul: The Shaping of the Private Self*, London, Routledge, 1990; see also his earlier *The Psychological Complex: Psychology, Politics and Society in England, 1869–1939*, London, Routledge & Kegan Paul, 1985.

19 W. R. Arney and J. Neill, 'The location of pain in childbirth', *Sociology of Health and Illness*, 4, 1982, pp. 109–17.

20 S. Nettleton, 'Power and pain: the location of pain and fear in dentistry and the creation of a dental subject', *Social Science and Medicine*, 29, 1989, pp. 1183–90; see also Nettleton's chapter in this volume, pp. 73–90.

21 W. R. Arney and B. J. Bergen, 'Power and visibility: the invention of teenage pregnancy', *Social Science and Medicine*, 18, 1984, pp. 11–19.

22 D. Armstrong, *Political Anatomy of the Body: Medical Knowledge in Britain in the 20th Century*, Cambridge, Cambridge University Press, 1983.

23 D. Armstrong, 'The patient's view', *Social Science and Medicine*, 18, 1984, pp. 737–44.

24 M. Foucault, *The Order of Things*, London, Tavistock, 1970, p. 387.

3

ON ANTI-MEDICINE AND CLINICAL REASON[1]

Thomas Osborne

One reason why Foucault's writings have often met with such a hostile reception in the Anglo-American world lies in the assumption that they are the idiosyncratic outpourings of a rather bizarre individual bearing a never fully articulated personal agenda. The cult of Foucault has clearly contributed to this effect – something that has been continued after Foucault's death by biographies like James Miller's *The Passion of Michel Foucault* (1992); Foucault himself took evident enjoyment in giving somewhat mystifying interviews about his theories.

An important antidote to this personalizing tendency – an antidote in line with Foucault's own belief in the 'death of the author' – is to emphasize the congruence of Foucault's work with wider patterns of enquiry in philosophy, the social sciences and historical sociology conducted by his predecessors and contemporaries. Foucault's work on insanity was widely perceived to fit in with the ethos of 'anti-psychiatry' evident in a wide range of public and scholarly concerns in the 1960s and early 1970s. Addressing *The Birth of the Clinic*, one of Foucault's earliest works and one of the least well known, Thomas Osborne helpfully contextualizes and historicizes it. By so doing, Osborne not only clarifies its aims and themes but shows that it was far from peculiar for a historically minded French philosopher, developing an agenda of questions in the 1960s, to be concerned with the emergence and the status of knowledge in the biomedical sciences.

The contrast between British and French styles of thought is relevant here. It may be argued that Anglo-American philosophy of science was blinded by an obsession with physics as the archetypal case of science: biomedical knowledge was typically viewed as epistemologically softer, inferior, and of no independent interest. The situation was different in French philosophical circles. Above all, one of Foucault's mentors, Georges Canguilhem, had produced a major investigation of the normal and the pathological, which highlighted the unique features of biomedical knowledge and investigated the rise of interest in such issues via earlier figures like Claude Bernard and Emile Durkheim.

As Osborne shows, *The Birth of the Clinic* has been influential not least in focusing attention upon the rather special modes of biomedical truth, inseparable from particular programmes of social investigation and regulation. In these aspects his essay should be read alongside the contributions to this volume by David Armstrong and Nikolas Rose.

I

Let us use the term anti-medicine to distinguish that mode of thought – or rather, that ethos – which regards the history of medical reason as a slow descent away from enlightenment towards disenchantment and despotism.[1] What unifies this ethos is the claim that the medicine of the past two centuries or so has been conducted increasingly (as Max Weber might have put it) 'without regard for persons' – hence, the frequent critiques of hospital medicine, biomedicine, doctor-centred medicine, the medical model and so forth.[2] Sometimes an underlying principle is invoked to explain this state of affairs: 'medicalization' (Illich), 'professionalization' (Parry and Parry), or 'scientization' (Pelling).[3] Characteristically, allusion to this medical model is accompanied by a plea, whether trumpeted proudly or left implicit, for a 're-enchanted' medicine; one that would *not* be governed by a medical model. A kind of anti-medical model perhaps; humanist, caring, individualizing, preventative, progressive, person-centred, phenomenological, ideographic, or whatever.

This terminological usage is not, however, intended to invoke an ethos that rejects medicine wholesale, that is literally against medicine altogether. Indeed, not infrequently, a component of anti-medical analyses is a kind of sentimentalism – often amounting to a form of nostalgia – with regard to medicine. Anti-medicine is less an all-embracing philosophy than a kind of schema, a way of thinking that is drawn upon selectively by different sets of people in different contexts. An after-dinner speaker bemoaning the spread of technology and calling for an enhanced attention to the individual, a medical historian using the theme of a medicine devoted to death as a principle of empirical coherence, a general practitioner calling for the provision of an ideographic medicine outside the hospital, a medical sociologist denouncing the medical model or the machine metaphor; all these are instances of the anti-medical ethos. But this is not to presuppose wholesale agreement or homogeneity among the proponents of anti-medicine; the same individuals might adopt different stances in other contexts.

Lastly, it should not be thought that anti-medicine is a wholly negative affair, that it is a priori wrong or misguided. On the contrary, writers have produced rich accounts of medicine from such anti-medical perspectives. One thinks particularly of Reiser's work on the history of medical technologies (the whole premise of which is that medicine has been moving further and further away from the person of the patient) or the justly influential work of Jewson who argued that modern medicine is governed by an object-centred cosmology rather than a person-centred one.[4]

II

Michel Foucault, on the other hand, never put forward a general theory of medicine grounded in an anti-medical ethos. It is certainly true that medicine is invoked often enough in his works. This invocation, however, takes a variety of contexts. For example, in *Madness and Civilization*[5] there is much discussion of medical approaches to something akin to madness, even before the advent of the psychiatric profession. Indeed, as Foucault makes clear, the detachment of forms of organic intervention and physical treatment from the founding category of 'unreason' was itself a historical achievement in epistemological terms. In Volume 1 of *The History of Sexuality*[6] medicine appears above all in its function as a normalizing discourse. In later volumes medicine appears in a different context again – as an arena for the promotion of various techniques for the 'care of the self'.[7]

In *Discipline and Punish*,[8] Foucault devotes some of his most celebrated comments to the development of the hospital as a disciplinary institution. Is not this, then, an anti-medical emphasis? And one which has influenced others? Bryan Turner, for example, has outlined a model of medical activity according to which medical surveillance brings about the 'disciplinary individuation of patients within the hospital bureaucracy'.[9] And David Armstrong has extended this disciplinary model even further, so that even the more subjective, community-centred forms of medicine that he has described in such fine detail come under this theoretical rubric of discipline, surveillance and panopticism. Armstrong thus writes of the parallels between medical and panoptic power: 'The prisoner in the panopticon and the patient at the end of the stethoscope both remain silent as the techniques of surveillance sweep over them.'[10]

But this kind of emphasis, invigorating as it is, perhaps amounts to an overgeneralization from the pages of *Discipline and Punish*. For while it is true that Foucault does have occasion in that work to use the example of the hospital to illustrate the nature of discipline, it is nevertheless the case that medicine and the hospital serve as surfaces of emergence or points of application for certain *general* disciplinary technologies. Discipline, warns Foucault, 'should be identified neither with an institution nor with an apparatus; it is a type of power, a modality for its exercise . . . a technology'.[11] As a technology, it can be taken over by institutions – schools, hospitals – as (in Foucault's words) 'an essential instrument for a particular end'. What Foucault's perspective seems to exemplify, then, is less the basis of a general theory of medicine than an analysis of the heterogeneous applications of discipline – *one* of which is, indeed, medicine. But he gives no hint that medicine should be described *in toto* and as a form of knowledge as being the mere effect of discipline.

Foucault's *The Birth of the Clinic*[12] seems to offer a different perspective again. A good deal of perplexity appears to surround this most neglected of Foucault's works. In what follows, I hope to show that *Birth of the Clinic* can be used to throw some light on some of the limitations of contemporary forms of anti-medicine and to offer, perhaps, a minimal kind of basis for a more nuanced perspective on the nature of medical power.[13]

III

As Alan Sheridan explains in his Translator's Note to *Birth of the Clinic*, when Foucault refers to the clinic he is thinking of both the clinical method and the teaching hospital.[14] Yet the emphasis of the book is far more on the method than on the institution. But what is this method, or, as Foucault terms it, this 'way of seeing'? Obviously, a whole cluster of associations can be linked to it. The most important element in the mythology of the clinic is no doubt a particular emphasis on the individual patient. The clinician is a medical scientist who works with the real thing – patients. Foucault himself glosses this mythology in his preface to the book. The archetype of clinical reason, he argues, takes the form of

> a simple confrontation of a gaze and a face . . . a sort of contact prior to all discourse, free of the burdens of language . . . constantly praised for its empiricism, the modesty of its attention, and the care with which it silently lets things surface to the observing gaze without disturbing them with discourse.[15]

The notion of the clinic refers to a kind of practice or empirical orientation towards the fact of individuality; a kind of ethos that specifically opposes itself to what might be called scholastic forms of thought, that is forms of *post hoc* rationalization or theorization. This is a point that had been highlighted by Georges Canguilhem – whose influence haunts every page of *Birth of the Clinic* – when he attempted to specify the central attributes of medicine as a mode of activity or thought:

> it seemed to us that, despite so many laudable efforts to intro-
> duce methods of scientific rationalization, the essential lay in
> the clinic and therapeutics, that is in a technique of establishing
> or restoring the normal which cannot be reduced to a single
> form of knowledge.[16]

How, then, might one account epistemologically for the possibility of this clinical ethos? Perhaps the answer must be that one cannot account for it in narrow epistemological terms alone. For the clinic – apparently beyond discourse[17] – is itself a kind of anti-epistemology, more of an *aesthetic* than a form of knowledge.[18] Hence the privileging of the 'obviousness' of perception, a visual focus upon the hard surface of things, and an attentiveness above all to individuality, particularity, uniqueness, the description of difference. Foucault's task, then, is nothing less than to lay bare the conditions of possibility for the emergence of such an eccentric paradigm of knowledge.

Indeed his very choice of empirical terrain in *Birth of the Clinic* points to this kind of preoccupation. Like other authors, Foucault associates the clinical revolution of the eighteenth century with the convergence of new forms of observation of patients (associated with hospital structures, *in situ* education, etc.) and the correlation of symptoms of patients in hospital with the findings of pathological anatomy. The key figures here are also those of other histories; Bichat or Laennec, but also Corvisart, Cabanis, Pinel and Broussais. What emerged above all was a medicine orientated to the individual case; the production of a clinical description involving a presentation of symptoms and other factors relevant to the patient's history (swellings, effusions, breathing, colour of tongue, daily occupation and habits, nature of appetite, quantity of urine, nature of stools, relevant moral factors, etc.) and an account of findings at autopsy. The English-language classic in this field would be a work such as Bright's *Reports of Medical Cases* (1827), which sought 'by recording a number of Cases, to render the labours of a large Hospital more permanently useful by bringing together such facts as seem to throw light upon each other'.[19]

The distinctiveness of Foucault's approach here is twofold. First, he proceeds perspectively. In methodological terms, he seeks to describe the heterogeneous conditions of possibility present at the birth of clinical medicine. Rather than recounting the composite stages through which medical evolution passed, the book proceeds, as it were, piecemeal, only ending with the formation of what it is seeking to describe. This way of doing things has certain consequences. It means, for example, that the narrative of *Birth of the Clinic* is a more or less orthodox version of a kind of history made well-known by the French school of historical epistemology.[20] But this style of doing things means that the burden of explanation falls, not upon an exhaustive description of each stage of medical thought, but upon making *intelligible* each significant moment of transformation,[21] giving an epistemological value to particular developments in thought. Some important elements are, then, omitted from the discussion. Take, for example, the domain of tertiary spatialization discussed by Foucault in the first chapter of *Birth of the Clinic*.[22] This is not a 'level' of medical practice to be followed through equally at all stages. Rather, tertiary spatialization is only really given consideration in an epistemological context, that is in relation to the eventual formation of clinical discourse itself. This can be seen by taking the example of what Foucault calls the 'medicine of epidemics'.[23] The theory of epidemics, claims Foucault, was fairly isolated in epistemological terms (having *une destinée singulière*). The epidemic, he says, is opposed at every point to the predecessor of the clinic, the 'medicine of species'. Unlike the species, the epidemic is widespread, involving populations, yet unique and unrepeatable, involving the integration of considerations of series, time, causality and historical and geographical space. Above all, epidemics are a matter of *police*; they entail the requirement of a political status for medicine, both sensitive to the contingency of the individual fact and capable of targeting the mass of the population as a particular kind of object. The medicine of epidemics, then, is significant for Foucault's account because it provides a condition of possibility for the emergence of clinical medicine *per se*; partly because it provides the basis of a possible epistemological break from the medicine of species, and partly because it is an already constituted example of a form of knowledge – like that of the clinic itself – which is concerned, at the level of the population, with the isolation of the individual fact.

The second side of the distinctiveness of Foucault's account is his emphasis on discursive or linguistic determinants, coupled with his theorization of the notion of the 'gaze'. Both of these emphases take Foucault's account some distance away from the habitual themes of anti-medicine. Instead of reducing the medical revolution of this period to particular areas or emphases – surgery, the hospital, physical examination, professional organization, or common sense[24] – he locates the basis of clinical originality above all in a new orientation towards language and its object. As he makes clear in his preface, the clinical transformation in medicine was far from being a question of rationalization, scientization or even of the quantification of medical discourse. His very chronology militates against such an emphasis. For an author such as Shryock, for whom Paris medicine in the 1790s is equally significant, it was the period of statisticalization that was important.[25] For Foucault, on the other hand, whose analysis stops at 1816 with the publication of Broussais' *Examen des doctrines médicales*, clinical discourse is essentially a question of a certain *qualitative* precision of description.[26] Meckel's quantifications with weights and measures are contrasted with Bichat's excursions with the 'celebrated hammer' which opened up the brain to a particular kind of medical gaze. Hence Foucault argues that 'the precise but immeasurable gesture that opens up the plenitude of concrete things, combined with the delicate network of properties, to the gaze, has produced more scientific objectivity for us than instrumental arbitrations of quantity'.[27] The apotheosis of the clinic lies, then, with a mode of patient, laborious, qualitative description that is simultaneously a 'way of saying' and a 'way of seeing'; a form of discourse and a particular kind of gaze.

So what of the gaze itself? What does Foucault mean by this term? In *The Archaeology of Knowledge*[28] Foucault criticized his use of this term (*regard medical*) since it seemed to imply a subject of knowledge. This is indeed the sense in which it has been taken up by some of Foucault's own followers, notably Armstrong, for whom the gaze is a kind of founding subject of surveillance. But in fact, looking at the pages of *Birth of the Clinic*, there seems to be little support for this approach in that Foucault's actual deployment of the term there seems to represent less the intentionality of perception than a particular, historically substantive, style of perception. As such, the gaze does not originate from a particular kind of subject but is itself rather the effect of a certain kind of discursive constellation.[29] For example, an epistemological consideration of Bichat's thought indicates a particular modality in the relation of the subject of knowledge to the structure of the perceived. For Bichat, the task of 'analysis' was not performed by the speaking subject – in the previous clinical form, Foucault says, what was seen was reduced to what he calls its 'stability' by the doctor. In this sense, one had not confronted pathology until one had offered up a complete description of it. So the task of the subject became less to speak than to watch the disease, as it were, speaking on its own account. Hence the disease itself became 'analysis'. Later on, and ultimately in the work of Laënnec, it was language itself which became akin to vision – hence the image that Foucault uses of the 'speaking eye'.[30] It is this discursive constellation of the gaze that makes it possible for the act of teaching to take place at the bedside. Here, in what might be called the mature clinic, the gaze becomes a form of describing where the act of speaking (teaching) can be mapped onto the acts of seeing (perception) and knowing (clinical discovery). What is at stake in this notion of the gaze thus always seems to be a matter of alignments between different forms of perceptual appropriation. Again, in Laennec's work, for example, the gaze actually becomes akin to the sensory immediacy of touching (the 'glance') even if, as Foucault argues, for Laennec, touching, too, is effectively a form of seeing, so that even the use of an instrument like the stethoscope remains, as Foucault puts it, under the 'dominant sign of the visible'.[31]

The point to be made here is only that the notion of the gaze is not deployed in *Birth of the Clinic* as a kind of *deus ex machina* predetermining everything that happens. Nor does the gaze represent a reductive mode of perception, as an anti-medical perspective might encourage us to expect. On the contrary, the gaze is productive of individuality, uniqueness, particularity. Yet if, as a particular mode of perception, the gaze only sees what is obvious, then, for what is only obvious to be visible or significant in the first place, a certain 'labour in thought'[32] – the laborious fabrication of clinical medicine itself – has been historically required. The apparently (to our eyes) spontaneous perception in the clinic was not the product of necessity, but of an epistemological labour. If a fully formed clinical medicine can be said to be the object of *Birth of the Clinic*, then it is this labour – a process without a subject, certainly – that is the subject-matter of that work.

IV

Birth of the Clinic is not an anti-medical endeavour; Foucault's intro-
ductory disclaimer to the effect that his work is not for or against this
or that kind of medicine should be taken perfectly seriously.[33] This
can best be illustrated in the two areas where it seems most implausible: in relation to Foucault's analyses of death and of the hospital.

Birth of the Clinic is largely concerned with pathological anatomy
and its founding figure, Bichat. Surely this emphasis could be connected to a theme that is prominent in anti-medicine? Karl Figlio, for
example, has expressed his admiration for Foucault's handling of this
issue: 'We see here a metaphysics of death of the sort Illich thought
was so important to the establishment of modern medical thought'.[34]
But Foucault's interest in death can be thematized in a different way,
without reference to the author of *Medical Nemesis*. In fact, two themes
stand out.

First, this discussion undoubtedly bears upon the question of
vitalism as it appears in the works of Georges Canguilhem. Here a
prominent place was given to Bichat in the formation of the modern
conception of life in the biological sciences. For Canguilhem, the
espousal of vitalism (not so much a doctrine, he says, as a morality)
was connected to his contention, quoted above, that the most fundamental aspect of medicine was the confrontation with the pathological: its clinical side. Canguilhem associates the very possibility of
life with the capacity to fall sick and to confront sickness with the aid
of treatment.[35] It is the possibility of disease, he argues, that gives life
its specificity. Foucault, in *Birth of the Clinic*, does not refute this
contention, but he does add an ironic further dimension to it. He says
that beyond life and disease, we must situate a third term – death.[36]
In the nosographic view of things prior to Bichat, Foucault argues,
life and disease stood in opposition, as mutually exclusive terms.
Bichat, however, broke for good with the medicine of species when he
argued that the knowledge of disease was a condition for the understanding of life. Now, disease and life no longer stand in conceptual
opposition; rather the one can act as an epistemological surface for
the appearance of the other. Foucault demonstrates the conditions or
costs of this contention: pathological anatomy. It is only from the
standpoint of death – literally, by standing day and night at the
dissecting table – that one can gain a stable purchase on disease (from
the standpoint of death as a 'teeming presence' within the
individual), and hence on the specificity of life. Foucault notes:

> With Bichat knowledge of life finds its origin in the destruction
> of life and in its extreme opposite; it is at death that disease and
> life speak their truth; a specific, irreducible truth, protected
> from all assimilation to the inorganic by the circle of death that
> designates them for what they are.[37]

Thus it is this third term, death, which provides the exclusive point of
access and indispensable condition of possibility for any vitalist
philosophy. Hence Foucault's ironic neologism – mortalism.

Second, the question of death is related to the possibility of a science
of individuality itself. It is in death – on the dissecting table – that the
individuality of disease is finally isolated; and it is on the basis of
findings in corpses that the course of diseases within living individuals
can ultimately be known. Medicine has an exemplary status here
within what is in fact a far wider intellectual and cultural mutation.
For medicine, says Foucault, marked, at the empirical level, the first
opening up of that fundamental relation that binds man to his original
finitude.[38] What is at stake in this novel conceptual figuration of
death is an invigorated emphasis upon individuality; and correlatively death and individuality will now be irrevocably linked in
thought (from medicine to lyric poetry): death left its old tragic
heaven and became the lyrical core of man; 'his invisible truth, his
visible secret'.[39]

This is not of course an anti-medical analysis in that far from being a
negative thing, the clinical conceptualization of death is actually
constitutive, so far as Foucault is concerned, of the modern experience
of individuality.[40] And far from being a metaphysical experience,
death here is understood as being at the root of the very possibility of
positivism.

What, then, of that other site of anti-medical anxiety, the hospital?
Is not that institution potentially a malign, enclosing space which
divides the sick individual from personhood? Maybe so. But
Foucault's analysis should at least serve to draw our attention to the
fact that the original conceptualization of the clinical hospital was
itself founded on a reaction to, and a critique of, the previous – pre-
clinical – form of the hospital as a reductive, carceral space. For
instance, at the time of the Revolution,

> the hospital appears in many respects to be an obsolete structure.
> A fragment of space closed in upon itself, a place of internment
> for men and diseases.[41]

And so, for example,

> the abolition of the hospitals was demanded by the Mountain,
> the extremist party, who regarded them as an institutionaliza-
> tion of poverty and who believed that one of the tasks of the
> Revolution must be to make them unnecessary.[42]

What was required for an enlightened medical activity was not a
series of spaces of confinement but a *free field*, a kind of community
space coterminous with the national territory itself, unhindered by
artificial and distorting institutional obstacles. In fact, right up to the
fall of Robespierre, the dream of replacing the hospital – not yet a
machine à guérir so much as a dumping-ground for the incurable – by
organizing public assistance in the community retained its force. But
what in fact emerged was a compromise; not a free field nor a return
to the old form of the hospital but effectively a new kind of medical
space, a modification of the hospital more attuned to the revolutionary dream of a 'medicine in liberty'. This would be a different
kind of hospital where the unveiling of knowledge (clinical discovery
and teaching) could take place alongside the activity of treatment and
cure. As such, the clinical hospital – as a site for the unhindered
emergence of truth and treatment – was to be, if anything, self-
consciously *not* a hospital (in its *ancien régime* guise) but rather something as close as possible to a free space.[43]

None of this is meant to imply that the hospital, because of these
origins, has been beyond criticism. It is rather that the critique of the
hospital as potentially a carceral form of institution was present at the
inception of the modern hospital itself; that the critique of the hospital
was midwife at the birth of the clinic.

V

What, then, are the consequences of these brief considerations for the
ethos of anti-medicine? The consequences are not, certainly, all that
dramatic. Although there is nothing within the 'admirable, moving
pages' of *Birth of the Clinic* capable of refuting on an empirical level the
claims of anti-medicine, a reading of that work might at least induce a
certain uneasiness about using an anti-medical perspective for
gaining a conceptual purchase on medical evolution as a whole. This
is simply because it is difficult to resist the impression when reading
the book that most of the themes of anti-medicine are actually
internal to the structures of clinical thought, that clinical reason

contains, as it were, within itself the very possibility of its own critique. Foucault himself hints at this on the very last page:

> When one carries out a vertical investigation of this positivism, one sees the emergence of a whole series of figures – hidden by it, but also indispensable to its birth – that will be released later, and paradoxically used against it.[44]

Foucault is thinking here primarily of the philosophical implications of the birth of clinical positivism. But can we pick out some parallel themes which might be relevant directly to medicine itself? Might not the ethos of anti-medicine disclose certain points of alignment with some of the governing forms of clinical reason?

We might single out, in this context, a certain resistance within clinical thought to that *bête noire* of anti-medicine, the very notion of a medical model. What is a model? It is a blueprint, or a schema, a template which one places upon the evidence at hand. Yet clinical thought seems actually to be predicated upon a certain resistance to this notion of a model. Clinical thought – at least as an ideal – operates through a kind of controlled intuition which, as *Birth of the Clinic* shows, is more than just a myth, even though this form of intuition does have given historical conditions of possibility. Early on in the book, when describing the collectivizing emphasis of the medicine of epidemics, Foucault gives us a gloss of this particular aspect of clinical knowledge:

> What now constituted the unity of the medical gaze was not the circle of knowledge in which it was achieved but this open, infinite, moving totalization, ceaselessly mobile and enriched by time, whose course it began but would never be able to stop – already, a clinical recording of the infinite and variable series of events.[45]

The clinic, then, might be described in terms (which irresistibly recall certain anti-medical themes) of a genuine, accumulative empiricism, ever searching to deepen the probity of its perception towards ever-finer modulations of individuality.

Anti-medicine (prompted, above all, one suspects, by the model of bacteriology) resists the reification of disease entities. Yet there is within clinical thought a certain anti-essentialism about disease which itself seems to prefigure this very theme. Part of the distinctiveness of clinical thought, according to Foucault's account, is that it is a kind of medical rationality where the being of the disease has disappeared.

Disease, for the clinic, no longer has an objective essence but is now grafted onto the very structures of the body. Configuration and localization become one. Hence the notion of the lesion – organic damage; disease as less an entity attacking the organism than a phenomenon *of* the organism itself. Part of what is at stake here is a certain sensitivity on the part of clinical consciousness to individuality – not just to the individual person, but to the individual fact, singularity, particularity:

> For the first time, the anatomo-clinical method integrates into the structure of the illness the constant possibility of an individual modulation . . . The disease . . . has, from the outset, a latitude of insertion, direction, intensity, and acceleration that forms its individual figure.[46]

Far from being a form of thought which subverts individuality, clinical thought is precisely the science *of* individuality. Hence, calls for an ever more profound turn to the individual may only be expressions of this clinical ethos itself. Foucault, too, is quite explicit here: 'The gaze is no longer reductive, it is, rather, that which establishes the individual in his irreducible quality', adding that 'the object of discourse may equally well be a subject, without the figures of objectivity being in any way altered'.[47]

Indeed, the possibility of a subjectification of the medical field (another anti-medical theme) also seems to be internal to this – clinical – logic in two main ways. First, because there is a curious space of possibility for a phenomenological emphasis within clinical thought. A phenomenological emphasis is there, waiting to be unleashed. The disappearance of the disease as entity entails the consequence that the doctor confronts the modulations of the volumes of the body, as it were, directly. And this is a mutation which leads, as Foucault argues, to the vaunting of 'the signifying powers of the perceived and its correlation with language in the original forms of experience'.[48] Hence, the injunction to get as close as possible – preferably without forms of mediation (*pace* Reiser) – to the authenticity of the object of knowledge: let the object, as it were, 'speak for itself', that is, as if it itself were a *subject*. Second, the possibility of subjectification is internal because clinical thought already privileges, in a sense, the structures of subjectivity over those of objectivity. For this primacy of the powers of the perceived itself tends to lead to an emphasis upon the subjectivity of the medical personage, the doctor. Thus the very possibility of clinical thought seems to rely upon an ethic of subjective perception – in fact, a veritable *aesthetic*. Foucault quotes Cabanis here:

> Since everything or nearly everything in medicine is dependent upon a glance or a happy instinct, certainties are to be found in the sensations of the artist himself rather than in the principles of the art.[49]

And Foucault adds:

> The technical armature of the clinical gaze is transformed into advice about prudence, taste, skill; what is required is 'great sagacity', 'great attention', 'great precision', 'great skill', 'great patience'.[50]

Hence the irreducibility of the object of clinical thought (lesions, patients, whole persons) tends inevitably towards a vaunting of the subject of medical knowledge, the doctor. The clinician is not, from the beginning, accorded the status of objective scientist but bears his subjectivity, his 'fine sensibility' (as Foucault puts it), as part of the very nature of his expertise.

VI

Does the above analysis – which has sought to undermine the sense of antinomy between critical culture and clinical rationality, and which has stressed a certain continuity between clinical thought and some of the tropes characteristic of anti-medicine – have any implications for those who are interested in medicine today? To be sure, no positive recommendations can be forthcoming. There is nothing in *Birth of the Clinic* to tell us unequivocally what is right or wrong and what should be done. But at the very least, that work may provide us with a basis for certain principles of *detachment*, various means of escaping from some of the more self-limiting present-day obligations of critical thought. Three such principles of detachment may briefly be considered.

First, *Birth of the Clinic* effectively enjoins us to abandon totalizing accounts of medicine. What Foucault has isolated is but one rationality within medicine – that of the clinic. And no doubt there are others. Studies of public health or obstetrics would no doubt reveal quite different rationalities at work. In any case, as Foucault has argued elsewhere, the clinic itself should not be viewed as a totality or a unity, but as a set of diverse and loosely linked relations between a number of distinct elements, some of which concerned the status of doctors, others the institutional and technical site from which they spoke, others their position as subjects perceiving, observing, describing, teaching, etc.[51]

The clinic thus comprises an assemblage or set of relations, rather than a series of stages, a growth-story, a totality in evolution, or a cosmology. Consequently, there can be no *single* anti-medical ethos, since medicine itself is not a unified totality. The forms of critique should, perhaps, be multiplied.

Second, *Birth of the Clinic* may lead us to question the tying together of medical enlightenment and the promotion of subjectivity which so often seems to be the correlate of anti-medical positions.[52] The promotion of subjectivity stands, as we have seen, in no absolute or necessary opposition to medical enlightenment itself. The *possibility*, in epistemological terms, for a critique of medicine potentially damaging to liberty and subjectivity has been present since the inception of clinical rationality itself. That critique has found its most cogent postwar expression in an anxiety concerning the main institutional apparatus of medical reason, the hospital. Perhaps what is at stake here is, to use Robert Castel's formulation, the operation of a retrospective illusion through which successive generations mark out their own Middle Ages from which only the negative characteristics are recollected.[53] Hence the critique of the hospital serves, perhaps, as a justification for practices which are actually continuous with the – enlightened – aims of that institution. A similar tale could be told about medical expertise. Again, the critique of medical expertise – its monological character, its organic fixation – can serve as justification for the promotion of subjectivity. Increasingly, the doctor has been urged to be a reflexive being, a personage uniquely able to work upon the patient's subjectivity. What is at stake here is, again, not the antinomy of the medical model so much as a deepening of the probity of clinical rationality. It is not the absence of expertise, the eclipse of the directive powers of the doctor, which is at issue, but rather an *expertise of subjectivity*: an expertise that is all the more profound, all the more sensitive, all the more irreversible for being tied to our very desires for freedom.[54]

Lastly, a reading of *Birth of the Clinic* might raise some doubts in our minds concerning the very attachment of medicine to a progressive, enlightened politics. Again, the creeping problematic of subjectivity within medicine has had an important role to play here.[55] What this has involved – notably as regards the area of chronic illness – is effectively an attempt at the re-enchantment of the medical domain; some kind of *return* to the 'sick man', his biography, his passions, his feelings, a return, above all, to the sense of *meaning*, to the experience of sickness, hitherto disenchanted by biomedicine. The aim here, however, is not only a re-enchantment of medicine but, more generally, a re-enchantment *through* medicine. The domain of medicine and sickness becomes a kind of privileged space for the coming to grips with, the labouring upon, the fabrication of, the self. The promotion of subjectivity here is not, then, simply a medical matter; it is rather that medicine has become a privileged site, a kind of social laboratory – no doubt one amongst many – for the pursuit of enlightened subjectivity in general.

As *Birth of the Clinic* shows, one component of the clinical aspiration was that medicine should have a politico-utopian resonance; what was called the 'medicine in liberty' was very much a political matter. Foucault describes how medicine was to take a key role in the project of enlightenment and – more than this – to *pronounce* upon enlightenment, to set forth the norms of liberty:

> The first task of the doctor is therefore political; the struggle against disease must begin with a war against bad government. Man will be totally and definitively cured only if he is first liberated.[56]

And this impossible dream itself entailed that:

> Medicine must no longer be confined to a body of techniques for curing ills and of the knowledge they require; it will also embrace the knowledge of *healthy man*, that is, a study of *non-sick man* and a definition of the *model man*. In the ordering of human existence it assumes a normative posture, which authorizes it not simply to distribute advice as to healthy life, but also to dictate the standards for physical and moral relations of the individual and of the society in which he lives.[57]

But the existence of this link between clinical reason and the issue of social melioration should not be posed in terms of ideology or domination as if the relation between medicine and politics, for example, could be exhausted by functions of social control.[58] Indeed, medicine has been historically linked just as often to strategies of enlightenment as to covert strategies of social control; and it is this enlightenment tradition that has, paradoxically enough, anti-medicine as its current expression. Nevertheless, neither medicine nor anti-medicine is any less a normative endeavour for being tied to the project of our emancipation – whether through subjectivity, the pursuit of liberty, or whatever. It may be worth considering whether the most desirable aspiration now is less to bring about a reaffirmation of this general project of what *Birth of the Clinic* labels a 'medicine in liberty', than, on the contrary, to see how this very attachment between medicine and emancipation might be disturbed. This would not mean necessarily leaving medicine as it is, nor turning a blind eye to the vagaries of medical power. It would, rather, require careful investigation into the ways in which medicine has been constituted as an ethico-political endeavour, the ways in which medicine has become a kind of exemplary space through which the hopes, dreams and resentments of society have been channelled and given expression, the ways in which we tie medicine to our dreams of liberty.

NOTES

1 Parts of this chapter consist of streamlined sections of my article 'Medicine and epistemology: Michel Foucault's archaeology of clinical reason', in *History of the Human Sciences*, 5(2), 1992, pp. 63–93. I would like to thank the editors of that journal and Sage Publications Ltd for allowing me to rework some of that material for this volume. Thanks also to Colin Jones.

2 See, broadly, N. Jewson, 'The disappearance of the sick man from medical cosmologies, 1770–1870', *Sociology*, 10, 1976, pp. 225–44; G. L. Engel, 'The need for a new medical model: a challenge for bio-medicine', in H. T. Englehardt, A. L. Kaplan and J. McCartney (eds), *Concepts of Health and Disease*, London, Addison, 1981; and E. Mishler et al., *Social Contexts of Health, Illness and Patient Care*, Cambridge, Cambridge University Press, 1981.

3 I. Illich, *Medical Nemesis*, New York, Pantheon Books, 1977; N. Parry and J. Parry, *The Rise of the Medical Profession*, London, Croom Helm, 1976; M. Pelling, 'Medicine since 1500' in P. Corsi and P. Weindling (eds), *Information Sources in the History of Science and Medicine*, London, Butterworth, 1983, esp. p. 379.

4 S. J. Reiser, *Medicine and the Reign of Technology*, Cambridge, Cambridge University Press, 1978; Jewson, 'Disappearance of the sick man'. Cf. other sociological works such as Mishler et al., *Social Contexts of Health, Illness and Patient Care*, esp. pp. 237–44; N. Hart, *The Sociology of Health and Medicine*, Ormskirk, Causeway, 1985, pp. 10–12; M. Stacey, *The Sociology of Health and Healing*, London, Allen & Unwin, 1988; and, most famously, Illich, *Medical Nemesis*.

5 M. Foucault, *Madness and Civilization: A History of Insanity in the Age of Reason*, London, Tavistock, 1967.

6 *The History of Sexuality 1: An Introduction*, London, Allen Lane, 1989.

7 *The History of Sexuality 3: The Care of the Self*, Harmondsworth, Penguin, 1990.

8 *Discipline and Punish: The Birth of the Prison*, Harmondsworth, Penguin, 1979.

9 B. S. Turner, *Medical Power and Social Knowledge*, London, Sage, 1987, pp. 37–8. This approach is taken further in B. S. Turner, 'The practice of rationality: Michel Foucault, medical history and sociological theory' in R. Fardon (ed.), *Power and Knowledge: Anthropological and Sociological Approaches*, Edinburgh, Athlone, 1985, pp. 193–213.

10 D. Armstrong, 'Bodies of knowledge: Foucault and the problem of human anatomy', in G. Scambler (ed.), *Sociological Theory and Medical Knowledge*, London, Tavistock, 1987, pp. 59–76. Cf. D. Armstrong, *The Political Anatomy of the Body*, Cambridge, Cambridge University Press, 1983.

11 Foucault, *Discipline and Punish*, p. 215.

12 M. Foucault, *The Birth of the Clinic: An Archaeology of Medical Perception*, London, Tavistock, 1973.

13 There are useful discussions in G. Gutting, *Michel Foucault's Archaeology of Scientific Reason*, Cambridge, Cambridge University Press, 1989, and P. Miller, *Domination and Power*, London, Routledge, 1987.

14 Foucault, *Birth of the Clinic*, p. vii.

15 Ibid., p. xix.

16 G. Canguilhem, *The Normal and the Pathological*, tr. C. R. Fawcett, New York, Zone, 1989 [main section dating from 1943], p. 34.

17 Foucault, *Birth of the Clinic*, p. xix.

18 The birth of the clinic is, in fact, historically contemporaneous with the birth of the category of the aesthetic itself; see T. Eagleton, *The Ideology of the Aesthetic*, Oxford, Blackwell, 1990, esp. ch. 1.

19 R. Bright, *Reports of Medical Cases*, reprint, London, Longman, 1987, p. 7.

20 The classic of this approach is G. Canguilhem's *La formation du concept de réflexe aux XVIIe et XVIIIe siècles*, Paris, PUF, 1955.

21 M. Cousins and A. Hussein, *Michel Foucault*, London, Macmillan, 1984, p. 3.

22 'Let us call tertiary spatialization all the gestures by which, in a given society, a disease is circumscribed, medically invested, isolated, divided up into closed privileged regions, or distributed throughout cure centres, arranged in the most favourable way.' (*Birth of the Clinic*, p. 16)

23 Ibid., ch. 2.

24 For these developments, see, among others, O. Temkin, 'The role of surgery in modern medical thought', *Bulletin of the History of Medicine* 25, 1951; E. Ackerknecht, *Medicine at the Paris Hospital, 1794–1848*, Baltimore, Johns Hopkins University Press, 1967; T. Gelfand, *Professionalizing Modern Medicine: Paris Surgeons and Medical Sciences and Institutions in the Eighteenth Century*, Westport, Conn., Greenwood Press, 1985; M. Ramsey, *Professional and Popular Medicine in France 1770–1850*, Cambridge, Cambridge University Press, 1988; and R. P. Hudson, *Disease and its Control*, Westport, Conn., Greenwood Press, 1985.

25 R. H. Shryock, *The Development of Modern Medicine*, London, Gollancz, 1948. It is noteworthy that the figure whom Shyrock considers of

particular significance as regards medical statistics is P. C. A. Louis, who does not rate a mention in Foucault's account. See ibid., esp. pp. 139–40.

26 On this see the opening comparison of texts by Bayle and Pomme: 'equally qualitative, equally metaphorical' (Foucault, *Birth of the Clinic*, p. xi).

27 Ibid., p. xiii.

28 M. Foucault, *The Archaeology of Knowledge*, London, Tavistock, 1972.

29 See esp. ch. 7, 'Seeing and knowing', of *Birth of the Clinic*.

30 Ibid., pp. 112–14.

31 Ibid., p. 165.

32 L. Althusser, *Reading Capital*, London, Verso, 1970, p. 45.

33 Foucault, *Birth of the Clinic*, p. xix.

34 K. Figlio, 'The historiography of scientific medicine: an invitation to the human sciences', *Contemporary Studies in Society and History* 19, 1977, p. 273.

35 G. Canguilhem, *La connaissance de la vie*, Paris, Vrin, pp. 83–100.

36 Foucault, *Birth of the Clinic*, pp. 143–4.

37 Ibid., p. 145.

38 Ibid., p. 197.

39 Ibid., p. 172.

40 Ibid., pp. 170–1, 195–9.

41 M. Foucault, *Power/Knowledge: Selected Interviews and Other Writings, 1972–1977*, Brighton, Harvester, 1980, p. 177.

42 Foucault, *Birth of the Clinic*, p. 43.

43 Ibid., pp. 82–5. Cf. Foucault, *Power/Knowledge*, p. 178.

44 Foucault, *Birth of the Clinic*, p. 199.

45 Ibid., p. 29 (translation slightly altered).

46 Ibid., p. 168.

47 Ibid., p. xiv.

48 Ibid., p. 199.

49 Ibid., p. 121. Cf. J. Jacob, *Doctors and Rules: A Sociology of Professional Values*, London, Routledge, 1988, esp. p. 34.

50 Foucault, *Birth of the Clinic*, p. 121.

51 Foucault, *Archaeology of Knowledge*, pp. 53–4.

52 See, for example, the works listed in Note 1. Above all, the link between medicine and subjectivity has been made from within the discipline of medical sociology: for an excellent consideration of the application of 'social' perspectives to medicine, see P. M. Strong, 'Sociological imperialism and the profession of medicine', *Social Science and Medicine* 13A, 1979, pp. 199–215. Cf. Thomas Osborne, 'The doctor's view: clinical and governmental rationality in twentieth-century general medical practice', Ph.D. dissertation, Brunel University, 1991. General practice is a field in which the question of subjectivity has been raised with particular clarity in relation specifically to the shortcomings of the hospital and of medical expertise.

53 R. Castel, 'Moral treatment: mental therapy and social control in the nineteenth century' in S. Cohen and A. Scull (eds), *Social Control and the State*, Oxford, Martin Robertson, 1983, p. 248.

54 Cf. N. Rose, *Governing the Soul: The Shaping of the Private Self*, London,

Routledge, 1990. The classic work in the literature on the doctor as reflexive being is M. Balint, *The Doctor, His Patient, and the Illness*, Pitman Medical, 1957.

55 See Armstrong, *Political Anatomy of the Body*; and W. Arney and B. Bergen, *Medicine and the Management of Living*, Chicago, Chicago University Press, 1984.

56 Foucault, *Birth of the Clinic*, p. 33.

57 Ibid., p. 34.

58 The seminal piece in this tradition would be I. K. Zola, 'Medicine as an institution of social control', *Sociological Review*, 20, 1972, pp. 407–504; cf. P. Conrad and J. Schneider, *Deviance and Medicalization: From Badness to Sickness*, St. Louis, Mosby, 1980.

4

MEDICINE, HISTORY AND THE PRESENT[1]

Nikolas Rose

Much of Foucault's thinking was concerned with what has traditionally been called the history of medicine. But, as other essays in this volume show, Foucault felt uncomfortable with the label 'historian' in so far as it signalled traditional attempts to trace continuities from antiquity to modernity. Believing in the importance of deep structures and in discontinuities, Foucault preferred to use designations like 'archaeologist of knowledge'. It is little surprise then that Foucault never wrote a 'history of medicine'. Rather, as Nikolas Rose maintains, he pre-occupied himself with certain foci of interest of a medical nature: the differentiation of the medical domain into specialties; the institutions within which medicine had been practised (indeed which *create* particular medical knowledges and technologies); the formation of distinct types of expertise; and the invention of particular shapes of inquiry.

Above all, perhaps, Rose shows that in Foucault's way of analysis these different discourses and technologies of medicine were inseparable from distinctive ways of constituting the human body, both in the eyes of the medical gaze and through the cognition of the individual subject. From his early *Birth of the Clinic* through to his late and unfinished *History of Sexuality*, Foucault maintained a twin concern with knowledges respecting large populations (for instance public health) and practices respecting individual bodies (for example diagnosis) and probed their interconnections. He likewise played upon the creative ambiguity of the idea of the medical subject, simultaneously *subjected* to the medical gaze but also in some measure self-directing (as in the idea of 'care of the self' to which Foucault gave prominence in the later volumes of the history of sexuality).

Perhaps the key consequence of these thrusts is that Foucault dissolved and, in some measure, reconstituted the domain and orientation of medical history – his phrase 'history of the present' is a mark of a shift of viewpoint. As Rose emphasizes, the traditional doctor-centred story is deconstructed and new territories assume greater salience, including sexuality, hygiene, the family, and the analyses of populations. To some degree, Foucault was charting what others have termed 'the medicalization of society' – of everything! But insofar as that label typically flags assumptions about the rise of medical dominance, it may be misleading if applied to Foucault, whose concerns were epistemological and discursive rather than directed to the rise of the professions.

Michel Foucault's 'fieldwork in philosophy' drew him repeatedly to medicine. Foucault encountered medicine as he sought to discern some of the central coordinates that have defined our contemporary experience of ourselves, and the present which we inhabit. Medicine was bound up with the delineation of the unique human being, the human person in his or her very individuality and vitality, as a possible object for *positive knowledge*; that is to say, as a territory which could be mastered by a form of truth regulated by rationalities proper to the codes of scientific reason. Medicine was perhaps the first positive knowledge to take the form of *expertise*, in which the human being was not only to be known but to be the subject of calculated regimes of reform and transformation, legitimated by codes of reason and in relation to secular objectives. Medical sites and personnel were bound up with the mutation of political thought into its modern *governmental* form, in which political authorities in alliance with experts seek to administer a diversity of problematic sectors, locales and activities in the population in the attempt to promote a well-being that has become inescapably 'social'. Medicine was linked to the secularization of the *ethical regimes* through which individuals come to describe themselves in the languages of health and illness, to question themselves in terms of norms of normality and pathology, to take themselves and their mortal existence as circumscribing their values. The history of medicine, that is to say, is bound up with the historicity of all the different ways in which we have come to understand what is involved in making us better than we are.

It would, however, be a mistake to try to put together something like a general 'history of medicine' from these encounters, let alone to place them within a story of the progessive 'medicalization of existence'. Foucault offers us a philosophical perspective that sets itself against such a wish for the general, the universal, the linear; it is one which encourages us to attend to, not to reduce, the *heterogeneity* of the events with which 'medicine' has been engaged. What we must discern is the diversity of medical values, the diversity of interventions carried out in the name of health, the diversity of ways of relating the language of medicine to the language of politics. This 'medical complex' has no essence, be it epistemological (the 'medical model'), political ('social control') or patriarchal. Rather, an account of this engagement of medicine with our present would need, first of all, to see clinical medicine as merely one component in a complex of forms of thought and practice which question aspects of individual and group life from the point of view of health, and in relation to which medical knowledges, medical experts and medical practices play a variety of different roles. In this chapter, I would like to sketch out some ways in which the researches of Michel Foucault might encourage others to investigate further the part that medicine has played in making up our present.

METHODS

Nothing would be more counter-productive than an attempt to crystallize a 'methodology' from Foucault's studies, a recipe that could then be 'applied' to diverse 'topics'. I do not offer these notes in that systematizing spirit. Rather, I would simply like to offer some reflections to those who wish to carry forward the lines of enquiry opened up by Foucault's researchers – to those who might wish to practise as 'historians of the present'.

Any investigation that would seek to diagnose our present 'medical complex' in terms of its historical constitution would need to begin with an act of decomposition. A historian of the present must decompose the great certainties in which medicine and our present are bound together – the valorization of health and of the sanitization of suffering, the powers ascribed to the medical personage in relation to the disquiets of body, soul and social order, the sense of ourselves as perfectible through the application of medical techniques. This decomposition would not be in service of a critique of medicine, a wish to replace one form of medicine with another or to replace medicine with something that was not medicine. Rather, it would aim to help us to diagnose the conditions under which these profound linkages between medicine and our contemporary reality were formed, and to carry out some kind of assessment of their costs and benefits. What we have come to call medicine is constituted by a series of associations between events distributed along a number of different dimensions, with different histories, different conditions of possibility, different surfaces of emergence. Drawing upon Foucault's own encounters with medicine, perhaps I can suggest five lines of enquiry along which such analyses might proceed.

Our modern medical experience is, first, constituted in certain *dividing practices*: the heterogeneous practices within which sickness has been distinguished from health, illness from crime, disease from fate, madness from sanity, idleness from incapacity and the like; and the diverse problematizations of existence in terms of degeneracy, efficiency, productivity and the like within which these forms of division were applied. Here one would locate a description of the configurations of processes within which persons and populations were produced as objects of medical attention, and were separated from those which would be the focus of other authorities and apparatuses – religion, law, education.

Second, medicine is a matter of *assemblages*: the combinations of spaces, persons, techniques within which medicine has been deployed – not merely in the hospital, the clinic, the dispensary, the consulting room but also the town, the factory, the army, the home, the schoolroom, the insurance system, the community. Here one would seek to characterize the complex and heterogeneous apparatuses – which Foucault termed *dispositifs* – in which activity has been problematized and acted upon in the name of health. In general one might say that, starting from the nineteenth century, medical activity has been organized into five great *dispositifs*: a medico-administrative apparatus for regulating social space, incorporating within itself a range of activities from the directly political to those involving architecture and urban planning; the transformation of the home and the family into a hygienic machine; the medical staffing of the population in the form of general practitioners and innumerable other medical agents; the varieties of the clinical and curative hospital; the apparatus of security which transforms fate into risk and enables individuals and societies to secure themselves against disease.

Third, our contemporary field of medicine is a site for the deployment of diverse forms of *expertise*: all the various types of knowledgeable persons who have made disease their business and made a business out of sickness and health. Here one would need to examine the involvement, at different times and around different persons and populations, of religious, architectural, medical, nursing, social, legal, psychological and administrative personnel. This entails not only an examination of the various rivalries between these different modalities (as, for example, between doctors and lawyers in the courtroom) but also research into the practical divisions of labour established between them (as, for example, between psychiatrists and clinical psychologists in the treatment of different forms of behavioural pathology). And further, it would involve an investigation of the diverse forms of legitimacy – in terms of objectivity, efficacy, humanity, rationality, efficiency and the like – which different types of expertise have claimed or been accorded.

Fourth, contemporary medicine has composed within itself an array of *technologies of health*: technical forms within which one seeks to enact the business of curing sickness or producing health. This is not a matter of the repeated discovery of a 'medical model'. The relation between subjects is different in the general practitioner's surgery, the hospital ward, the tuberculosis sanatorium, the medicine of public health, in the practice of medical inspection of schoolchildren, in campaigns for vaccination and inoculation, in the advice of the health visitor to the mother, in the rituals of traditional Chinese acupuncture, in the murmuring of the stress counsellor's session, in behaviour modification programmes for those with 'eating difficulties', in the techniques of rehabilitation, in the injunctions to 'self-health' and the instrumentalization of lifestyle in the name of health. These relations empower medical personages in diverse ways and attribute diverse responsibilities to them in relation to the process of healing or normalization; they locate subjects in different relations to the decisions and actions made about their problems, and require them to disclose, identify and reform themselves differently.

Fifth, medicine has a dimension that one might term *strategic*: the particular ways in which medical thought and medical activity have sought to realize themselves through campaigns of social hygiene, through the reform of medical institutions into liberal spaces of reason and cure, through the staffing of the population with medical officers of health, through medical inspection, health visiting and campaigns for inoculation, through the exhortation to a healthy diet and modifications of lifestyle. Along this dimension one would also need to consider the different ways in which political tasks have been problematized and political objectives have been specified in the vocabularies and grammars of medicine – and vice versa. And one would need to analyse the various enactments of the 'social vocation' of medicine, as, for example, in the medico-politics of degeneration in the late nineteenth century and in the opposed strategies of eugenics and welfare in the first half of the twentieth century.

This rough-and-ready analytic division is sufficient to make two simple methodological points. First, a historian of the present must refuse the distinction between a realm of reason conceived of as a system of representations and a realm of power conceived of as a system of functional dominations. Such a historian cannot conceive of separating the concept of an epidemic from the sites within which it is identified, charted, and policed. She cannot conceive of distinguishing the discourse of clinical medicine from the structuring of the medical spaces in which it is deployed, the technologies of diagnosis and intervention to which it fused, the positions of doctor and patient in which it is embodied. It is not a question of 'discourse/meaning' on the one hand and 'power/domination' on the other; on the contrary, it is a matter of the meticulous investigation of the varied and complex ways in which practices of truth situate persons in particular relations of force.

The second 'methodological' point is also a simple one. The territory of medicine is formed through the complex interconnections between events and processes with diverse temporalities. To that extent, to study the history of medicine from the point of view of the present is necessarily to be perspectival – to trace out, from the point of view of a problem that concerns one today, the diverse connections and liaisons that have brought it into existence and given it its saliency and its characteristics. Rather than a 'general history of medicine', then, the task for a historian of the present is the writing of a perspectival genealogy of problem spaces, rationalities, authorities and technologies.

In what follows, I shall attempt to illustrate some of these issues, through a discussion of four distinct but related themes: medicine as a 'social' science; technologies of medical truth; the apparatuses of health; and medicine and the sufferings of the self.

MEDICINE AS A 'SOCIAL' SCIENCE

Medicine and the body appear to be fundamentally linked. To conjure up the image of the doctor is simultaneously to visualize the sickbed on which the ill body is isolated, the case notes that individualize the progress of the condition in relation to medical norms, the charts and records – temperature, pulse, blood pressure, X-rays, path reports – that inscribe the state of the body as disciplined by medical technology, the drug protocols that aim to influence this or that organic function, indeed all that is embodied in the fundamental proposition of clinical medicine – the body itself is that which is ill. But a critical historian of the present should not take this primary spatialization of medicine as establishing the nature and limits of her task – to chart the rise to power and monopoly of clinical medicine, its 'medical model', its focus upon illness rather than health, on cure rather than prevention, on the corpse rather than the person, on the enclosed disciplinary space of the hospital rather than the real life of the human community. For medicine, since its inception, has been a profoundly 'social' science.

Medicine, for a historian of the present, must be analysed as constitutively social. To say that medicine is constitutively social does not mean that medicine has to be understood in a 'social context', that it has been subject to 'social influences', or that its activities have been 'socially determined'. Rather, medicine has been bound up with the ways in which, since the end of the eighteenth century, the very idea of *society* has been brought into existence and acquired a density and a form – society as a domain 'with a complex and independent reality that has its own laws and mechanisms of disturbance . . . its specific characteristics and variables'.[2] Society, as it is historically invented, is immediately accorded an organic form and thought in medical terms. As a *social body* it is liable to sickness: that is to say, it is problematized in the vocabulary of medicine. As a social body it needs to be restored to health: that is to say, its government is conceptualized in medical terms. And, in relation to these forms of government, medical personnel enter into relations with many other authorities who come to concern themselves with issues of sickness and of health, and medical techniques such as the segregation of the sick and the monitoring of contagion are accorded a special place.

To understand the part played by medicine in making up our present, we need to trace out the diverse relations that have been established between medical reason and political reason. From the moment that European political reason came to assume its modern governmental form, it had a medical dimension. Foucault and others have suggested that the form of political rationality which termed itself 'the science of police' can be seen as the moment when political power came to address itself to a new task – that of administering life.[3] As deliberations of statesmen, merchants and pamphleteers came to connect the political well-being of a nation to its *population* – its size, its strength, its well-being – a new set of tasks arose: how was the state of this population to be known; how could it be best administered to enrich the coffers of the state, secure the wealth of the population, ensure good order and public tranquillity.

There were 3,215 texts on 'the science of police' published in German-speaking lands alone during the seventeenth and eighteenth centuries; the police of health and cleanliness took its place amongst the police of religion, customs, subsistence, highways, commerce, beggars and the various other domains for which regulations were to be drawn up and enforced. By 1779, when Johann Peter Frank published the first of six volumes of his system for a comprehensive *medical* police, medicine had encouraged itself fully within the rationalities of government.[4]

Medicine was to be fully enmeshed in the two central axes of police. There was the axis of *statistics*, which mapped out the population as a territory to be known, with its rates of birth, illness and death, which were stable enough to be known yet varied across time and space – in the towns and in the countryside, in the different geographical regions of a territory, between the well-to-do and the labouring classes.[5] And there was the axis of *administration*, which sought to invent the mechanisms for regulating events in widely dispersed and heterogeneous locales, forms of conduct and types of difficulty, not merely to avert illness, but to promote well-being.[6] Thus medical thought and medical activity, through the rationalities that unified the inhabitants of geographical space as a social body, through the compilation of statistics of birth, death, rates and types of morbidity, through the charting of social and moral topographies of bodies and their relations with one another, played a key role in 'making up' the social body and in locating individuals in relation to this dense field of relations bearing upon the individual body. Medicine, that is to say, has played a formative role in the *invention of the social*.[7]

Medicine was to engage itself with one of the most fundamental sets of questions that troubled and provoked governmental thought during the nineteenth century and which inspired the invention of the basic administrative knowledge and techniques of modernity. This set of questions concerned the regulation of life in towns. Over the first half of the nineteenth century, medical police was to problematize the life of populations in towns in terms of health, and to devise a whole variety of schemes for its improvement. The diversity of tactics adopted ranged from grand schemes of architectural renewal of public space in the name of health and civility to a host of more mundane projects of social hygiene, sanitary reform and sewage arrangements, pure air and pure water, paving of streets and controls on burial of the dead. Of course, in one sense it was a concern with particular problems of illness that energized these campaigns of police. The epidemics that ravaged European cities in the eighteenth and nineteenth century struck terror into the inhabitants of the towns and those who would exercise government over them – cholera, typhus, what the 1842 *Report on the Sanitary Conditions of the Labouring Population of Great Britain* simply called 'fever'.[8]

The miasmic conception of epidemics as inhering in the relation between social space and human character lent itself to a medicine of social spaces: diseases were produced in certain types of social space, circulated around social space, alighted upon those predisposed by character or habits to succumb and ran its course in them. Disease could be spatialized, a topography of disease could be constructed and superimposed upon a topography of the towns to produce a disease map where the high points of infection could be seen to coincide with physical squalor and moral degradation. Hence medicine had a task that was directly political: the struggle against a disease had to begin with a war on bad government. From this time onwards the doctor, as Foucault points out, 'becomes the great advisor and expert, if not in the art of governing, at least in that of observing, correcting and improving the social "body" and maintaining it in a permanent state of health'.[9] And, from both grand enquiries into the health of populations and less flamboyant local and municipal collections of information on cases, diagnoses, addresses and districts, a 'medico-administrative' knowledge begins to develop, of a human and 'biological' space of society, of its health and sickness, of the relations of these to housing, to moral habits, to types of labour and the like. Thus it is medicine as much as philosophy which will provide the foundation of the 'positivist' sociology and social statistics of the nineteenth century.

But over and above this, one sees here the ways in which, for at least a century, the task of government was thought within a medical vocabulary. Medical rationalities provided the matrix within which government problematized the population – delinquency, criminality, indigence, inebriety were construed as sicknesses afflicting the social body, they were rendered thinkable in medical terms, as so many products of the foul moral miasma circulating at the heart of the great cities. This medicalization of rationalities of government was not merely a matter of metaphors, for it was embodied in a range of programmes of moral hygiene entailing opening up these swamps of vice to the purifying gaze of civilization. For if bad housing interacted with temperamental predispositions to produce *physical* ills, no wonder it produced the same effects upon the vulnerable *moral* constitution, especially that of the young. And, of course, this relation between medical and political reason was to be maintained into the first half of our own century. It was to exist – although with a reversed

56

direction of causality – in the theories of degeneracy that emerged towards the end of the nineteenth century. And it was to find its culmination in the eugenic movement with its politics of race and blood.[10]

TECHNOLOGIES OF MEDICAL TRUTH

The persons and populations with which medicine concerns itself do not merely exist, sickly and mutely awaiting its attention: they are formed by differentiation. Medical thought and medical practice always exist in relation to other forms of thought and practice – those of charity, assistance and social security, those of law and order, those of religion and the church. An analytic of medicine thus needs to examine the divisions within which its objects are formed, the *lines of differentiation* which define certain persons, groups, sites, locales as appropriate for medicine and others as not: the mobile divisions and relations between the sick and other troubling social categories, as, say, in the late nineteenth century when the tubercular, the neuropath, the inebriate, the indigent, the unemployable and the prostitute were all different manifestations of a degenerate constitution; the distinction between normality and pathology, as, for instance, in the new relation established between madness and everyday life during the first half of the twentieth century in the category of the neuroses, or the more recent realignment of the relations between illness and health in the lifestyle strategies of health promotion; the disputed linkages and differentiations between poverty and health – and between the poor and the sick – as in the debates in England in the 1930s on food, health and income, or those concerning 'inequalities in health' fifty years later.[11]

The problems and populations with which medicine will concern itself, that is to say, do not form naturally in some ancient space of communion between the medical personage wishing only to cure and the sufferer wishing only to be cured. Of course, the moment of the consultation has a long history, and one that needs to be documented and understood. But, as I have suggested above, from at least the nineteenth century, the persons and conditions with which medicine will deal have been produced within other social practices, and in a range of practical sites and encounters. Encounters within the legal system, between the juridical apparatus and the wayward child, the infanticidal mother, the perpetrator of a crime without reason. Encounters within the domestic space, with the hysterical wife, the ignorant mother, the undisciplined infant. Encounters within the apparatuses for the conservation of abandoned or ill-treated children: the foundling homes and systems of fostering. Encounters within the factory, with industrial accidents, with absenteeism and occupational illnesses. Encounters within the school system, with the various classes of children who cannot or will not learn their lessons – the maladjusted, the feeble-minded, the delicate. Encounters within the army, with those who cannot or will not fight, those who are too sickly to be recruited, or those who must be discharged as suffering from 'shell shock'. Encounters within the security system with those claiming pensions, benefits or insurance on grounds of sickness or disability.

The phenomena that will be the concern of medicine are formed within all these various apparatuses for managing the conduct of individuals: it is their problematizations and classifications that begin to demarcate the diverse and heterogeneous field of concerns that medicine will take as its own. These classifications and systems of segregation divide those objects, events and persons to be problematized in medical terms from those to be rendered intelligible through other modes of rationality. And they impose a certain pattern of unification upon the concerns of medicine, patterns which will, in important ways, delimit the objects about which medicine will be able to speak.

These lines of differentiation are not 'merely conceptual': they are practical. To differentiate is also to classify, to segregate, to locate persons and groups under one system of authority and to divide them from those placed under another. Placing persons and populations under a medical mandate – in the asylum, in the clinic, in an urban space gridded by medical norms – exposes them to scrutiny, to documentation and to description in medical terms. It is here that one can discover the conditions for the emergence of 'positive' knowledges of the human individual. This is, perhaps, the most general and significant point of method that emerges from Foucault's studies – for it goes to the heart of the history of truth. Truth, at least in the human sciences, arises out of the institutional and organizational conditions which gather humans together and seek to act upon them in order to produce certain ends. The history of truth, the constant schisms, oppositions, transformations and successions of rationalities, is to be understood as a 'practical matter' – that is to say, as always a matter of practices. We can best grasp the relation of truth to our experience of its effects through a study of what one might term *truth machines*: the machinery of forces, spaces and subjects which bring into existence and configure the space which truths inhabit, and for which truths themselves provide the fuel.

This 'machine' metaphor is rather misleading – it suggests something bright, shining, designed, engineered, gears smoothly meshing, inputs linked to outputs and so forth. The 'truth machines' that Foucault describes are assemblages of parts of different provenance, connected together in ways that are often the result of contingencies, producing unexpected yields in strange places. They thus resemble the fabrications of Tinguely or Heath Robinson rather than those of Audi; in the manner in which Foucault describes France's legal system as 'one of those immense pieces of machinery, full of impossible cog-wheels, belts which turn nothing and wry gear systems: all these things which "don't work" and ultimately serve to make things "work" '.[12] Gilles Deleuze, discussing Foucault's use of the notion of *dispositif*, thinks of them in terms of lines – tangled, multilinear ensembles of vectors and tensors making up a 'social apparatus'.[13] It is out of this regime of lines, this regime of spaces and gazes, that new knowledges of human individuality can be born – in the asylum, in the school, in the factory and, perhaps first of all, in the clinic.

Foucault's account of the birth of clinical medicine in *The Birth of the Clinic* is instructive in this regard. It exemplifies the ways in which that which is new comes about neither through the forward march of reason nor through the relations of 'meaning' in an abstracted realm of 'discourse' but within a 'clearing' opened up by the connections between diverse elements, practices and surfaces. The transformation of eighteenth-century hospitals into 'curing machines' was itself a complex occurrence involving shifts at many levels.[14] The increasing hospitalization of the poor during the eighteenth century was certainly related to the processes of urbanization and industrialization. It was also linked to changes in the laws of assistance which made institutionalization of the poor a condition of medical treatment. Yet, correlatively, the legitimacy of the hospital was thrown into doubt, as a place of the heterogeneous and confused gathering of different conditions and persons, a place of miasma and hence of danger: its very existence was questioned as incompatible with the imperatives of a liberal social order. To justify its existence it must become not a place of darkness but a place of light: a curing machine.[15]

As the hospital responded to these demands that it become a curing machine, it established new relations between patient and patient, between patient and doctor and between doctor and doctor. Following Deleuze once more, we could say that the hospital established certain 'lines of visibility', lines which distributed the visible and the invisible in particular ways. Out of this organizational force arose a new epistemology. An organizational form such as a hospital entails a certain structuring of light which brings certain objects into focus. This 'regime of light' makes visible *the case* as the unique intersection of a body and a life history: the case as the proper object of the cure.

Making visible, here, is meant in an entirely literal way, enabling time and space to be perceived, divided, inscribed, utilized. It was the collection of large numbers of sick people in a single institutional space under medical surveillance that enabled illness to be normalized. To make the hospital a proper liberal space required it to be organized according to a concerted therapeutic strategy. This entailed 'the uninterrupted presence and hierarchical prerogatives of doctors, through systems of observation, notation and record-taking'.[16] As the medical record meticulously inscribes the details of the individual history of the patient in a stable, transferable, comparable form, it renders the sufferings of the sick person knowable in a new way, in relation to the population of patients of which he or she forms an element. Doctors could now observe a whole series of instances of any particular condition. Observed empirical regularities could now be constructed between symptoms at different levels – a coated tongue, trembling of the lower lip, the tendency to vomit. Further, one could now, for the first time, observe the similarities and differences between symptoms in different individuals at any one time and over time. This provided the conditions for a statisticalization and normalization of diseases: a new classificatory system, which would reduce the uncertainty inherent in medical diagnosis by the location of the individual facts of any particular case within a field structured by norms. A symptom was now to become intelligible because it was a fact that could be assessed in terms of its convergence or divergence from such norms.

Of course, the conditions for the triumph of the empirical within the clinic were not 'merely' institutional; certain revolutionary transformations in systems of thought established the perspective from which the eyes and hands of doctors applied themselves to their objects. Sensationalist philosophies of knowledge, represented in France most notably by Condillac, encouraged a certain empiricism of values, according an epistemological dignity to the act of observation.[17] Statistical thought, associated with Laplace and Condorcet, made possible probabilistic forms of reasoning and thus transformed the evidential status of discrete and variable facts.[18] But it was within a particular *dispositif*, in a truth machine that arranged bodies, spaces, gazes, inscriptions within a certain regime of light, that sickness – and with it, health – became relocated in a thoroughly empirical domain of observable events and mathematical regularities. The empirical knowledge of the human individual was made possible here – as in the case of the asylum and psychiatry, the school and the psychology of individual difference – by the regulated organization of persons under the gaze of authority.

Truth, at least as far as the human sciences are concerned, is a technological matter. Thus it was the technical form of the clinic that permitted that 'exact superposition of the "body" of the disease and the body of the sick man' which Foucault describes at the opening of *Birth of the Clinic*.[19] The technology of the clinic brings together three elements of different provenance: vitalism, dissection and case histories. None of these elements was particularly new. Cases had been recorded before, as we have seen above, and symptoms traced from inception to death, without producing the epistemological shift in which the body itself became that which was ill. While the philosophy of vitalism enabled observations of lesions in tissues to be organized within a matrix of the body as a vital order, vitalism was not unique to Bichat. While pathological anatomy enabled the gaze of medicine to penetrate from the surface of the body to the depths of its tissues, bodies had been dissected before. But when these hetero-geneous elements – a mode of inscription, a kind of philosophy of life, a practice of cutting and looking – were assembled together in a particular configuration in the hospital, a clearing opened in which something new could appear. It was the fusion of pathological anatomy and the empirical experience of the hospital that enabled the progress of symptoms to be traced to their interior sources in a system of life: it allowed successive events to be followed not merely to the point of death but beyond it. Thus the signs recorded in the case history ceased to be merely 'superficial' and statistical; immediate dissection of the corpses allowed the link between sign and lesion to be solidified and deepened. It is true that the most fundamental experi-ence of modern medical thought is that in which 'the human body defines, by natural right, the space of origin and distribution of disease: a space whose lines, volumes, surfaces and routes are laid down, in accordance with a now familiar geometry, by the anatomical atlas'.[20] But no great leap of the human imagination gave birth to that experience, nor did it arise out of some mystical mutation in an abstracted realm of 'discourse'. An event in philosophy, here as elsewhere in the sciences of man, owes everything to the mundane material practices of looking, seeing, experimenting, calculating, measuring, and writing.

I have been trying to make a methodological point which is simple yet fundamental to the work of a historian of the present. The phenomena which medicine – and other human sciences – will 'think' as well as the very forms of thought itself, emerge out of the institutional and practical conditions of its operation. Thought, here, should not be understood in a contemplative sense – as medical 'theories' or medical 'discourse', medical 'concepts' or medical 'explanations'. Certainly one must attend to the changing rules that govern medical reason and its truth claims: the different codes of truth embodied in, say, the notions of the morbid processes within miasmatic theories of epidemics in the nineteenth century as opposed to the revised conceptions of illness that emerged with the notion of the body itself as a vital order whose normal processes serve to maintain it in health.[21] But forms of medical reason are articulated into more complex regimes of truth, entailing not merely explanation but also the material and conceptual means by which illness is rendered thinkable, describable, calculable, predictable.

An analysis of medical technologies of truth thus involves, for example, an investigation of the ways in which medical reason has come to require a diagnostic moment, and the diverse ways in which this diagnostic moment has been given form. This has entailed complex procedures through which actuality has been rendered thinkable: the collection of statistics on the distribution of morbid phenomena; the dissection of corpses and the drawing of the organs; the use of instruments, from stethoscopes to ultrasound, to chart and visualize the existence of the disease. It has entailed constituting certain phenomena as symptoms and connecting them in various ways to one another and to other processes to which they relate. Further, an investigation of medical truth would call for an examination of the *performative* character of medical judgement – that is to say, the ways in which medical judgements are integrated into systems of action in relation to pathology. And it would require an investigation of the various *legitimating* and *justificatory* mechanisms whereby medical truth claims are sustained, in relation to varying criteria – of which objectivity, rationality, efficacy, humanity are only some of the possibilities. A historian of the present needs to think of thought as itself 'technical'; the task is not one of interpreting 'discourse' in terms of the meanings embodied in systems of representation, but of analysing the *intellectual technologies* by which thought renders being amenable to being thought.

THE APPARATUSES OF HEALTH

Medicine is characteristically thought of as that activity which, since the nineteenth century, has been carried out in certain institutional locales, notably the hospital, the asylum and the consulting room. However, as I have suggested, these sites form only the most obvious and 'concentrated' zones for the practice of modes of diagnosis and intervention conducted in medical terms. The nineteenth century may have seen the invention of the modern 'clinical' hospital and a range of other enclosed locales such as sanatoria and isolation hospitals. But, in the dreams of medicine from the eighteenth century onwards, the hospital was to be the hub of a web of other medical activities, the focus for a medical corps spread throughout the population offering medical treatment 'in the open' and also accompanied by the recurrent theme of the dispensary, which would extend consultation and medication to patients without the need to intern them.[22]

The nineteenth century saw the establishment of a number of other apparatuses of health. As complex regimes of medical practice spread across urban space, the town became a multifaceted apparatus for fighting disease and securing health. The domestic environment – the home and family and all the relations amongst persons and activities within it – was constituted as a site subjected to scrutiny and administration in medical terms, principally through alliances and dependencies between doctors and mothers. Over the course of the twentieth century, a whole variety of places of medical scrutiny and health regulation were added, notably through the transformation of schools and factories into 'inspection machines' and institutions gridded by norms of health, and through the establishment of sites of institutional care for the old, the young, and the disabled. Further, each of these apparatuses was located within a new insurantial rationality, in which security for each and for all was to be maximized through the application of a calculus of risk.[23] In our own times, the ideal territory of the community serves as the basis for innumerable utopian projects for the reintegration of the practice of medicine, a territory to be traversed by community physicians, community nurses and numerous other professionals and dotted with micro-territories for the practice of medical cure and reform.

The pervasiveness of medicine in our modern 'liberal' experience owes as much to these other apparatuses of health as it does to the hospital and the medicine of the clinic. Each of the five great apparatuses of health – the medical administration of public space, the hygienic regulation of domestic life, the curative clinic, the medical staffing of the population, the insurantial mitigation of suffering – is bound up with a different set of relations between experts and subjects. Each apparatus embodies a different distribution of the rights of speaking and listening, of prescribing and obeying; different ways of making up the persona of the expert as a technician of health, linked to different images of the person of the sufferer and tied to different ways in which subjects themselves are urged to problematize aspects of themselves and their lives in the name of health and to act towards them according to a logic prescribed for them by experts.

The medicalization of social space and the hygienic transformation of the family can serve as two exemplars of the technical enactment of medicine's 'liberal' vocation. Within the rationalities of medical police, the town was constituted as a fundamental site for the operation of medical reason and medical technique. Police, in its earliest forms, was an 'anti-liberal' art of government – the population to be governed was ideally to be comprehensively known, rendered visible and transparent to the gaze of authorities and criss-crossed by detailed regulations for all aspects of life from the weight of a loaf of bread to the proper dress to be worn on the sabbath. These anti-liberal moments of medical government have not disappeared; the dystopian dream of a regulated calculus of social relations in the name of health recurs in certain moments of crisis – as, for example, in certain strategies for policing AIDS. But over the nineteenth century, the government of conduct in the name of health was to assume a more liberal form, that is to say, it operated according to a division between a 'public' domain to be rendered pure, clean, healthy and sanitized by authoritative action, and 'private' spaces to be governed not by reducing freedom but by regulating it.

In the name of the health of the social body, public space was to be reconstructed through town planning in order to penetrate the dark and fetid locales where disease bred untouched by the purifying effects of light, air and civility.[24] This medico-administrative government of public space was not merely a matter of medical offiers of health, sanitary reformers and the policing of food and drink. It also entailed the development of spatial technologies of health, in the form of a new set of relations between medicine and architecture. In the schemes of planning space, at the the macro-level of the towns and in the micro-territory of the design of buildings – prisons, asylums, schools, homes, bathrooms, kitchens – one sees the desire to make space healthy. Architects and planners seek to enact a medical vocation, by organizing the relations between persons, functions, objects, effluents, activities in order to minimize all that would encourage disease and to maximize all that would promote health. This dream of the healthy body – the healthy city, the healthy home – has, perhaps, done more than most to embody a medical aspiration within the territories upon which we manage our individual lives. Yet it is an enlightened dream; one in which the relations between experts and subjects are essentially liberal. On the one hand, a certain image of what humans are, and what humans can and should be – rational, healthy, normal – is embodied within each scheme for the programming of space. On the other, space is organized only as a field of possibilities, and within the vectors and tensors, visibilities and invisibilities, probabilities and improbabilities established by this field of organized space, individuals are to conduct themselves freely.

This liberal vocation of medicine was also to be manifested in the ways in which it sought to construct private space, in particular the domestic environment of home and family, in a form conducive to the promotion of both physical and moral health.[25] From the eighteenth century onwards, within the great apparatus of alliances and descent that was its time-honoured role, the family will consolidate itself as an apparatus for securing 'the healthy, clean, fit body, a purified, cleansed, aerated domestic space' and doctors 'will have the task of teaching individuals the basic rules of hygiene which they must respect for the sake of their own health and that of others: hygiene of food and habitat, exhortations to seek treatment in case of illness'.[26] The initial wave of the medical offensive on the family bears on the care of children and their conservation, especially that of babies. The focus, in England as well as France, is first upon the wealthier classes, whose lineage is threatened by the death rates consequent upon wet nursing and poor domestic hygiene: the mother is to be brought into a kind of alliance with the doctor that will secure her role as against the patriarchal authority of the father, but at the price of transforming her into an agent of medical supervision of the domestic sphere: a system of medical care organized around the child, within which the family is to bear both some of the moral responsibility and some of the economic cost for illness and health.

Throughout the nineteenth century the campaigns to medicalize the family, by enjoining the mother to take responsibility for the health of her child and her spouse, were embodied in many forms: in journals, in philanthropic interventions, in schemes of model housing, in feminist campaigns to encourage marriage and the responsibilities of fathers and much else. The key point here concerns the ways in which these campaigns sought to make the family into a quintessentially 'private' space, yet ensure that it accepted its responsibilities for securing the 'public' objectives of the social health. As Foucault puts it:

> The family is assigned a linking role between general objectives regarding the good health of the social body and individuals' desire or need for care. This enables a 'private' ethic of good health as the reciprocal duty of parents and children to be articulated on to a collective system of hygiene and scientific technique of cure made available to individual and family demand by a professional corps of doctors qualified and, as it were, recommended by the State.[27]

Medical expertise here reveals its capacity to act as the relay between political objectives and individual desires and responsibilities, thus constructing 'private' spaces that will simultaneously come to secure social goals: acting as an exemplar for all those other forms of expertise that will follow, and which will ensure that, in a liberal society, individual well-being will assume an inescapably social form.

MEDICINE, ETHICS AND THE SELF

In 'the great disputation on sickness and health' in *The Magic Mountain*, Thomas Mann contrasts two ethics of suffering and redemption.[28] For the humanist, and Freemason, Ludovico Settembrini, modern medical science, the embodiment of reason and humanitarianism, is to fight back epidemic disease and pestilence through hygienic reform. The triumph of reason is, at the same time, the triumph of the principles of health over sickness and virtue over vice – in short, the triumph of a social morality, the morality of the normal man. For the Jesuit, and revolutionary, Leo Naptha, this ethic of the normal man and the triumph of reason is banal and vulgar. Human spirituality and human freedom are not bound to a veneration of the healthy body, but to an acceptance, an embracing, a mastery, of bodily suffering. Disease is indeed very human, for the essence of man is to be ailing:

> There were those who wanted to make him 'healthy', to make him 'go back to nature', when the truth was, he had never been 'natural'. All the propaganda carried on today by the prophets of nature, the experiments in regeneration, the uncooked food, fresh-air cures, sun-bathing, and so on, the whole Rousseauian paraphernalia, had as its goal nothing but the dehumanization, the animalization of man . . . the more ailing he was, by so much more was he the more man.[29]

Against the principle and value of the normal person, the healthy person, let us pit the abnormal, the genius, the mad, the sufferer, the outcast – for the normal have lived upon their achievements since time began.

No doubt there are still some who, like the pious Christians of the Middle Ages, would drink the water in which they had bathed the wounds of the afflicted, as a manifestation of reverence for the transfigurative nature of suffering. But for the most part, in our own times, care has become a matter of cure and normalization, and even supervision of the dying has become a project in which those who suffer are to be reclaimed to a humane and social world. Our present is suffused with the ethic of the humanist, the ethic of the normal social person, which is intrinsically an ethic of the healthy body. All aspects of our care for ourselves are to be judged in terms of a logic of health and reorganized in terms of a quest for normality. As the secular value of health replaces older non-corporeal or theological virtues and becomes one of the principal dimensions according to which we seek to compose a style of life for ourselves, the remit of medicine extends beyond the dimension of illness and cure and into the management of normality itself.

Sociologists have proposed various explanations for this transformation, for example medical entrepreneurship or the collapse of religious faith. However Foucault's own account seems to offer a particularly productive path for future research. If, in our present times, medicine has come to play such an important role within this ethical complex, it is in part because it has come to link the ethical question of how we should behave to the scientific question of who we truly are and what our nature is as human beings, as life forms in a living system, as simultaneously unique individuals and constituents of a population.

The Birth of the Clinic has at its heart a consideration of the reorganization of our relationship to individuality, to suffering and to death that has made this new regime of the self possible. The mutation in medical thought and practice that is traced in the book marks, claims Foucault, an ineradicable chronological threshold. The underside of disease – illness – comes to light, offers itself to the gaze, to language and to the practice of the cure in the same moment as it distributes itself in the enclosed but accessible volume of the body. This mutation has epistemological and ethical dimensions which are not confined to the territory of illness. Clinical experience and the anatomo-clinical method have a decisive *epistemo-ethical* significance, in constituting 'man' as an object of knowledge, in making possible a science of the human individual as a complex of specifiable processes and attributes that can be diagnosed, calibrated, compared and generalized. Foucault suggests that in the same way that a positive knowledge of individual human mental life became possible only on the basis of the experience of unreason – of madness – so a positive knowledge of human corporeal life becomes possible only on the basis of integration of death into medical thought.

When the positive knowledge of the individual inaugurated by the clinic internalized illness within the body of the sick person, it initiated that springtime of reason which would progressively seek to eliminate the metaphysical and spiritual significance of suffering in favour of a propaedeutic of health and an ethic of happiness. When language and vision connect death to life, when death becomes embodied in the living bodies of individuals, then science can take the 'natural order' of the body as an object of knowledge. Thus we should not be surprised that health has replaced salvation in our ethical systems, that the doctor has supplanted the priest, that the discourse of medicine has become saturated with questions concerning the meaning of life. For while medicine constantly reminds the inhabitants of our present of the possibilities of disease and death that they carry within them, it offers them the possibility of vanquishing the sufferings of the flesh, or at least postponing them, through the instrumentalization of life by medical criteria and procedures:

> The importance of Bichat, Jackson and Freud in European culture does not prove that they were philosophers as well as

doctors, but that, in this culture, medical thought is fully engaged in the philosophical status of man.[30]

Foucault's early writings on medicine thus link up with his last writings on ethics and technologies of the self. For this philosophical engagement of medicine is a very practical matter: the doctor as an expert in the arts of living. The infusion of medical values into ethical judgements can be located in relation to the successive ways in which humans have been urged to engage in practices of self-formation, to master themselves, improve themselves and regulate themselves in the name of certain problems and through the use of certain techniques. At a time when we have lost faith in the sanctity of moral codes, have no wish to be bound by legal imperatives and are forced to rationalize our fate in terms of our choices, the new ontology of ourselves constituted by medicine appears to offer us a rational, secular and corporeal solution to the problem of how we should live our lives for the best; of how we might make the best of our life by adjusting it to our truth, by letting medicine enlighten our decisions as to how to live it.

In her classic text *Illness as Metaphor*, Susan Sontag seeks to strip medicine of its metaphorical significance, both to free disease from the weight of representation that it has come to carry and to free the experience of the sufferer from the burden of morality imposed when disease is in some way linked to personality, to diet or to forms of life.[31] She dreams of a time when a disease will be no more than it is – a biological malfunction susceptible to biological methods of treatment. But Foucault's researches enable us to recognize this dream as the final point of the very trajectory which, over the last two hundred years, has progressively demythologized suffering and sought to discipline sickness in the name of health. In its name we have come to celebrate normality, but simultaneously to live under the constant dread of all that which would threaten it. And in the very same movement as illness becomes amenable to an explanation in terms of the biology of the body, medical experts come to take up their role as masters of lifestyle. In the subsequent search for a normality conceived in terms of health, we have come to experience ourselves and our lives in fundamentally medical terms. Like Hans Castorp upon his Magic Mountain, our stay in the sanatorium is not limited to a brief and terminable episode of illness. It is a sentence without limits and without walls, in which, apparently of our own free will and with the best of intentions on all sides, our existence has become bound to the ministrations and adjudications of medical expertise. For a historian of the present, to recognize this is not to condemn it, not to participate in that fashionable scorn which cultural critics, in the Jesuitical tradition of Leo Naptha, like to pour upon the banality of an ethics 'beyond good and evil'. It is merely to open the possibility of posing certain questions about the costs of organizing our experience of ourselves in this way.

CONCLUSIONS

An engagement with medicine, from a range of different angles and perspectives, is thus part of what Foucault terms, in *The Use of Pleasure*, an analysis of 'the *problematizations* through which being offers itself to be . . . thought – and the *practices* on the basis of which these problematizations are formed'.[32] Foucault's work may be historical, but it is aimed at the heart of our present, and the field that defines the possibilities of our experiencing, recognizing and valuing ourselves in that present. The present here figures as a field of heterogeneous vectors and forces in which objects and actions can appear, make sense, enter into relations with one another.

In addressing the history of that present, Foucault's researches aim to disturb and fragment our understanding of the lines of descent that have made us what we are. But this rejection of unities was not done in the name of a post-modern metaphysics that celebrates diversity. Rather, Foucault's studies proceed in the light of a more sober and, dare one say, more historical conviction that that which 'is' is much less determined, much more contingent, than we think. We do not merely need to abandon the comforting thought that our present is the outcome of a process of History. We also need to jettison all those forms of narcissistic historicism that read the past in terms of the present that it has become, the present here being portrayed as a culmination of everything that is 'progressive' in that which preceded it.

This is not to engage in some game of 'deconstruction', nor to delegitimate that which we take to be pure by revealing its 'impure' origins. Rather, in delineating the complex contingencies that have made up the territory we inhabit and the horizons of our experience, in showing us that things could have been different, such analyses encourage us to weigh up the costs as well as the benefits of the present we inhabit. They thus allow us to dream of a time in which our times could be different again. Perhaps Gilles Deleuze captures this relation between Foucault's philosophy and his historical investigations most aptly:[33]

> If Foucault is a great philosopher, this is because he uses history for the sake of something beyond it: as Nietzsche said: acting against time, and thus on time, for the sake of a time one hopes will come.

NOTES

1 Thanks to Thomas Osborne and Gary Wickham for helpful comments on an earlier draft of this paper.

2 M. Foucault, 'An ethics of pleasure' in S. Lotringer (ed.), *Foucault Live: Interviews 1966–84*, New York, Semiotext(e), 1989, p. 261. Cf. G. Kendall and G. Wickham, 'Health and the social body' in S. Scott et al. (eds), *Private Risk and Public Danger*, Aldershot, Avebury Press, 1992.

3 On police, see M. Foucault, 'Governmentality' in G. Burchell, C. Gordon and P. Miller (eds), *The Foucault Effect*, Hemel Hempstead, Harvester Wheatsheaf, 1991, pp. 87–104; and P. Pasquino, 'Theatrum Politicum', ibid., pp. 105–18.

4 G. Rosen, 'Cameralism and the concept of medical police', *Bulletin of the History of Medicine*, 27, 1953, pp. 21–42.

5 I. Hacking, *The Emergence of Probability*, Cambridge, Cambridge University Press, 1975; I. Hacking, *The Taming of Chance*, Cambridge, Cambridge University Press, 1990.

6 A. Small, *The Cameralists: Pioneers of Social Policy*, New York, Burt Franklin, 1926.

7 Cf. J. Donzelot, *L'invention du social*, Paris, Fayard, 1984.

8 E. Chadwick, *Report on the Sanitary Conditions of the Labouring Classes of Great Britain*, ed. M. Flynn, Edinburgh, Edinburgh University Press, [1842] 1965.

9 M. Foucault, 'The politics of health in the eighteenth century' in M. Foucault, *Power/Knowledge: Selected Interviews and Other Writings, 1972–1977*, Brighton, Harvester, 1980, p. 177.

10 Cf. M. Foucault, *The History of Sexuality 1: An Introduction*, London, Allen Lane, 1979, pp. 148–50.

11 Cf. J. Boyd Orr, *Food, Health and Income*, London, Gollancz; P. Townsend and N. Davidson, *The Black Report: Inequalities in Health*, Harmondsworth, Penguin, 1982.

12 M. Foucault in *Le Monde*, 21 October 1978, cited in C. Gordon, 'Afterword' in Foucault, *Power/Knowledge*, pp. 229–59.

13 G. Deleuze, 'What is a *dispositif*?' in *Michel Foucault, Philosopher*, tr. T. J. Armstrong, Hemel Hempstead, Harvester Wheatsheaf, 1992, pp. 159–68.

14 M. Foucault, B. Barret-Kriegel, A. Thalamy, F. Béguin and B. Fortier, *Les machines à guérir: Aux origines de l'hôpital moderne*, Paris, Institut de l'Environnement, 1976.

15 Foucault, 'Politics of health', pp. 178ff.

16 Ibid., p. 180.
17 M. Foucault, *The Birth of the Clinic*, London, Tavistock, 1973, ch. 6.
18 See esp. I. Hacking, 'How should we do the history of statistics?' in Burchell et al., *The Foucault Effect*, pp. 181–95.
19 Foucault, *Birth of the Clinic*, p. 3.
20 Ibid.
21 See esp. G. Canguilhem, *The Normal and the Pathological*, New York, Zone, 1991.
22 Foucault, 'Politics of health', p. 180; cf. D. Armstrong, *The Political Anatomy of the Body*, Cambridge, Cambridge University Press, 1983.
23 F. Ewald, 'Insurance and risk' in Burchell et al., *The Foucault Effect*, pp. 197–210.
24 P. Rabinow, *French Modern: Norms and Forms of the Built Environment*, Boston, Mass., MIT Press, 1989.
25 Foucault, *History of Sexuality 1*; J. Donzelot, *Policing the Family*, London, Heinemann, 1979.
26 Foucault, 'Politics of health', pp. 173–6.
27 Ibid., p. 174.
28 T. Mann, *The Magic Mountain*, Harmondsworth, Penguin Books, [1924] 1960.
29 Ibid., p. 466.
30 Foucault, *Birth of the Clinic*, p. 198.
31 S. Sontag, *Illness as Metaphor*, London, Allen Lane, 1979.
32 M. Foucault, *The History of Sexuality 2: The Use of Pleasure*, Harmondsworth, Penguin, 1986, p. 11.
33 Deleuze, 'What is a *dispositif*?', pp. 164–5.

5

INVENTING MOUTHS
Disciplinary power and dentistry[1]

Sarah Nettleton

It is a basic assumption of Foucauldian analysis – as it has been of much radical sociology of knowledge over the last generation – that the body is not a natural datum. By consequence, disease is not a self-evident thing which medicine unproblematically treats. They are in different degrees and in various ways 'invented' or 'constructed'. Different schools of historical and sociological interpretation have emphasized distinct factors in the making of such 'inventions': 'labelling theory' has been influential, stressing the power of words to create realities and showing how supposedly neutral and scientific terminology routinely carries moral charges, resulting in scapegoating and stigmatization. The diagnosis 'hysteria' is an obvious example.

Foucault's distinctive approach to such problems was to emphasize the symbiotic relations between knowledge and power (*savoir* and *pouvoir*), in a manner perhaps somewhat reminiscent of the Marxist notion of the unity of theory and practice. In other words, the objects of science and medicine were not simply there waiting to be studied but were realized by certain viewpoints (the gaze) and certain technologies of intervention (experiments, modes of data collection and recording, kinds of interrogation). Psychoanalysis affords a case Foucault often used of the creation of such a technology of power. Sarah Nettleton shows the applicability of Foucauldian analysis to the creation of the objects and the discourses of dentistry. The transition from mere tooth-drawing to the science of dentistry that has developed during the last century has involved not merely new scientific knowledge (bacteriology and so forth) and better instruments, but the elaboration of new conceptualizations of the mouth as a disease focus and of the dentist as an agent of public hygiene. The dentist's chair might serve as a superb microinstance of a 'laboratory of power'.

A certain sort of bluff empirical historian might be tempted to scoff at such Foucauldian analyses, implying that they make heavy weather of the simple business of fixing bad teeth. A cogent counter-argument would run that dentistry occupies such a disproportionately large part in the public phobic imagination that some interpretative schemes like Foucault's of the power relations involved in dentistry is positively indispensable. Here it is noteworthy that teeth and dentistry have figured large in Freudian psychoanalytic symbolism: see David Kunzle's 'The art of pulling teeth in the seventeenth and nineteenth centuries: from public martyrdom to private nightmare and political struggle', in M. Feher (ed.), *Fragments for a History of the Human Body 3* (New York: Zone, 1989), pp. 28–89.

INTRODUCTION

The aim of this chapter is a simple one. It is to use some of Foucault's ideas to gain an understanding of how the mouth and teeth came to be the focus of a discipline and profession that was distinct and ultimately separate from medicine. In the pursuit of this aim we can assess the usefulness of Foucault's work. By applying it to a historical instance hitherto unexplored in this way, we can both (a) assess the value and relevance of Foucauldian analyses and (b) offer new insights into the emergence of dentistry. Indeed, it will be seen that the way in which the mouth and teeth have come to be policed does, in fact, offer a fine exemplar of a key theme in Foucault's work, that is disciplinary power.

It must be stated at the outset that this is above all an empirical study. All historical studies draw on material in the light of their current interests, values or theoretical perspectives. This study is no different in that it uses Foucault's work to direct the collection and interpretation of material. However, it differs from conventional studies of the past in that its prime task is to describe the dental discourse and its associated objects within their own temporal specificity. With this in mind this chapter will do three things.

First, it will provide an outline of conventional dental histories. Second, and against this backdrop, an alternative, Foucauldian account of the emergence of dentistry will be presented. Thus the main body of the chapter seeks to describe the discursive context in which the mouth and teeth were invented. Herein we have the crux of the argument. That is, that mouths, dental diseases, and teeth are not pre-existent natural entities, but rather objects realized through the discourse which surrounds them. Here the term discourse refers to more than words. The terms discourse and discursive practices encompass a whole assemblage of activities, practices, events, instruments and settings. Thus a dental discourse refers to not only what is said about the mouth with teeth but also the instruments used, such as the probe and the mouth mirror, and the differential settings of dental activity such as the bathroom or the dental surgery. In addition to the delineation of the dental discourse a third issue, or rather question, will be raised. How is it possible that sociologists have come to study and teach matters which pertain to the mouth and teeth?[2] In other words, how is it that sociology has come to form an element in the discourse of dentistry? The answer to this question will become evident by the end of the chapter.

CONVENTIONAL HISTORIES

Histories of the profession of dentistry have tended to focus on legislation and innovation. Legal enactments sought to secure the trained dentist's monopoly to practice. For example, the 1858 Medical Act and the Dentists Acts of 1878, 1921 and 1956 have been identified as major developments. Advancements of knowledge and skills, together with innovations in technical dental equipment, such as porcelain teeth, anaesthesia, amalgam-filling, vulcanite, the drill, the X-ray and so on, have also been documented. This often involves acknowledging the work, and the works of, a number of men, for example Ambroise Paré who published a text in 1579, John Hunter in 1771, Robert Blake in 1798, James Fox in 1803, Thomas Bell in 1829 and John Tomes in 1859. Overall, it is argued that such developments eliminated empiricism and quackery and resulted in the establishment of the learned and practised dental profession that we have today.[3] There has been a progression from unscientific to scientific knowledge:

> It is in this dark background formed by ignorance and empiricism that we should view dentistry around the year 1840. Judged by present-day standards dentistry as practised during these years presents a very bleak and disappointing picture; it is as well to remember that the early history of dentistry as of many professions is enveloped in an aura of quackery, charlatanism, public apathy and lack of scientific knowledge.[4]

Among these Whig accounts it is possible to identify two types of historical explanation. These are the functional and the causal approaches. The first, functional, approach, argues that 'a profession comes into being when there is a need for it'.[5] The need for dentistry, it is argued, arose because of the ever-increasing problem of dental decay. This, in turn, was due to increased sugar consumption.[6] The causal approach reasons that modern dentistry is a consequence of what has gone before; its present state can be explained in terms of developments in the past. During an address to members of the British Dental Association in 1949, Cohen noted that in the future it will

> be seen that the first half of the nineteenth century saw the sowing of the seeds which were to grow into such flourishing plants in the second half of the nineteenth century, the seeds of dental education, dental politics and dental societies.[7]

Moreover, it would only be by learning from the past that we could hope for achievements in the future: as Lewin-Payne put it, 'each generation has added a few stones to the cairns of dental knowledge'.[8]

Spanning both these approaches it is possible to detect a temporal shift from essentially individualistic histories to those which are more social in their orientation. In 1877 Hill argued that 'dentistry as a profession was created out of the labours of individuals whose prime concern is service'.[9] He offers a detailed day-by-day account of the events, meetings, letters, lectures, etc. initiated by certain dentists, which he maintained had produced and shaped the dental profession. However, by 1968 Richards offers a history that does not only note the role that individuals played in shaping the dental profession but also invokes broader contextual factors, for example demographic changes and the shift from the country into towns.[10]

Some more recent studies take the social and economic context into account when seeking to explain the growth of the profession and have found the uncritical progressive descriptions of the past inadequate. Dussault[11] explains the state of contemporary dentistry not just as a culmination of technological advances and impressive discoveries, or as the outcome of the activities of men of great integrity, but rather as a consequence of political struggles for power and control. The state of dentistry in the 1980s is, he argues, a result of collective occupational control strategies. Again from an occupational control perspective, Larkin assesses the dentists' claim to have sole control over what they consider to be specialized knowledge and the associated clinical functions.[12]

We have seen that explanations for the emergence of dentistry are relative to the author's historical context. Hitherto, however, they have all assumed that dentistry was an inevitable and necessary result of a physical deterioration of teeth, an increasing need for treatment and that dentistry today was the result of activities, inventions, discoveries and events that took place in the past. More recent studies have attempted to take a broader, more contextualized view, with some exposing the role of social interests, rather than the role of altruism which had been emphasized in the earlier dental accounts. Both approaches have, nevertheless, depicted a continuous and progressive story emphasizing the move from incorrect to correct knowledge and the significance of a concentration of power and control in the hands of the profession. They ignore the mouth and teeth, which are assumed to exist independently of the practice and discipline of dentistry. By contrast the problematization of the dental object, the mouth with teeth, provides the starting point of this analysis.

INVENTING MOUTHS

To reiterate the argument introduced above, this chapter is not a history of the past, but a history of the present. That is, it does not attempt to reconstruct the past through the conceptual and intellectual lens of the present. Rather than making assumptions on what 'we know now' about the need for dental treatment, or the extent to which the population was ravaged by dental disease, or the levels of pain which dental patients must have suffered, we will consider dental objects, concepts and theories and dental practices within their own temporal specificity.

When we consider the theories and activities of dentists and, perhaps more significantly, public health medicine towards the end of the nineteenth century, we can begin to appreciate the conditions that made possible the establishment of the mouth as a discrete entity. For it was at this time that the mouth came to be significant in relation to the rest of the body. But first, to facilitate an appreciation of the relevance of these occurrences, it is instructive to reflect on Foucault's notions of 'exile enclosure' and 'plague'.

In *Discipline and Punish* Foucault describes two ideal-typical responses to disease which he labels exile enclosure and plague.[13] In the former, those people who were diseased would be physically removed from the community and not permitted to mix with the general population. Disease was monitored by exclusion and so ensured a pure community. The epitome of this might be the leper colony, or to a lesser extent the hospital. An alternative response, termed plague, would be to establish a system of order within the existing population where disease would be met not by the removal of ill people, but rather by order, surveillance, observation and writing. The plague, envisaged as a possibility at least, would define ideally the exercise of disciplinary power. It is worth quoting Foucault at this point:

> But there was also a political dream of the plague, which was exactly its [exile enclosure's] reverse: not the collective festival, but strict divisions; not laws transgressed, but the penetration of regulation into even the smallest details of everyday life through the mediation of the complete hierarchy that assured the capillary functioning of power; not masks that were put on and taken off, but the assignment to each individual of his [sic] 'true' name, his 'true' place, his 'true' body, his 'true' disease. The plague as a form, at once real and imaginary, of disorder had as its medical and political correlative discipline. Behind the disciplinary mechanisms can be read the haunting memory of 'contagions', of the plague, of rebellions, crimes, vagabondage, desertions, people who appear and disappear, live and die in disorder.[14]

A community in which disease is ever-present is not dealt with by dividing the sick from the well, by removing and isolating diseased persons, but by a whole range of analysing and monitoring techniques. Thus it was the plague that gave rise to 'disciplinary projects' – of which public health medicine and dentistry are exemplars.

In the nineteenth and early twentieth centuries, clinical medicine was dominated by the hospital, and by acute and interventionist care. Concurrently there was another field of medicine, which comprised a system reminiscent of Foucault's plague, namely the public health movement. Public health involved not the treatment of disease but the control and assessment of its causes, which were at first predominantly environmental factors and then increasingly matters of personal hygiene and social contact.[15]

The prime focus of general medicine after the eighteenth century was the clinical examination – wherein the patient's anatomy was scrutinized in the space of the hospital. The prime focus of public health medicine was the community – wherein bodies were monitored and observed in a variety of sites, such as schools and clinics, to ensure their adherence to the rules of hygiene, diet and exercise. The medical response within the former was intervention, whereas in the latter it was prevention. Such differences were illustrative of what Foucault calls the 'old dispute' between 'active' and 'expectant medicine'.[16] Dentistry was created within the context of expectant medicine, that is the practices of public health, rather than, as has often been supposed, being carved out as a highly technical, specialized sub-branch of clinical medicine. Public health and dentistry had a very different focus from that of medicine; they had a shared cognitive base. While medicine focused on the three-dimensional space of the body, the attention of public health and dentistry traversed the body and scrutinized the space between the physical body and the environment. It is in this latter space that dentistry first discovered its object – the mouth.

AETIOLOGIES OF DENTAL DISEASE

This argument can be more readily appreciated by way of an explora-tion of nineteenth-century debates on the aetiology of dental disease. At that time three arguments were postulated: one saw dental disease as the outcome of 'vital forces'; another saw dental decay as being due to parasitic processes; and a third emphasized chemical process. Towards the end of the century, the first theory, which interpreted diseases of the mouth in relation to internal bodily functions – the teeth forming part of the living organism[17] – became unpopular and, according to Tomes, 'met with few adherents'.[18] At the same time the parasitic argument, which emphasized the actions of the acids and germs present in the mouth, which in turn served as an incubator, gained relatively more currency. However, it was theories on the chemical interaction on the teeth of elements and substances that were to be found beyond the body which came to hold the greatest sway. In fact, by the 1890s, the second and third arguments were combined. It was claimed that Miller's *Micro-Organisms of the Human Mouth* correctly described the origins of dental disease. Tooth decay, he wrote, was 'a chemico-parasitic process consisting of two distinctly marked stages, decalcification or softening of the tissue, and the dis-solution of the softened residue'.[19] This process was due to the 'effect of external causes, in which the vital forces of the individual play no part'.[20]

Thus, the dental debates focused on the environment. It was the external agents and substances that might transgress the body that were of concern. The environment and not simply the body had to be monitored. Such notions were, of course, congruent with the ideas and activities of the public health movement whose concern was to ensure order and prevent the transmission of diseases which might occur if bodies were mixed together. Thus the mouth did not form part of the anatomy that had to be treated and removed to the hospital, but rather the mouth was to be managed and monitored; it was to be subjected to a network of surveillance.

Ideas of contagion were prevalent at that time. The texts on public health saw the mouth as a vulnerable region between the internal body and the external sources of pollution. The mouth had to be protected from those of external threats. Boyd wrote in his book *Practical Preventive Medicine* about the significance of those

> portals through which infective agents enter the body . . . the principal body orifices play an important part, particularly the orifices of entrance rather than those of exit . . . the mouth and nose are the portals of entrance of the greatest importance from the number of the infective agents which are introduced through them.[21]

The mouth formed an important dimension of personal hygiene. The latter, according to the Chief Medical Officer, had by this time come to form the 'centre of gravity of our public health system'.[22] Indeed, in 1906 Hyatt had observed that 'it is not an exaggeration to say that two-thirds of the ills of mankind would be – no, will be – banished as soon as the teeth and mouth receive the care and attention they require'.[23] A characteristic feature of dental disorders was 'that they bring innumerable evils in their train, not least of which is that lowering the door's vitality thus opening wide a door for other diseases to enter'.[24]

By the early twentieth century attention to dental health was to form but one component of a wider concern for healthy bodies. Health and physical well-being had undoubtedly emerged as one of the central objectives of government. Bodies were to be maintained to ensure their maximum production for society as a whole. This is not only in a utilitarian sense (although utilitarian theories contributed to the establishment of the government's aims and objectives) but it formed part of a politico-strategic exercise which might, potentially, subject everyone to the policing of health. Bodily portals became crucial in the monitoring of bodies, and the techniques of regulation and surveillance contributed to the fabrication of the mouth and teeth. Indeed, dental surgeons became guardians of the oral cavity and its contents.[25] Dentists were not simply surgeons – tooth-drawers and menders – as the title dental surgeon would suggest, but they were custodians who watched, monitored, recorded and compared mouth and teeth.

THE EXERCISE OF DISCIPLINARY POWER

The dentist was as much a tooth-judge as a tooth-drawer. The duty of the dentist was not just to invade the mouth but to monitor and regulate and thus to contribute to the policing of bodies. It had become the dental profession's 'obvious and primary duty to seek prevention of diseases rather than rely on even a certain measure of arresting the once established process'.[26] Cunningham, who was an advocate of routine dental examinations, had also expressed the view that 'it is our duty as well our right to agitate for the due recognition of preventive and remedial dentistry as an essential part of state medicine and public hygiene'.[27]

Miller, writing in 1907, argued that the dental profession must aspire to secure 'the greatest good for the greatest number of people'. In realization of this aim, he continued, dentistry fulfilled three criteria. First, 'dental science exists not for the dentist but for the people'; second, it must exercise its practices over everybody and, third, its priority must be prevention and care rather than treatment.[28] Hence it was the discourse of prevention that 'invented' the mouth. Prevention activities, like those of the plague, comprise observing, recording, comparing and monitoring, and it was these that established dentistry and its object as but one of the many institutional sites where disciplinary power was exercised. The public health movement gave rise to a disciplinary project, that of dentistry.

Discipline, in the Foucauldian sense of the word, implies a technique of power which provides procedures for training, coercing, using and thus transforming bodies. There are three interrelated instruments of disciplinary power. *Hierarchical observation*, first, refers to those sites, such as schools and prisons, where individuals can be observed. Such institutions serve as 'laboratories of power' in that they form apparatuses within which observation and training can take place – for example the toothbrush drill in the school. In 1910 Denison-Pedley advised, 'basins should be provided with water taps over them and unbreakable cups, a toothbrush for every child with its own number and racks where they may be placed with names and numbers on'.[29]

A second instrument of power is *normalizing judgement*, which involves the way in which actions of individuals are compared with others. Actions can be assessed and measured, and through the application of value measures a norm could be established and conformity induced by way of correction. The norm came to form a

81

crucial device for the exercise of discipline and, as Foucault notes:

> The judges of normality are present everywhere. We are in the society of the teacher-judge, the doctor-judge, the educator-judge, the 'social worker'-judge; it is on them that the universal reign of the normative is based; and each individual, wherever he may find himself, subjects to it his [sic] body, his gestures, his behaviour, his aptitudes, his achievements.[30]

To this list of judges, we can legitimately add the dentist judge.

The third instrument of discipline, which combines both hierarchical observation and normalizing judgement, is the most important. It is the *examination*. The examination, Foucault writes, permits 'the subjection of those who are perceived as objects and the objectification of those who are subjected . . . in this slender technique are to be found a whole domain of knowledge, a whole type of power'.[31]

The examination linked the formation of knowledge to the exercise of power. Foucault set out three aspects of the examination that achieved this association between power and knowledge. First, 'the examination transformed the economy of visibility into the exercise of power'.[32] The principle of compulsory visibility assures that power is exercised over all subjects, and so ensures a knowledge of them. The dental examination was crucial to the dental system as it potentially rendered all mouths to inspection; each mouth could be subjected to systematic examination. The regular dental examination placed each patient in a situation of perpetual observation and so facilitated a knowledge of the whole population.

Second, 'the examination also introduces individuality into the field of documentation . . . [and] leaves behind it a whole meticulous archive'.[33] Details of teeth were derived from the patient's mouth by the dentist who then recorded, classified and documented the information for each case. A record of each individual was kept in the dental case notes. Each tooth and each tooth surface – palatal, buccal, mesial, distal, occlusal and lingual – was recorded in meticulous detail on a specially designed card, which would then be fed into a central data system. The epidemiological record cards would in turn serve the process of normalization. Thus the techniques of observation and assessment that dentistry used functioned on two levels: the collective level of the population and the individual level of each patient's mouth. The dental examination formed the juxtaposition of these two levels of discipline.[34] Each mouth could be rendered to detailed scrutiny, every six months and, if the patient's mouth and teeth were such that they did not conform to the dental norm, they could be corrected. This might involve intervention; for example, the dentist putting amalgam in the carious tooth, or training in the correct way in which to hold a toothbrush, or by way of counselling in dietary habits. Indeed, such activities are the very stuff of disciplinary power. Thus the techniques of writing within the examination constitute each individual's mouth with teeth as a both describable and analysable object and create a comparative system that make possible the measurement of overall phenomena.

The third feature is that 'the examination, surrounded by all its documentary techniques, makes each individual a "case" '.[35] Within each dental surgery, the dentist would keep a set of record cards about each of their patients. Each patient who enters the surgery becomes a 'case' within the dental system. The features of each case, which include age, sex, address, as well as details of teeth structure and cleanliness, are kept, so that each individual can be described, judged, measured and compared with others.

DIFFERENT MOUTHS IN DIFFERENT SPACES

There is a relation between what is seen in the examination and what is described, that is, there is a 'correlation between the visible and the expressible'.[36] It is not a case of what is seen can then be described; rather, what is described can then be seen. Herein we have an essential characteristic of the *gaze*: 'in the clinical gaze', writes Foucault, 'what is manifested is originally what is spoken'.[37] The central postulate of 'modern medicine' was that all that is visible must invariably be expressible, and yet, paradoxically, the opposite was the case in that all that was expressible was visible.[38] 'To describe . . . is to see and to know at the same time, because by saying what one sees, one integrates it spontaneously into knowledge.'[39] Consequently, what is said or, indeed, what activities are carried out, is crucial to the possibility of valid knowledge about things. There is, in fact, an alliance between words and things. Thus, what is significant about what is said, is not who said what, or the extent to which such statements represent the speaker's thoughts, or even the prevalence of such statements, but it is the fact that once certain things have been said they are 'thereafter endlessly accessible to new discourses and open to the task of transforming them'.[40]

In the nineteenth century the policing of bodies and the disease of epidemics gave rise to a 'ceaselessly supervised environment'[41] and the scrutiny of bodies in the domain of the hospital. These activities established the pathological phenomenon that we know as pathological anatomy, wherein 'the illness is articulated exactly on the body, and its logical distribution is carried out at once in terms of anatomical masses'.[42] Foucault argues that to locate disease and illness within the anatomy, however, is a temporary thing and that 'there have been, and will be, other distributions of illness'.[43]

Since the nineteenth century there has been a shift in the localization of disease and illness from the pathological to the psychological and the social.[44] This is not so much to say that the pathological has been displaced but rather that it has been superimposed. The origin of truth, that is the attention of the gaze, has been deflected from the pathological lesion to the mind and more recently to the characteristics of the social space in which the body resides. To return to our example of dentistry: the disciplinary techniques used by dentists to generate healthy mouths were, like the mouth itself, contextually specific. Dental discourse has changed since the nineteenth century when the dental object was first invented. Indeed, since that time the transformations that have occurred within the discourse of dentistry have created new dental objects; they have invented new mouths. The implementation of dental programmes and the exercise of disciplinary techniques associated with dentistry are inextricably related to the formation of dental knowledge. This is what is meant by power/knowledge; there is a correlative relation between what is knowable or thinkable and the techniques of dental disciplinary power.

These transformations of dental discourse might best be understood in terms of varying spatializations in which the mouth and teeth came to be located. The Foucauldian notion of spatialization implies the space of the configuration of the disease and the space of the location of illness.[45] Put simply, as the dental gaze has shifted, so too, has its object of concern. Contrary to traditional accounts of dentistry, the development of the profession has not involved a progressive accumulation of the knowledge of the pre-existent mouth, rather there have been a number of identifiable shifts in dental discourse which have transformed dentistry's very object of study. That is, there is a correlative relation between the different techniques of dentistry and the constitution of mouths.

A more thorough analysis of dentistry has revealed that the spatializations associated with dental activities have attained differential privileges at different times.[46] These are illustrated in Table 1, which sets out dental disciplinary techniques at both the collective and individual levels, the spatializations associated with these techniques and the objects that were invented in those spaces. The rows represent different historical contexts: row 1 refers to the turn of the twentieth century; 2 to the interwar years and 3 to the period from the 1950s to the present day.

Table 1 Disciplinary techniques and dental objects

| | Techniques | | Space | Object |
	(Population)	*(Individual)*		
1	Numerical data on teeth	Visual inspection	Physical	Mouth/Teeth
2	Epidemiological data	Listening/speaking	Psychological	Mind/Mouth Complex
3	Survey of attitudes, beliefs and circumstances	Supporting/ negotiating	Social	Subjective Person

In the late nineteenth and early twentieth centuries the mouth and teeth were located in a *physical space*. The mouth, as we have seen, had been discovered in the context of the public health discourse, which had focused on the environment and hygiene, and was subjected to monitoring and observation by way of, for example, dental check-ups and toothbrush drills. Such disciplinary techniques carried out in the dental surgery and the school confirmed the mouth and the dental patient as a physical entity. For example, dental health education at that time aimed to alter the actions of a passive body. Education was about the inculcation of habits and routines that would impose order and would ensure the sanitation of the socio-physical space. The body was a malleable entity and if it underwent adequate training, could be so fashioned that in conjunction with other bodies it would carry out habitual and uniform actions.

The key to such training, it was argued, was to start young because, if habits were correctly taught, the child would 'become so thoroughly habituated to those health habits that omission would cause discomfort'.[47] Tooth brushing was one such health habit. Children were taught in meticulous detail how to use the toothbrush in their mouths. The finite details of tooth brushing were, and still are, defined and refined. Turner, for example, articulated the following method:

> With the bristles of the brush pointing upward and the end of the thumb on the back of the handle, brush the roof of the mouth and the inside of the gums and surfaces of the teeth with a fast in-out-stroke, reaching back on the gums as far as you can go. Go back and forth across the roof of the mouth with this in-out-stroke at least four times. Hold the handle of the toothbrush in your fist with the thumb lying across the back of the handle and brush the gums and teeth with an in-out-stroke, using chiefly the tuft end or the toe of the brush. Reach back in the mouth on the gums below the last tooth on both sides and brush with a fast, light, in-and-out stroke.[48]

During the interwar years there was a shift from the purely anatomical to a *psychological space*. The dentist could no longer simply train the physical body because now the patient also possessed a mind. The dentist's object was affected by psycho-physiologically based emotions: wants, fears and drives. This is not to say that dentistry's object had, at this time, been established as a person in possession of an independent mind who was capable of making their own decisions and interpretations. This was not to occur until much later. The patient's mind was only used by the dentist to ensure cooperation. As Stedman wrote in 1930,

> for the dentist it is particularly necessary that his [sic] method of going about his work, his choice of subjects of conversation, and the line of treatment he adopts, shall be appropriate to the mentality of the patient. To this end a knowledge of psychological theory cannot but be of service.[49]

At this time a complex relationship was established between the mind and the mouth. The techniques adopted for the education of the patient or, for example, the control of pain, and the methods used for overcoming fear were not only about refining and perfecting physical or technical methods, they were also those which were associated with and attuned to the patient's mental orientation. The dental object was not just a physical entity which could be sculptured, but it was also a complex organism, the actions of which were determined by instincts, emotions, drives and feelings.

Within our final spatialization the dental objects of the mouth and teeth have a social dimension. Dental decay, for example, now serves as a mirror to social circumstances.[50] Pain does not necessarily have its origins in anatomical changes; idiopathic pains, for instance, are to be found in certain social groups.[51] Dental health education is not just about telling, but must be enabling, providing people with supportive environments and helping them to be active in their given social circumstances. Dentistry's object is now located in a multi-dimensional *social space*. Patients' subjective accounts, their experiences and their ideas about their mouths and teeth are now fundamental to dental knowledge and are fabricated through the techniques of counselling, the survey and qualitative social research.[52] Today, the dental gaze rests not upon that inert object of the mouth; rather, the mouth simply provides a starting point for a much broader gaze which encompasses people's lives, their experiences and their social circumstances.

At this point we can turn to the third and final strand of this chapter. A question raised above was: how was it possible for the sociologist to be part of the dental discourse? The answer now seems evident. The concerns of dentistry – disease, dental pain, fear of dentistry and effective dental health education – today have their origins not only in the structure of the mouth, or in the substances in the environment, or in the mixing of physical bodies, but also in social relationships and people's social contexts. Today the exercise of power and the correlative formation of knowledge involves the exploration of that social space. As certain things have been identified, the means are devised to reveal their origin. Once things are revealed, they are at the same time hidden. During the nineteenth century this pertained to the pathological anatomy, today, however, it also implies social circumstances. In relation to the mouth and teeth, once the patient's views have been acknowledged to be important the task of the dentist is to refine the means by which such knowledge can be accessed.

Knowledge *develops* in accordance with a whole interplay of *envelopes*; the hidden element takes on the form and rhythm of the hidden content, which means that, like a *veil*, it is *transparent* . . . The individual senses lie in wait through these envelopes, try to circumvent them or lift them up; their lively curiosity invents innumerable means, including even making shameless use of the sense of shame (witness the stethoscope).[53]

It is here that the sociologist can be of assistance, just as in the inter-war years the psychologist became an important participant in the dental quest for 'truth'.

CONCLUSION

We have seen that dental knowledge and the activities of the dental profession have not occurred independently of the dental object. A range of mouths have been realized within the discourses of dentistry. While dental discipline resides in the school and in the home,[54] it is the dental examination that has remained the prime site of dental power, although, as we have seen, the techniques employed within it have changed. The words mouth and teeth have remained but their meanings have been shifted within their physical, psychological and social spatial locations. The mouth with teeth is not a pre-existent entity but an object that has been realized through the discourse of dentistry.

NOTES

1 This chapter summarizes arguments dealt with at greater length in S. Nettleton, *Power, Pain and Dentistry*, Milton Keynes, Open University Press, 1992.
2 See for example D. Locker, *An Introduction to Behavioural Science and Dentistry*, London, Routledge, 1989.
3 See for example B. R. Townend, 'The beginnings of dentistry', *British Dental Journal*, 63, 1937; D. Richards, 'Dentistry in England in the 1840s: the first indications of a movement towards professionalisation', *Medical History*, 12, 1968; and E. G. Forbes, 'The professionalisation of dentistry in the United Kingdom, *Medical History*, 29, 1985.
4 Richards, 'Dentistry in England', p. 138.
5 L. Lindsay, 'Notes on the history of dentistry in England up to the beginning of the nineteenth century', presented to the Conference on the History of Medicine, Geneva, 1925, reprinted by the British Dental Association, p. 268.
6 For example, J. L. Hardwick, 'The incidence and distribution of caries throughout the ages in relation to the Englishman's diet', *British Dental Journal*, 108, 1960, pp. 11–12; C. Hillman, 'Dental practices before 1855: the predisposing, enabling and limiting factors', presented to the Lindsay Club in June 1985, copy kept by the British Dental Association; S. W. Mintz, *Sweetness and Power: The Place of Sugar in Modern History*, New York: Viking Press, 1985; and A. Quick, A. Sheiham and H. Sheiham, *Sweet Nothings: The Information the Public Receive about Sugar*, London, Health Education Council, 1985.
7 R. A. Cohen, 'British dentists and dentistry in the first half of the

nineteenth century', reprinted from the *Birmingham Medical Review* by the British Dental Association, 1949, p. 3.

8 J. Lewin-Payne, 'Milestones in the history of British dentistry, 1855–1860, 1877–1880, 1919 and after', *British Dental Journal* 45, 1924, p. 137.

9 A. Hill, *The History of the Reform Movement in the Dental Profession during the Last Twenty Years*, London, Trubner, 1877, p. 356.

10 Richards, 'Dentistry in England', p. 137.

11 G. Dussault, *The Professionalisation of Dentistry in Britain: A Study of Occupational Strategies 1900–1957* London, unpublished Ph.D. thesis, 1981.

12 G. V. Larkin, 'Professionalisation, dentistry and public health', *Social Science and Medicine*, 14A, 1980, pp. 223–9.

13 M. Foucault, *Discipline and Punish: The Birth of the Prison*, Harmondsworth, Penguin, 1979.

14 Foucault, *Discipline and Punish*, pp. 197–8.

15 See for example G. Newman, *Annual Report of the Chief Medical Officer of the Board of Education 1910*, London, HMSO.

16 M. Foucault, *The Birth of the Clinic: An Archaeology of Medical Perception*, London, Tavistock, 1973, p. 17.

17 C. S. Tomes, *A System of Dental Surgery*, London, Churchill, 1887, p. 258.

18 Ibid.

19 W. D. Miller, *The Micro-Organisms of the Mouth*, Philadelphia, S. S. White, 1890, p. 151.

20 Tomes, *System of Dental Surgery*, p. 286.

21 M. F. Boyd, *Practical Preventive Medicine*, London, W. B. Saunders, 1920, p. 29.

22 Newman, *Annual Report*, p. 15.

23 T. P. Hyatt, *The Teeth and their Care*, New York, King Press, 1906, p. 35.

24 R. Denison-Pedley, *The Care of Teeth during School Life*, London, Churchill, 1910, p. 4.

25 As noted in G. Newman's Chief Medical Officer's report, 1910.

26 H. J. Pickering, 'The condition of school children's teeth: its results and suggested remedies', *British Dental Journal*, 21, 1900, p. 625.

27 J. Cunningham, 'On the dental aspects of public health' in *Transactions of the British Dental Association*, London, John Bale & Sons, 1888, p. 95.

28 W. D. Miller, 'The education of the dentist', *British Dental Association*, 28, 1907.

29 Denison-Pedley, *The Care of Teeth*, p. 12.

30 Foucault, *Discipline and Punish*, p. 304.

31 Ibid., pp. 184–5.

32 Ibid., pp. 187.

33 Ibid., p. 189.

34 Although Foucault is not explicit about the procedures of disciplinary power in *The Birth of the Clinic*, he does draw attention to the juxtaposition of what he calls 'immediate level' observations and 'higher level' (collective) observations and the 'ceaseless movement between these two levels'. He states:

What defines the act of medical knowledge in its concrete form is not, therefore the encounter between doctor and patient, nor is it the confrontation of a body of knowledge and a perception; it is the systematic intersection of two series of information, each homogeneous but alien to each other – two series that embrace an infinite set of separate events, but whose intersection reveals, in its isoluble dependence, the *individual fact*.

(p. 30; emphasis in original)

35 Foucault, *Discipline and Punish*, p. 191.
36 Foucault, *Birth of the Clinic*, p. 113.
37 Ibid., p. 108.
38 Ibid., p. 115.
39 Ibid., p. 114.
40 Ibid., p. xix.
41 Ibid., p. 32.
42 Ibid., p. 4.
43 Ibid., p. 3.
44 See also W. R. Arney and B. J. Bergen, *Medicine and the Management of Living: Taming the Last Great Beast*, London, University of Chicago Press, 1984, for an illustration of this.
45 Foucault, *Birth of the Clinic*, p. 4.
46 For more detail see Nettleton, *Power, Pain and Dentistry*.
47 G. S. Millbery, 'Contribution of the dentist to health education', *Journal of the American Dental Association*, 11, 1924, p. 552.
48 C. E. Turner, *Hygiene, Dental and General*, St Louis, C. V. Mosby, 1921, p. 288.
49 H. Stedman, 'The psychology of children in relation to dental practice', *British Dental Journal*, 51, 1930, p. 1164.
50 See for example A. S. Blinkhorn, 'The caries experience and dietary habits of Edinburgh nursery school children', *British Dental Journal*, 152, 1982; C. Carmichael et al., 'The relationship between social class and caries experience in five-year-old children in Newcastle and Northumberland after twelve years of fluoridation', *Community Dental Health*, 1, 1984.
51 As described by C. Feinmann, 'Psychogenic facial pain: presentation', *Journal of Psychosomatic Research*, 27, 1983, pp. 403–10.
52 See for example S. Nettleton, 'Understanding dental health beliefs: an introduction to ethnography', *British Dental Journal*, 161, 1986, pp. 145–7. The editorial of this same issue drew readers' attention to the paper saying that

it calls on a sociological research method, ethnography, which is described as the study of individuals' perceptions, beliefs and actions within the context of their daily lives. It behoves us all to read this short paper carefully, for it may contain the secret that will enable us to attract even the most reluctant person to seek regular dental care.

(p. 121)

53 Foucault, *Birth of the Clinic*, p. 166.
54 S. Nettleton, 'Wisdom, diligence and teeth: discursive practices and the creation of mothers', *Sociology of Health and Illness*, 13, 1991.

6

POWER AND HUMANITY, OR FOUCAULT AMONG THE HISTORIANS

Randall McGowen

Though Foucault wrote about the past, he declined to call himself a historian – he tended to speak of himself as an archaeologist, notably of course in *The Archaeology of Knowledge*, and historians have generally taken him at his word. *Madness and Civilization* has been particularly vilified by Anglo-American historians, ostensibly for its empirical failures; but most of Foucault's writings have been accused of playing fast and loose with the evidence, or rather of dogmatizing in contempt of the data. It is debatable whether Foucault believed that historians had got the past wrong, or whether he was attempting to create a form of truth about the past that circumvented conventional history, on the grounds that it was a misconceived discourse.

Randall McGowen investigates the charges historians have levelled against Foucault. He demonstrates that the common barrage of accusations – that Foucault radically oversimplifies, fails to note exceptions, or is selective in his use of evidence – tends to fall wide of the mark. But a deeper critique of Foucault's reading of history warrants serious discussion. Was Foucault a 'Whig in reverse'? That is, did he, with the benefit of hindsight, embrace a conspiracy theory in which certain impersonal or depersonalized forces were ceaselessly and malignly extending their clutches? If Whiggism sees history as the story of rationality, freedom and progress, did Foucault see history as the growth of rationality, confinement and control? And, perversely perhaps, if Foucault were to be said to be offering a vision of history as the triumph of evil forces, does that entail his denying agency even to the groups that star in traditional demonologies – kings, popes, the ruling class, Freemasons, Jews or whoever? McGowen's careful account shows that these would be tendentious readings of Foucault. Foucault's 'pessimism' stems from a realistic appreciation of the fact that change in history never springs from gratuitous acts of good: all change has its reasons, and all modes of rationality involve structures of power. Foucault's essential insight lies in exposing the mythology underlying Whiggish, liberal or even Marxist assumptions that social development can culminate in the truly free and independent individual. This is a demonstration which has important implications for the history of insanity, medicine and the body.

As an author who has exerted an immense influence over the direction of recent scholarship, Michel Foucault has been a prophet little honoured among historians. Yet it is difficult to find a provocative historical debate that has not been touched by his investigations, whether in the case of madness, medicine, the prison, sexuality, or the nature of modern power. Despite this obvious debt, Foucault's name is usually greeted with scorn and hostility by practising historians. In part, the Anglo-American tradition of historical scholarship has always been sceptical of theory. But Foucault arouses passions far more intense than this customary suspicion would explain. The outraged cries of historians only confirm his unerring ability to expose particular values and assumptions that are foundational for historical practice today. The issue is not merely one of method; it concerns the question of humanity, of who we are as historians and of the way in which we describe our relation to people in the past.

Allan Megill, in characterizing the relationship between Foucault and the discipline of history, adopts a familiar story of the tension between a radical thinker and the settled practices of 'normal' scholarship. In his account, the gulf separating the two is unbridgeable. Yet Megill recognizes the influence Foucault has exercised and offers an ingenious way of finessing the contest. 'Though Foucault is solitary', Megill writes, 'he has none the less become part of a collective machinery of research, reflection, and argument. Though he is not *of* the discipline, he is important *to* it.'[1] Megill presents a more sophisticated version of an older argument that history benefits from the theories of imaginative thinkers who blaze a new path, sending up sparks and starting wild fires. The historians follow in their wake, limiting the conflagration and bringing order to the newly cleared land. This account is true to the profession's sense that there is danger as well as glamour in the practices of original thinkers, while routine history is safe and sane. The trouble with such accounts is that they deflect the force of the criticism implied in Foucault's work. In drawing the line between disciplinary history and unorthodox speculation so decisively, Megill has regulated the encounter. Yet the issue is not so easily decided. Foucault, like Marx or Weber, produced historical narratives. They all wrote history, however uncomfortable such a claim may make historians trying to evaluate their work. They did something more than history, too, but that recognition cannot be used summarily to discount the historical activity in which whey engaged. The confrontation with such thinkers must always be dangerous for historians, or else the profession is merely policing its own boundaries.

Foucault, in some of his more provocative remarks, contributes to the atmosphere of mutual suspicion. He denies being a historian even as he admits that his studies are 'of "history" by reason of the domain they deal with and the references they appeal to'.[2] He describes his investigations as 'philosophical fragments put to work in a historical field of problems'.[3] But while he struggles against disciplinary history and the constraints imposed by its methods and rules, he appeals to a principle that sounds more like what a historian than a philosopher would say. 'I try', he says, 'to historicize to the utmost in order to leave as little space as possible to the transcendental.'[4] Historians tend to make such a claim against theorists, but seldom has it been pursued with such meticulous thoroughness. And at the same time it has become part of a radical strategy for questioning the present. 'To give some assistance', Foucault declares in explaining his wider project,

> in wearing away certain self-evidences and commonplaces about madness, normality, illness, crime and punishment; to bring it about, together with many others, that certain phrases can no longer be spoken so lightly, certain acts no longer, or at least no longer so unhesitantly, performed; to contribute to changing certain things in people's ways of perceiving sensibility and thresholds of tolerance – I hardly feel capable of attempting more than that.[5]

We do not usually associate Foucault's name with modest enterprises, but he frequently used such language to describe his own activity, an activity that was deeply involved with historical materials and narratives.

Why, then, have historians reacted with such intensity to his work? He has been criticized for his use of evidence, for the seeming obscurity of his style, for his popularity and partisanship. But many other historians have been attacked for some or all of these reasons. Foucault has at times been disarmingly frank when acknowledging the limits of his work and the changes of direction in his research. Historians have not been swayed by such admissions. They scent something else in Foucault's thought. The most serious and frequent charges concern his discussions of power and humanity. Both his method and his conclusions produce much anxiety surrounding these themes. On the one hand Foucault is charged with employing a naively reductionist and functionalist notion of power to explain the

rise and operation of a range of institutions. Historians have complained that this conception of power is too monolithic and unrelent-
ing. In discovering what appears to be the same power behind every
policy or practice, in diminishing the difference between repression
and opposition, Foucault seems to allow no space for the operation of
human agency. He even undercuts the possibility of the kind of
radical criticism he tries to practise. This analysis of power leads
directly to the second and more serious charge levelled against
Foucault, that he is an anti-humanist. Humans in his accounts
become no more than victims of an ever-expanding power, at most
targets for manipulation and repression. But Foucault is not simply a
methodological anti-humanist. What particularly disturbs historians
is that Foucault criticizes the efforts made over the last several
centuries to improve the human situation. Indeed, they read Foucault
to say that it was exactly those efforts made to 'liberate' humanity and
to alleviate suffering that have advanced the programme of domination. They can find in his work no distinction between actions done to
hurt and to help humanity. The most sweeping charge is that he is a
symptom of the erosion of belief in justice, reason and charity that
threatens the survival of humane and democratic society.

Much of the criticism of Foucault has centred upon his discussion
of power. His preoccupation seems at times so peculiar and obsessive,
so to defy common sense, that it cannot be taken seriously. Yet he
could reply that it is we who are obsessed with power. He is interested
in our representations of power, the metaphors we use to describe it,
the narratives we tell of struggling against and overcoming it. In
particular he writes about the manner in which we imagine a subject,
who seeks to liberate the truth of her or his identity or desire from the
grip of power. These stories are some of the most important ways we
define individuals and their relations to society. In the familiar
accounts we find power portrayed as violent and repressive, coercive
and destructive. It seeks to control and repress. And in the modern
world it has found its fullest and most negative form in the increasingly centralized power of the state. Campaigns are frequently
mounted against the repressive power of the state or society. Successes
are celebrated when the state is forced to roll back some control or
circumscribe its own activity. These episodes reinforce our conviction
that power is evil, that it can be shut off, and that the most valued
human attributes and relationships occur outside of power. Modern
consciousness has arisen within a particular thematics of power and
liberation.

In no sense does Foucault simply reject the terms of this narrative, but he seeks to explore its consequences. He is suspicious of power and sometimes writes of it in extraordinarily negative terms. This has led some of his critics to read his portrayal of power as employing the familiar perspective that treats power as negative. Yet even these authors find something unsettling about Foucault's approach to the issue. He seems to carry it too far. Power is suddenly discovered everywhere. It has invaded even those points where we ground resistance and in whose name we fight. Power seems to have rendered humanity impossible. Many historians view Foucault as a particularly subtle exponent of the 'social control' school of history. He finds reform, too, suspect; he discovers a broader programme of control at the heart of the reform campaigns. But Foucault seems intent upon compounding the sinister interpretation offered by earlier representatives of this approach. They at least offered a comprehensible story which placed class interest at the heart of the historical process. However simplistic their accounts, they excited anger and produced demands for change. Foucault's history of the prison seems to foster only confusion, paranoia, and despair. The bleakness of *Discipline and Punish* has led to the charge that Foucault merely produces a 'reverse Whiggism', giving us, instead of a tale of progress, a narrative of ever more total subjection. In this work, power seems to expand without human agency; it serves no interest but its own internal logic. Since every move only more securely implanted power, his history of the prison offers no evidence of resistance to its advance. Each reform only reveals the clever operation of power to deepen and entrench its hold. Historians have felt confident in dismissing an account that appears to repeat endlessly the story of repression.

Like the charge of anti-humanism, this account of Foucault's description of the prison is not simply mistaken. Foucault does find power operating in ways and through reforms that traditional historical accounts have represented differently. But he does far more than expand the usual terms of 'social control' history. He is also suspicious of our familiar descriptions of the operation of power. These descriptions, in the words of Jana Sawicki, postulate that 'power is possessed', that it 'flows from a centralized source', and that it is 'primarily repressive'. Foucault, on the other hand, argues that 'power is exercised rather than possessed', that it is 'not primarily repressive, but productive', and can be 'analysed as coming from the bottom up'.[6] The analysis of power, Foucault argues, has been handicapped by the continuing fascination with the moments of violence and repression. Power is associated with what is distasteful and obnoxious. Foucault responds that 'the interdiction, the refusal, the prohibition, far from being the essential forms of power, are only its limits, power in its frustrated or extreme forms. The relations of power are, above all, productive'.[7] Power is a field within which relationships are constituted. 'When I speak of power relations', he said in an interview,

> I am not referring to Power – with a capital P – dominating and imposing its rationality upon the totality of the social body. In fact, there are power relations. They are multiple; they have different forms, they can be in play in family relations, or within an institution, or an administration . . . It is a field of analysis and not at all a reference to any unique instance.[8]

In proposing these assumptions, Foucault is trying to distance himself from an older discussion of power. But in doing so, he is not trying to construct a new theory of power. Such an enterprise would be difficult if not impossible. Totalizing theories have proved a 'hindrance to research'. Instead he offers us an 'analytics' of power. He practises a kind of 'local criticism'.[9] Foucault seeks to multiply our ways of talking about power, to keep the concept in play, to avoid being frozen in one position or another. His is a strategy marked by small reversals and modest displacements, although he never loses sight of the whole field.

The particular targets of Foucault's thought are the institutions, practices, and names that are accepted as natural. 'All of my analyses', he has said, 'are against the idea of universal necessities in human existence. They show the arbitrariness of institutions.'[10] It is the hold of particular ideas upon our minds that concerns him as much as the controls placed upon our bodies, even as he argues that the two are intimately related. 'In fact', he writes, 'power produces, it produces reality; it produces domains of objects and rituals of truth.'[11] Foucault takes as his subject the practices, the institutions and the knowledges that fill our world with taken-for-granted objects and concerns. 'We have, then', he explains,

> power structures, fairly closely related institutional forms – psychiatric confinement, medical hospitalization – that are bound up with different forms of knowledge, between which it is possible to draw up a system of relations based not on cause and effect, still less on identity, but on conditions.[12]

For Foucault the central question is always: what permits some things to be said and not others. By this he does not simply mean what pre-conceptions shape our knowledge, but what existing power arrange-ments constitute the conditions under which something can be said. This strategy contains Foucault's answer to those who have said that his discussion of the prison bears little relationship to the actual history of the institution, to either the halting and problematic character of its creation or the experience of those confined. He wants to explore the conditions that permitted the concept of the 'criminal' to arise, as well as track the ways in which this notion circulated through the debates about what should be done with this figure. The prison and its experts produce the reality of the offender who in turn anchors both the knowledge and the institution. Eventually all of society is swept up in these changed relations as the discourse of criminality spawns a welfare apparatus dedicated to surveying the community for the slightest traces of incipient deviancy.

The interpretations of his work offered by his critics fail to register the subtlety of Foucault's own project. They have proved unwilling to follow him in his careful exploration of power. It is ironic that the very model of repressive power that Foucault opposes has become the model he is accused of employing. Since his work is read into the 'social control' controversy, only particular aspects of his investiga-tion register while the central thrust of his argument is entirely missed. This misreading of Foucault thus becomes one more testi-mony to the capacity of a particular discourse about power to sustain a sense of reality. He began by setting aside the usual perspective from which we approach power, that of the autonomous subject. When his critics respond with anguish at this measure, but interpret it as a mistake, by their complaints they symptomatically lend support to Foucault's argument that conceptions of freedom and human agency are produced in relation to a particular conception of power. Foucault's investigations arouse such anxiety because the security of our older notion of freedom is imperilled.

What has made this investigation so disconcerting is that Foucault discovers power operating in places where we did not expect it and in forms that had escaped our observation. It is less the face of power that disturbs us than the way in which he has robbed us of certain comforting conclusions about humanity. He discloses the subtle ways in which a yearning to be outside power has been produced by a particular regime whose operation is obscured as a result of that desire. In addition, it confuses us about the power that we possess.

His criticism involves a painful disenchantment of the world as we learn that there is no one moment when power is overthrown and that the subject is never merely the innocent victim of power. But in offering these conclusions, Foucault is trying to open up different modes of criticism and alternative models of resistance. His theory strips us of familiar weapons but also empowers us in other ways. He is raising objections to the way in which we describe human agency and the role we assign to ideas in shaping historical events.

Foucault employed these more general insights about the nature of power in a series of investigations into the forms of power that emerged in Europe between the sixteenth and the nineteenth centuries. These studies are detailed and limited. 'I have not', he says in answer to critics of his prison book, 'gone into detail on *all* kinds of power exercised in the eighteenth century. Instead, I have examined, in a certain number of model eighteenth-century institutions, the forms of power that were exercised and how they were put into play.'[13] Still, the outlines of a more general argument are clear. The political struggles of the seventeenth century and the Enlightenment fostered notions of sovereignty and individual rights, employing the language of laws, rules and popular will to describe the freedom of the citizen in society. But these centuries also saw 'the production of an important phenomenon, the emergence, or rather the invention, of a new mechanism of power possessed of highly specific procedural techniques, completely novel instruments, quite different apparatuses'. While the principles of freedom were articulated in a struggle against the figure of the monarch, new principles and practices of power developed that were opaque to the discourse of rights. The prison was an institution that illustrated the change with peculiar directness. 'Power', writes Foucault, 'is no longer substantially identified with an individual who possesses or exercises it by right of birth; it becomes a machinery that no one owns.'[14] Modern power has disappeared from view, not because we are unaware of its effects, but because we continue to expect illegitimate power to assume a particular form, that of the monarch or the execution. What such formulations ignore is that the humanitarian campaign to reform the prison aimed 'not to punish less, but to punish better'.[15]

Foucault notes that these new modalities of power tend to operate at two extremes, on the one hand by individualizing and on the other by treating populations as a whole. He has developed several different approaches to tracing out this power. For instance, he read widely in the manuals concerned with the 'police' of populations that appeared in the eighteenth century. 'The police', he explains, 'become the very *type* of rationality for the government of the whole territory.'[16] Governments were no longer content with mere obedience; they desired a large and productive population. They became concerned to promote the health of the people, less from any particular concern for humanity than from a regard for the strength of the state. This change of focus entailed a transformation of governmental power which appears 'no longer in the form of control by repression but that of control by stimulation'.[17] In these developments Foucault found the inauguration of 'power techniques oriented towards individuals and intended to rule them in a continuous and permanent way'. A series of state and private initiatives took as their target new areas of concern: 'what the police sees to is a live, active, productive man.'[18]

However, Foucault cautions against regarding the state as the primary focus of these changes. Modern regimes operate less at the command of a central agency than through a 'micropolitics' at the extremities. There is no controlling hand; instead there are numerous moments of regulation. This power is not opposed to the principle of individualism: on the contrary, it employs and heightens it. 'As power becomes more anonymous and functional,' writes Foucault, 'those on whom it is exercised tend to be more strongly individualized.'[19] The peculiarity of modern power is that it operates by producing the subject, a subject that is both the target of yet other strategies and meticulously contained in the details of the discourse. In this sense those who read Foucault as focusing too much upon the state mistake the main lines of his argument. 'I don't think', he argues,

> that we should consider the 'modern state' as an entity which was developed above individuals, ignoring what they are and even their existence, but on the contrary as a very sophisticated structure, in which individuals can be integrated, under one condition; that this individuality would be shaped in a new form, and submitted to a set of very specific patterns.[20]

The state was not the engine of change even if at times it benefited from the new technologies and disciplines. It was as much subject to the wider processes as it was master of them.

Foucault developed the notion of 'pastoral power' to describe another aspect of this emerging arrangement. The very conjoining of these two words which carry such different connotations implies a shift of tone if not emphasis in his work. 'The care for individual life', Foucault says of eighteenth-century developments, 'is becoming at this moment a duty for the state.'[21] Society increasingly proclaims that the benefit of the individual is its goal, that it acts only to secure this end. Agencies and legislation announce that their concern is to protect and improve life. They take up the health and happiness of the individual as their primary purpose. 'Now it is over life, throughout its unfolding,' writes Foucault, 'that power establishes its domination.' These concerns mark a different 'intensification of the body' from that which could be found in the regimes of torture and execution. Power 'provided itself', he explains, 'with a body to be cared for, protected, cultivated and preserved from the many dangers and contacts, to be isolated from others so that it would retain its differential value'.[22] The traditional pastoral concerns of the clergy became generalized and redirected: 'the word *salvation* takes on different meanings: health, well-being (that is sufficient wealth, standard of living), security, protection against accidents.'[23] These practices gain a hold upon the subject, but not in any way that a model of power as repression can describe. They foster, among other things, a particular cultivation of the self, one that centres upon the quest for security, happiness and pleasure. 'This type of discourse', Foucault suggests,

is in fact a formidable tool of control and power. As always, it uses what people say, feel, and hope for. It exploits their temptation to believe that to be happy, it suffices to cross the threshold of discourse and remove a few prohibitions.[24]

Pastoral power claims the loyalty of the subject precisely because it promises to foster and respect the liberated individual whom it pretends to have discovered. Foucault responds that this subject, who is supposedly the antithesis of power, is inextricably caught up in and moulded by regimes of power.

Perhaps we can now reconsider the objections made by historians to Foucault's account of the prison. The most frequently repeated charge is that he ignores the multiple causes of events, the contingent character of particular historical outcomes and the role of human agency. Those who talked and wrote about reform, as well as the magistrates and members of parliament, never made 'control' their sole concern. The reforms that resulted were often compromises achieved after heated debates and were in no sense foregone conclusions. And in its actual operation the reformed prison was often far removed from the conception in the minds of the reformers. What particularly bothers historians is that this model of power seems to leave no room for humanity, and this in a double sense: as a source of value, and as a programme for promoting the good of others. 'Whereas for Foucault', writes David Garland, one of his most careful critics,

> leniency in punishment is understood as a ruse of power, allowing a more extensive form of control to take hold, for these other accounts it is viewed as a genuine end that was sought after, along with others, for reasons of genuine benevolence and religious conviction . . . The ethical values and compassionate concern that others present as the causes of penal change are, for Foucault, at best the 'incidental music' which accompanies change, at worst, a euphemistic covering device for the new forms of power.[25]

These objections are not simply causal in character; they resonate with other concerns. Garland's use of the word 'genuine', along with his appeals to compassion and benevolence, point to the central issue. What is at stake is a particular model of human action and a particular standard for judging human conduct. Garland implies that if we cannot reduce benevolence to some other force or interest, then we must admit that the actors control their ideas and mean their actions. Even more, we must see in their wrestle with ideas and values the central arena for determining change. Thus, subtly, our attention is shifted from what these debates produced to the question of whether the participants were sincere in their beliefs. We pass over the difficult questions of the extent to which ideas cause anything and of the relation between ideas and intentions. These criticisms presume a model of history in which people mean what they say, that intentions exert control over language, and that the solution to these puzzles lies in the interiority of the subject.

Such criticism misrepresents Foucault's discussion of power. We have already seen that for Foucault there is nothing simple about the description of 'a whole network of relationships of power'.[26] The complex interaction of power, truth and subject in Foucault is never simply the discovery of power behind every phenomenon. Yet Garland is right in noting that Foucault fails to examine intentions and to consider the mental and moral character of individuals. But this is not a 'mistake'; it is part of a strategy. 'My objective', writes Foucault, 'has been to create a history of the different modes by which, in our culture, human beings are made subjects.'[27] Foucault resists the demand that he search for the meaning of penal reform in a wider intellectual context. He does not approach the question of

101

meaning as if it involved a mystery that gave itself up only to those scholars who possess the right attitude or techniques. Foucault reads texts differently; he is not deferential to some deep truth that they might contain. He seizes a document in order to wrestle from it readings that it resists. He respects a concept for the power that it expresses as well as for the truth it claims. The challenge is to unsettle this truth claim by examining the conditions that constitute its naturalness. Foucault deliberately reads along the surface of a text with a seeming naivety that is in fact cunning and relentless. Far from being a reductionist, he resists the easy gesture of reduction. His is a more arduous task of deciphering the operation of power in and through discourse. Foucault is constantly attentive to nuance. He constructs his account with a care and attention to detail that can frustrate the casual reader. There is a necessary relationship in Foucault's work between his general theoretical concerns and the methods he employs to study a specific institution. For example, it is not enough to assert that the penal reformers were driven by a 'genuine benevolence' in their advocacy of more lenient punishment. Foucault asks whether this idea of leniency already figured in some other power configuration. This relationship may not have been acknowledged by the reformers, which is certainly not to say that they were hypocrites. Rather they were blind in some sense, or looked too intently in another direction, and so missed implications and consequences (perhaps the most important) of their proposals.

Humanity was the name given to an expanding number of causes in the nineteenth century. It was a common ideal that tied together a widely dispersed field of activities, everything from schooling the young and assisting the mad to aiding the poor and showing greater kindness to animals. It produced innumerable campaigns, often to the side of more straightforward political contests. Yet these causes invariably extended the scope and scale of state activity. Among other things these movements established a style for formulating social problems and a procedure for dealing with ever more various groups of people. 'Through these different practices,' writes Foucault, 'psychological, medical, penitential, educational – a certain idea or model of humanity was developed, and now this idea of man has become normative, self-evident, and is supposed to be universal.' Social reform produced an ever greater regulation of life precisely by promising increased security and happiness. Historians typically approach such causes as if the central issue involved one of origins and intentions: where did the movement come from? Whose interests did it serve? What class did the humanitarians represent? They seldom question the term 'humanity'; they ask instead whether a group deserves the distinction that goes with a title like that of humanitarian. Foucault sets out to challenge the unspoken consensus that sustains such questions. 'What I am afraid of about humanism', he says, 'is that it presents a certain form of our ethics as a universal model for any kind of freedom.'[28]

Perhaps these issues will come into sharper focus if we try to apply Foucault's scheme to a different kind of humanitarian cause. A campaign that proved of immense if ill-defined significance for nineteenth-century England was the struggle against slavery. Unlike the contests over penal reform or poor relief, this movement worked to secure liberation from an unambiguous form of oppression. This cause had so noble a goal, one so transparently 'right', that historians have approached it with caution. 'Clearly the rise of anti-slavery sentiment', writes David Brion Davis in a book that otherwise seeks to demonstrate the hegemonic function of the cause, 'represented a major advance in the moral consciousness of mankind.'[29] The anti-slavery campaign presents a clear challenge to revisionist historians who are critical of middle-class reform movements. It is easier to write critically of prisons or asylums than it is of the abolition of slavery. Yet these causes were all of a piece. 'About the time that slavery was being transformed', writes Thomas Haskell, 'from a problematical but readily defensible institution into a self-evidently evil and abominable one, new attitudes began to appear on how to deter criminals, relieve the poor, cure the insane, school the young, and deal with primitive peoples.'[30] The anti-slavery movement created a paradigm for these other efforts. It generated a language and a set of symbols that developed in directions few could have anticipated at the outset.[31] It garnered immense prestige and gave birth to an equally powerful mythology. It earned a retrospective popularity and sanctity that scarcely could have been foreseen in the first dark days when the struggle commenced.

Foucault himself never addressed the anti-slavery campaign. He tended to focus upon sources from mainland Europe in general and the French experience in particular. But he devoted much of his research to reform causes, and so it is interesting to see if his perspective can cast light upon a vexing historical debate. In recent years the anti-slavery movement has come in for intense historical investigation. Scholars have brought to the subject a more critical attitude towards nineteenth-century England. Since the abolition of slavery is

103

so undeniably valuable an achievement, it has frustrated some historians that they must credit the middle classes for its success. They have argued instead that while the cause was noble, the English supported it because it served narrower class interests or performed a vital ideological function. In order to support this argument they have insisted upon ever finer distinctions until the terms of the dispute threaten to disappear entirely. The revisionists have been caught in a contradiction between their desire to affirm the humanitarian project and their wish to deny credit for it to those most active in the cause.

Foucault might begin an investigation of the movement by setting aside the types of questions that have troubled recent historians. He would come at the issue more obliquely. In particular, he would take as his central focus the term that both traditional and revisionist historians agree upon, 'humanity'. In a seemingly naive fashion he might ask: what happened when this word was spoken? This campaign is interesting precisely because of its effect upon the perception of power. The discourse of the anti-slavery movement revolved around three figures – the slave, the slave-owner, and the humanitarian. Each of these characters gained definition within the terms of a discussion that was about power, its form and intentions. The abolitionists succeeded in abolishing slavery in the West Indies. But their efforts produced other consequences as well. They contributed to a narrative that defined corrupt power in relation to self-interest, and the cause of humanity as a pure campaign that disclaimed any connection to power.

The slave-owners were defined by the absolute power they possessed. The abolitionists easily identified this power with an older style of tyranny and despotism. This meant first and foremost the control over life and death, but it assumed its particularly graphic form in the shape of the whip. 'The whip is itself', wrote William Wilberforce, 'a dreadful instrument of punishment; and the mode of inflicting that punishment shockingly indecent and degrading.' He returned time and again to this phrasing, complaining of 'the brutal outrage of the cart-whip . . . the indecent, degrading, and merciless punishment of the West Indian whipping.'[32] The excessive character of this power was established in relation to anxieties about particular aspects of the slave's condition. The slave system, according to the reformers, fostered a series of violations, transgressions that would activate humanitarian concern for other groups over the next century. In other words, only particular practices gained visibility as abuses. Most obviously, it perpetrated violence done to the body.

But it also tolerated sexual licence and permitted the destruction of family ties. Owners indulged their vicious passions at the expense of female slaves. Here was a scandal so serious that it could only be suggested in the most circumspect manner. But slavery also disrupted family life by separating husbands from wives, and parents from children. Finally, the slave system neglected the souls of the slaves by failing to instruct them in Christianity. These three concerns constituted the specific indecencies inextricably tied up with the practice of slavery. They amounted to a tyranny such as no human should enjoy over another. But the specific condition that produced this catalogue of abuses was the existence of a power that sacrificed the human body, family, and soul to self-interest. Power founded upon interest was corrupt and corrupting. It made the slave a simple object for the realization of private ambitions and desires. The evils of slavery flowed from an ill-regulated and misdirected power.

The tragic consequence of the slave system, according to the humanitarians, lay in its reduction of the slaves to a condition less than human. When Wilberforce described the regime he talked about the 'terror of the whip', which drove the slaves to work 'like brute animals'. 'Lower than this it is scarcely possible for man to be depressed by man.' These were the effects traced to a sordid power. 'It is idle and insulting', he wrote,

> to talk of improving the condition of these poor beings, as rational and moral agents, while they are treated in a manner which precludes self-government, and annihilates all human motives but such as we impose on a maniac, or on a hardened and incorrigible convict.[33]

The abolitionists insisted that power corrupted by reducing its victims to a less than fully human condition. 'Remember', wrote George Thompson, 'what they might have been, and what they are. They might have been virtuous; but they are deeply sunk in vice. They might have been enlightened; but they are enshrouded in thick darkness.'[34] The slaves could only take on reality in this discourse on the basis of an incapacity and negativity that defined their identity. Their humanity was at best potential.

It followed from this characterization that the slave's situation was described in terms of what the victim's body felt, rather than what the slave thought or said. For this reason, violence loomed large in every statement; it was the language that the reformers heard most clearly. 'Discretionary punishments', a circular of the Abolition Society read, 'are usually inflicted on the naked body with the cart-whip, an instrument of dreadful severity, which cruelly lacerates the flesh of the sufferer.' The Society called upon its readers 'to listen to the cry of the wretched Negro'.[35] But it was an inarticulate cry. Slaves were identified on the basis of their impotence and their suffering, not their labour or their speech. Indeed their weakness came to efface all the other attributes they might have possessed. The humanitarians focused upon the pain, suffering, degradation, and cruelty the slaves endured. In order to raise the slaves up they must first be pictured in the most miserable terms. In their absolute suffering they found a purity that was beyond reproach. But it was a purity earned by being outside of power and the victims of power. The irony was that, as they suffered, they were so degraded by the experience that they might even be unconscious of their plight. The slaves gained standing in this argument on the basis of what they lacked. At the same time there was a truth to their suffering and the goal of eliminating it that seemed to overwhelm all other considerations. Suffering possessed a 'truth' that spoke beyond what the sufferer said about it, spoke through the victim to the one who observed and understood it.

Both the master and the slave shared a deficiency that did not afflict the humanitarians. Each was warped by the regime, became less than human as a result of a particular relationship to power. The slaves lived in a 'low and ignominious condition' that was entirely the consequence of the self-interested tyranny of the master's power. As a result, the slaves could not escape the stain of this situation by their own unaided efforts. They were hardened and brutalized by it. But, surprisingly, so were the slave-owners. Wilberforce claimed that their style of life corrupted them. It supplied them with a temptation to abuse power that no human could resist. The wrong relationship to power changed human nature for the worse, and it did not matter whether one was perpetrator or victim. 'Knowing this fraility of our common nature', Wilberforce wrote, 'and its disposition to abuse absolute power, we ought not to deliver the weaker party altogether into the power of the stronger.' 'In truth,' he continued,

West Indians must be exempt from the ordinary frailties of human nature, if, living continually with those wretched beings, and witnessing their extreme degradation and consequent depravity, they could entertain for the Negroes, in an unimpaired degree, that equitable consideration and that fellow-feeling, which are due from man to man; so as to sympathize properly with them in their sufferings and wrongs, or form a just estimate of their claims to personal rights and moral improvement.[36]

Power distorted one's sensibilities and played upon one's human frailties. It was dangerous as well as immoral to exercise the kind of power that masters possessed.

The position of the humanitarian was defined by a different relationship to power, one which endowed this figure with capabilities and responsibilities quite unlike those that belonged to the slave or master. The critique of the slave regime constructed a counter-image of a benevolent power, one that protected the body, respected family life, fostered sexual morality and saw to the instruction of the soul. This programme was sanctioned by a unique capacity to know others. The humanitarians recognized suffering and were sensitive to it. They knew how to give it voice and act upon it. The plight of the slaves, like the suffering of animals, was inarticulate until understood by the deep sympathy of the humanitarian spirit that translated and interpreted it. 'Think of these things,' argued Thompson, 'and let your zeal be enkindled and your pity excited, that your exertions may henceforth be commensurate with the miseries of these unhappy beings, and your own responsibility.'[37] Indeed, the abolitionists often spoke of themselves as being in the grip of a compulsion to act, so that the act did not spring from their own will but from the need of the people on whose behalf they acted. The impotence of the slave demanded the response of the reformers. The deficiency of the afflicted excited the overflowing humanity of the feeling person. A peculiar relationship of positive and negative existed, where the negative condition of the slave elicited the positive action of the humanitarian in a seemingly smooth and frictionless transition. 'We are bound,' proclaimed an Abolition Society circular, 'without hesitation or delay, to come forward.' When Thomas Fowell Buxton thought to himself of the 'poor slaves', he felt instantly called to his duty. He expressed the obligation in religious terms: 'make me an instrument in thy hands for the relief, and for the elevation of that afflicted people.'[38] But one can read the prayer in other terms as well. The desire to be made an instrument of God was not original, but the direction of the activity marked a new departure. Buxton's hope was to be freed from the burden of self-interest by service to God in the cause of humanity. Such a campaign worked to root out ambition, vanity, and interest. In this fashion the humanitarian, too, was constituted within the discourse of anti-slavery, but as one who employed power benevolently, disavowing self-interest and the desire for power. As the case of the slave-owner demonstrated, power and interest combined to create evil. The humanitarian proposed to sever this link in two ways, by not seeking power for personal ends, and by using power only to realize the interests of the 'other'.

One conspicuous feature of the humanitarian's power and position was the element of self-denial. The focus was insistently placed upon the negative condition of the victim that warranted the ever more strenuous obligation to interfere. There was no limit to the responsibility to help. It permitted the reformers to speak for the slaves, to represent them in a fully human state, since they could not so represent themselves. The humanitarians made of themselves a relay in a philanthropic regime, and the proof of their self-effacement lay in their willingness to serve the good of the other. What they emphasized was the intensity of the feeling and the irresistible nature of the call. Suffering was so pure that it ennobled the cause of those who sought to alleviate it. It provided a commission for those who acted in its name. In contrast to patriarchal charity, which identified power and goodness, humanitarian charity sought to prove its virtue by effacing the connection to power. This model for a new kind of authority and for a novel form of action created a commitment so overpowering that its terms went unexamined. Thus it obscured the process by which this identification was achieved and the cost it might occasion for the victim. The appeal to humanity made it possible to imagine a sympathetic link that leapt across cultural differences. The existence of such a capacity might even be said to demand such exertions in order to establish one's own goodness. But the precondition for such an appeal to be made was the denial of its own power.[39]

The state stood in a peculiar relationship to such movements. Their participants denied traditional political ambitions. They sought instead to prove their disinterest as a measure of their merit. Their campaign involved an effort to move a reluctant government to action. State action was a vital but subordinate instrument unfortunately required in order to realize the humanitarian goals. Yet, ironically, the victory of the abolitionists produced a 'most daring use of state power', as successes in humanitarian struggles often did.[40] The anti-slavery campaign affected the direction and capacity of government even if it was not simply about such power. The state did not intend these effects; it was not 'behind' the humanitarian cause. But it was a beneficiary of its success, and this in several senses. The state became involved in new areas of social life, but it did so in response to a demand that arose outside the political realm and in the name of a cause superior to mere political power.

Now Foucault, as we have seen, would have us take these movements as central to the production of new relationships, identities, and forms of authority. The common themes and strategies they share are best captured in the appeal to 'humanity', an appeal that presents itself as universal in its claims and liberating in its ambitions. What remains striking about this notion of humanity is that while reformers proposed freedom and individual autonomy as their goals, they constantly described an imperfect world in which programmes were needed, actions called for, in order to achieve that individuality and autonomy. The freeing of the slaves was only part of a wider project, one whose ambition was the profound transformation of the individual. Each group that gained recognition achieved this status only when identified with a deficiency that society was required to remedy. When action was taken it was done in the name of helping individuals rather than gaining power over them.

This description of the anti-slavery movement avoids any discussion of whose interest lay behind these changes and any attempt to situate the particular actors who participated in the campaign. It does not involve an exhaustive search for the origins of the movement. This is in order to sharpen other questions, such as what kinds of relationships were produced within the discourse of humanity, and what kinds of policies were demanded and on what terms. It seeks to unsettle the categories that have been accepted as describing the reality of the past. That the humanitarians, in overthrowing one regime, helped to foster the development of other power relations with their own dark consequences should come as no surprise. To point out that the activities of the abolitionists produced other results along with the freeing of the slaves is not to imply any simple judgement of them or their action. It is neither to praise nor to condemn them to say that we must now struggle with the arrangements they helped to inaugurate. What this means in particular is that we must wrestle with the narrative of power they proposed. Their conception of power permitted them to identify their own activity as outside of power, uncontaminated by its corruption, even as they denied power to those who suffered. This description had profound consequences for how they and others understood the operation of the power they possessed. This outcome was not consciously intended, nor was it all part of a hypocritical conspiracy. The abolitionists were not masters of the meaning system in which they participated, nor could they foresee all the effects of their actions.

Foucault has tried to make us aware of what we have long known but still uncomfortably confront, that one of the most powerful arguments supporting current institutional arrangements is a mood of self-congratulation on what seems to be our self-evident humanity: that prisons are better than the gallows, that free labour is better than slave labour. Foucault would demand of us: what are we doing when we make such claims: who are we to make such statements? Foucault does not set out to overthrow the notion of humanity, but to examine more carefully the way it presents itself. He seeks to expose not only those moments when the rhetoric of humanity leads to self-deception, but when it in fact constitutes 'humanity' as the target of a set of dangerous practices. In this sense, the charge of anti-humanism hits its mark; our story of humanity was meant to be consoling, and Foucault has robbed us of that consolation. Foucault's position is that there is no end of power, no privileged place outside of power even in the most seemingly benevolent relationship. But this also means that even as victims we are not powerless. Rather, the task of politics is vigilance, criticism, and struggle. 'The intellectual's role', Foucault once said,

> is no longer to place himself 'somewhat ahead and to the side' in order to express the stifled truths of the collectivity; rather it is to struggle against the forms of power that transform him into its object and instrument in the sphere of 'knowledge', 'truth', 'consciousness', and 'discourse'.[41]

Historians may well be uncomfortable to have Foucault in their midst, but perhaps one day we will learn to value this discomfort.

NOTES

I would like to thank Tres Pyle and Howard Brick for their comments on this essay.

1 A. Megill, 'The reception of Foucault by historians', *Journal of the History of Ideas*, 48, 1987, p. 134.
2 M. Foucault, *The History of Sexuality 2: The Use of Pleasure*, New York, Pantheon, 1985, p. 9.
3 M. Foucault, 'Questions of method', in G. Burchell, C. Gordon and P. Miller (eds), *The Foucault Effect: Studies in Governmentality*, London, Harvester Wheatsheaf, 1991, p. 74.
4 S. Lotringer (ed.), *Foucault Live: Interviews 1966–84*, New York, Semiotext(e), 1989, p. 79.

5 Foucault, 'Questions', p. 83.
6 J. Sawicki, *Disciplining Foucault: Feminism, Power, and the Body*, New York, Routledge, 1991, pp. 20–1.
7 L. Kritzman (ed.) *Politics, Philosophy, Culture*, New York, Routledge, 1988, p. 118.
8 Foucault, *Politics*, p. 38.
9 M. Foucault, *Power/Knowledge: Selected Interviews and Other Writings, 1972–1977*, New York, Pantheon, 1980, pp. 80–2.
10 M. Foucault, 'Truth, Power, Self: An Interview', in H. Gutman, P. Hutton and L. Martin, *Technologies of the Self*, London, Tavistock Publications, 1988, p. 11.
11 M. Foucault, *Discipline and Punish: The Birth of the Prison*, New York, Pantheon, 1977, p. 82.
12 Kritzman, *Politics*, p. 265.
13 Ibid., p. 39.
14 Foucault, *Power/Knowledge*, pp. 104, 156.
15 Foucault, *Discipline and Punish*, p. 82.
16 Lotringer, *Foucault Live*, p. 260.
17 Foucault, *Power/Knowledge*, p. 57.
18 Kritzman, *Politics*, pp. 60, 79.
19 Foucault, *Discipline and Punish*, p. 193.
20 H. Dreyfus and P. Rabinow (eds), *Michel Foucault: Beyond Structuralism and Hermeneutics*, Chicago, Chicago University Press, 1983, p. 214.
21 Foucault, 'Truth', p. 147.
22 M. Foucault, *The History of Sexuality 1: An Introduction*, New York, Pantheon, 1978, pp. 138, 107, 147, 123.
23 Dreyfus and Rabinow, *Foucault*, pp. 214–15.
24 Lotringer, *Foucault Live*, p. 142.
25 D. Garland, 'Foucault's *Discipline and Punish*: an exposition and critique', *American Bar Foundation Research Journal*, 1986, pp. 870, 877.
26 M. Foucault, 'The ethic of care for the self as a practice for freedom' in J. Bernauer and D. Rasmussen (eds), *The Final Foucault*, Cambridge, Mass., MIT Press, 1983, p. 3.
27 Dreyfus and Rabinow, *Foucault*, p. 208.
28 Foucault, 'Truth', p. 15.
29 D. Brion Davis, *The Problem of Slavery in the Age of Revolution 1770–1823*, Ithaca, Cornell University Press, 1975, p. 455.
30 T. Haskell, 'Capitalism and the origins of the humanitarian sensibility', *American Historical Review*, 92, 1987, p. 339.
31 See for example R. Anstey, *The Atlantic Slave Trade and British Abolition 1760–1810*, New Jersey, Humanities Press, 1975, pp. 411–13; S. Drescher, 'Cart whip and billy roller: anti-slavery and reform symbolism in industrializing Britain', *Journal of Social History*, 15, 1981, pp. 3–24.
32 W. Wilberforce, *An Appeal to the Religion, Justice, and Humanity of the Inhabitants of the British Empire on Behalf of the Negro Slaves in the West Indies*, London, 1823, pp. 13, 35.
33 Wilberforce, *Appeal*, p. 12.
34 Quoted in E. F. Hurwitz, *Politics and the Public Conscience*, New York, Barnes & Noble, 1973, p. 140.

35 Ibid., pp. 114, 116.
36 Wilberforce, *Appeal*, p. 32.
37 Quoted in Hurwitz, *Politics*, p. 140.
38 Ibid., pp. 116, 120.
39 For a slightly different development of this argument, see my 'A powerful sympathy: terror, the prison, and humanitarian reform in early nineteenth-century Britain', *Journal of British Studies*, 25, 1986, pp. 312–34.
40 Quoted in Hurwitz, *Politics*, p. 18.
41 M. Foucault in D. Bouchard (ed.), *Language, Counter-Memory, Practice*, Ithaca, Cornell University Press, 1977, pp. 207–8.

7

BODIES IN SPACE
Foucault's account of disciplinary power

Felix Driver

Preoccupied as they are with the varied components of the constitution of knowledge, Foucault's writings have appealed to sociologists, anthropologists, linguists, historians and, not least, geographers. Indeed, because Foucault was so lastingly interested in comprehending power in terms of the spatial networks and relations that power presupposed and through which it operated, geographers particularly have drawn upon his works. Himself a geographer, Felix Driver here complements David Armstrong's essay by probing the relations between the human body (itself a spatial form defined by bodies of knowledge like medicine) and certain kinds of disciplinary space that confer command over such bodies. The prison is the obvious example, analysed brilliantly in *Discipline and Punish: The Birth of the Prison*.

Foucault's chief instance in that book, the penitentiary, offers a case of carceral power. In his essay, however, Driver builds on Foucault's frequent insistence that power is to be viewed not as negative but as a positive and enabling force or web of relations; hence he examines other forms of institutional space created in the nineteenth century explicitly dedicated to creative uses of control. Reformatories, youth colonies and other kinds of corrective educational establishments offer good illustrations of the more subtle deployment of the remedial and improving social ordering of space.

In thus showing the versatility of disciplinary topographies in administrative hands, Driver, while offering a critique, effectively takes the sting out of the anti-Foucauldian critique of those who would impugn *Discipline and Punish* merely because the ideal-type Benthamite Panopticon there discussed at length was rarely actually implemented. That may have been so, but, as Driver demonstrates in detail, concern for the control potential created by the official ordering of space has been, and remains, high on the agenda of all disciplines, like pedagogy and penology, dealing with large populations in confined spaces – to say nothing of hospitals, medical practices and other, more medical instances of power. Foucauldian insights into the potency of spatial ordering carry a validity that transcends the particular institutions upon which he focused.

FOUCAULT AND THE SPACES OF HISTORY

Amongst academic historians, the work of Michel Foucault has been received with a mixture of indifference, scepticism and downright hostility.[1] A few, to be sure, have been more generous; but in general, Foucault's writings on madness, health, punishment and sexuality have been regarded as beyond the disciplinary pale. Banished from the kingdom of History proper, they have received a warmer welcome amongst philosophers, although professional opinion remains sharply divided. In recent years, debates over modernity and postmodernism have inspired new readings of Foucault's work amongst cultural theorists and geographers, particularly in the United States. Ironically, what they frequently find attractive in Foucault's work is precisely its powerful sense of history; its obsession with discontinuities, practices, concrete details and complex genealogies. If Foucault is now widely seen as a philosopher of modernity, it is important to recall that much of his work was framed by what Peter Dews describes as an 'individual historical vision'.[2] This sense of history sets Foucault apart from other philosophers of his generation; the comparison with Derrida, for example, is instructive. Foucault addresses general questions by analysing specific moments, setting out to create 'philosophical fragments in historical building sites'.[3]

Foucault's sheer enthusiasm for historical documents was plain throughout his writing, in his archaeologies of the human sciences, in his genealogies of power and his studies of the techniques of the self.[4] Foucault's history was a history without nostalgia; there was no longing for a return to a mythical past, no dream of origins, no comforting vision of transcendence. In place of a continuous history, centred around the human subject, he proposed a decentred history, history in a space of dispersion.

> Nothing in man [he insisted], not even his body, is sufficiently stable to serve as the basis for self-recognition or for understanding other men. The traditional devices for constructing a comprehensive view of history and for retracing the past as a patient and continuous development must be systematically dismantled. Necessarily, we must dismiss those tendencies that encourage the consoling play of recognitions.[5]

The Nietzschean rhetoric is perhaps overdone, but the anti-humanist message is clear: how are we to write a history without the transcendental subject? A history, that is, which accounts for the constitution

114

of subjects, as much as of knowledges, discourses and practices, 'without having to make reference to a subject which is either trans-cendental in relation to the field of events or runs in its empty same-ness throughout the course of history'.[6] This suspicion of universals was a theme to which Foucault constantly returned throughout his work. Rather than reducing discourses and practices to simple essences or fundamentals, he wanted to explore their heterogeneity. As he mischievously observed in 1982, 'nothing is fundamental. That is what is interesting in the analysis of society'.[7] Foucault looked to history as a way of challenging the assumption that our conceptions of such things as madness, sexuality, crime and health spring directly and self-evidently from our experiences. Foucault's history dis-concerts; it offers a means of criticizing the present, without the possi-bility of a return to the past.

Foucault's histories do not present us with linear narratives. They are concerned less with the flow of individual intentions, actions and consequences than with discourses, practices and effects. We might characterize many of his historical inquiries as maps rather than stories; a new kind of cartography, to borrow a phrase from Gilles Deleuze.[8] Evidence for such a view may be found throughout Foucault's work, especially in his constant recourse to the language of space; in the emphasis on exclusions and boundaries in *Madness and Civilization*, medical and social spaces in *The Birth of the Clinic* ('This book is about space, about language, and about death; it is about the act of seeing, the gaze')[9], discursive spaces in *The Archaeology of Knowledge*, and diagrams or figures of power in *Discipline and Punish*. Critics differ in their interpretations of Foucault's spatial fixation. Some have argued that Foucault's sensi-tivity to space represents a decisive break from the historicism of much social theory, providing a new model for a postmodern geography. Others contend that Foucault's spatial metaphors were all too often used uncritically.[10] My own argument would be that space was indeed central to Foucault's concerns, although geography was not. This can be demonstrated in several ways. First, I would suggest that Foucault's spatial perspective represents a radical version of historical modes of inquiry, rather than an alternative to them. His genealogies attempt to bring grand narratives of truth and reason back to earth, as it were, grounding them in the realm of bodies, powers and spaces: 'Once knowledge can be analysed in terms of region, domain, implantation, displacement, transposition, one is able to capture the process by which knowledge functions as a form of power.'[11] Second, Foucault's constant use of terms such as *dispositif* (usually translated as 'apparatus') was supposed to highlight relations of connection rather than of causation, simultaneity rather than succession. Power, in Foucault's analysis, does not exist prior to discourses and practices, on some other plane or level; rather, it operates through them. Third, spatial concepts lend themselves to an analysis of power relations in terms of strategic encounters, battles, terrains, colonizations and campaigns. Foucault certainly found these terms useful as metaphors; but their significance was more than metaphorical, because they highlighted the central role of the body, or rather bodies, in power relations. Foucault believed that 'space is fundamental in any exercise of power' mainly because he regarded the control of bodies as fundamental.[12] Fourth, when Foucault wrote about spaces, he often focused on particular institutions – the clinic, the prison, the hospital, the asylum – which help to constitute, or make visible, particular aspects of modern subjectivity. These were the sites within which various forms of knowledge and power were inscribed on bodies and souls. What was perhaps unclear was how these spaces were to be situated within a broader social whole; how the various kinds of spaces were to be related. It has been suggested, for example, that in Foucault's work, 'power and knowledge operate in the space of the body, not of geography'.[13] This is an important point to which I shall return.

In the rest of this chapter, I shall consider aspects of Foucault's account of disciplinary power. It would be misleading to treat Foucault's disparate statements on power as if they made up a coherent and consistent general theory, without recognizing the very different contexts in which they were made. In his books, especially in *Discipline and Punish*, Foucault explored particular aspects of discourses of power in specific settings; in his interviews, on the other hand, he was frequently tempted to express his views on power more freely. In both, he was less concerned with establishing a new theory of power than with challenging those which already existed. As Foucault's writings on power continue to stimulate lively debate, I should emphasize that in what follows I am less concerned with the overall logic, or otherwise, of Foucault's work than with its utility for specific kinds of historical research. (I shall also say little about the normative and ethical dimensions of Foucault's account of power.)[14] With this aim in mind, we might apply to our subject what Foucault himself once rather teasingly said of Nietzsche:

The only valid tribute to thought such as Nietzsche's is precisely to use it, to deform it, to make it groan and protest. And if commentators then say that I am being faithful or unfaithful to Nietzsche, that is of absolutely no interest.[15]

POWER AND THE DISCIPLINARY SOCIETY

It is clear from many of his comments in essays and interviews that Foucault was uneasy about his reputation as a theorist of power. In much of his writing on power, as on other subjects, he was at pains to emphasize the limitations of general theories. The only thing that could be said about power in general, he once remarked, is that it is an open-ended, more or less coordinated 'cluster of relations'.[16] Rather than seeking the essence of power in some simple theoretical formula, Foucault posed apparently more modest questions about *how* power is exercised in particular sites and settings. At the same time, however, Foucault did make some far-reaching criticisms of existing theories of power, and if these did not amount to a coherent alternative, they did at least offer new perspectives on the problem.[17] Instead of portraying power as the property of any particular group or institution, Foucault preferred to describe it as a heterogeneous ensemble of strategies and techniques. He was thus sceptical of any approach which mapped power onto an abstract model of class relations. ('I believe that anything can be deduced from the general phenomenon of the domination of the bourgeois class. What needs to be done is something quite different. One needs to investigate historically, and beginning at the lowest level, how mechanisms of power have been able to function.')[18] Rather than confining his analysis to key institutions such as the state, he emphasized that power took many forms, often at its most effective where it was least visible. ('We must escape from the limited field of juridical sovereignty and state institutions, and instead base our analysis of power on the study of the techniques and tactics of domination.')[19] Finally, rather than seeing power always in negative terms, as prohibitive, Foucault asked how power could function as a positive force, creating, shaping, moulding subjects and subjectivity. ('What makes power hold good . . . is simply the fact that it doesn't only weigh on us as a force that says no, but that it traverses and produces things, it induces pleasure, forms knowledge, produces discourse.')[20] This was the general perspective which inspired Foucault's account of the emergence of modern systems of punishment in *Discipline and Punish*.

In *Discipline and Punish*, Foucault set out to explore the changing rationale and techniques of punishment in modern Europe. His analysis was framed in terms of three distinct 'regimes' of power: the monarchical, the contractual and the carceral. (This approach shared some of the features of Foucault's earlier work on discursive formations in *The Order of Things* and *The Archaeology of Knowledge*, although now he was as interested in the actual techniques of punishment as in their theoretical rationale.) The monarchical regime is exemplified in the opening pages of *Discipline and Punish* by the horrifying spectacle of public torture and execution. The contractual regime is read through the writings of reforming jurists, such as Beccaria, who called for a more efficient and transparent system of criminal justice. The carceral regime is associated with the disciplinary institution, pre-eminently the prison, where the inmate was trained in new ways of behaviour. For Foucault, each of these regimes depended on different mechanisms of power. The public execution, for example, ritually reaffirmed the power of the sovereign. The reforming jurists, in contrast, put their faith in the law itself as a 'technology of representation', a means of transmitting appropriate messages about the calculable consequences of criminal acts. The theorists of the carceral regime, in their turn, looked to disciplinary training as a means of producing docile, obedient individuals. Instead of representing punishment as a kind of exchange value modulated according to the criminal act, the carceral regime was designed to produce reformed individuals. The modern prison, in Foucault's account, was the place where the 'semio-techniques' of the law were superseded by the disciplinary techniques of surveillance.

Foucault interprets the movement between these regimes of punishment as a shift in the way in which power gains hold of human beings. Within the monarchical regime, power was exercised at a distance, exceptionally and capriciously; within its successors, power was supposed to operate routinely and universally, throughout the social body. The contractual regime, according to Foucault, offered a new economy of the power to punish in a universe of juridical subjects. He argues, however, that its semiotic techniques were ultimately superseded by the disciplinary technology of the prison, designed to produce obedient objects. In the carceral regime, individuals were instead to be trained into new habits, new patterns of conduct; their bodies subject to a *dressage* of disciplinary routines, their conduct monitored as closely as possible. 'In the first instance,' argues Foucault, 'discipline proceeds from the distribution of individuals in space . . . each individual has his own place; and each place its own individual.'[21] Classifications, timetables and routines organize activity in space and time; prisons are divided by cells, landings and wings, just as schools are managed by classes and hospitals by wards. These arrangements are carefully designed to ensure the increasingly efficient surveillance of individual conduct and the exercise of what Foucault calls normalizing judgement. The new techniques of moral regulation depend on a more calculative attitude towards human behaviour; new modes of power go hand in hand with new forms of knowledge.

Discipline and Punish has attracted considerable criticism from historians. Was the movement between punitive regimes as clear-cut as Foucault implies? Did he take into account the gap between the reformers' intentions and actual outcomes? What about the differences between different institutions, in different times and places? What of conflicts between policy-makers, administrators, guards and the prisoners themselves? All of these questions are of course vitally important for historians. To be fair, Foucault has anticipated or responded to many of them, acknowledging, for example, that historical changes are always complex and uneven, that unintended consequences are a chronic feature of all projects of social reform, that there were important differences between different institutions and that conflicts and struggles played a critical role in the development of institutional practices.[22] However, to accept the importance of all these things for the history of prisons and prison reform is not necessarily to undermine Foucault's own project. For Foucault was not attempting to reconstruct the history of the prison system in all its complexity. Instead, his aim was to trace the emergence and consolidation of a set of disciplinary strategies which, he argues, provided the basis for a new regime of punishment. It is important to recall that Foucault was concerned more with practices than with closed institutions *per se*; with techniques of training which are found at their most concentrated within institutions, but are also present in all sorts of other social settings. Rather than offering *Discipline and Punish* as a history of prisons or penal policy, Foucault intended it to be read as a chapter in the history of 'punitive reason'.[23]

The differences between these readings of *Discipline and Punish* may be illustrated by the controversy over Foucault's account of the Panopticon, Bentham's bizarre scheme for a model prison. Some critics have taken Foucault to task for suggesting that the Panopticon, an institution which was never actually built, should be seen as a symbol of a new disciplinary regime. Others have complained that the Panopticon model cannot faithfully express institutional realities, especially given the myriad ways in which inmates may escape the gaze of officials.[24] To some extent, this criticism simply misses Foucault's point. The Panopticon is not presented by Foucault as an 'expression' or a 'reflection' of the reality of institutional life; rather, it is a paradigm, a model, in which many disciplinary strategies are concentrated. In *Discipline and Punish*, for example, Foucault describes the Panopticon as a 'diagram of a mechanism of power reduced to its ideal form . . . a pure architectural and optical system [abstracted from any] obstacle, resistance or friction'.[25] Foucault's account of 'panopticism' is thus to be read as a model of a disciplinary programme, not as a description of actual disciplinary institutions.[26] Why does Foucault regard it as exemplary? Because it embodied principles and techniques which were increasingly influential in the discourses of social policy: a faith in the moral powers of design; an emphasis on the surveillance of individual conduct; and an attempt to cultivate a sense of self-discipline amongst those to be trained – the habitual criminal, the demoralized pauper, the unreformed delinquent.

Although Bentham's Panopticon scheme attracted little support amongst his contemporaries, the principles it embodied were to exert an important influence on projects of moral regulation during the eighteenth and nineteenth centuries. It was in the sphere of institutional policy that strategies of surveillance and reformatory training were developed with most effect. Bentham himself had no doubt about the moral powers of architecture. (As he had proclaimed in drawing up his Panopticon plan: 'Morals reformed – health preserved – industry invigorated – instruction diffused – public burden lightened – economy seated as it were upon a rock – the Gordian knot of the Poor Laws not cut but untied – all by a simple idea in Architecture!')[27] In recent years, historians of prisons, asylums, hospitals and reformatories have confirmed that this faith in institutional design as a technique of moral discipline was remarkably widespread. This is suggested by the very terms they have used – the 'moral architecture' of the asylum, the 'moral geometry' of the prison, the 'moral space' of the reformatory, the 'moral universe' of the hospital, the 'school as machine'.[28] Contemporary reformers made a variety of assumptions about the mechanisms which linked the design of space with the pattern of individual behaviour. Within Bentham's plan, for example, the psychology of associationism provided a materialist framework for understanding the process by which individual sensation, perception and conduct were connected; a means by which the inmate could be trained to be the agent of his own reformation. The Panopticon in a sense combined what Foucault terms the 'semio-techniques' of the contractual regime (which presumed an economy of signs centred on the rational, calculating individual) with the disciplinary techniques of the carceral regime (which presumed a political technology based on disciplinary training).[29] Yet Foucault's general argument in *Discipline and Punish* is that the former were superseded by the latter, as the dreamworld of the Enlightenment gave way to the corporeal mechanisms of the prison. In so far as it consigns the 'semio-techniques' of the reforming jurists to a kind of historical no man's land, this view presents a rather one-dimensional account of the genealogy of Victorian discourses of social policy.[30] It also neglects the continuing significance of religious frames of reference in discourses of moral reformation. As Ignatieff has argued, penal reformers continued throughout the nineteenth century to attach importance to 'symbolic persuasion' (surely a kind of 'semio-technique') as much as to 'disciplinary routinization'.[31]

If Foucault's account of the relationship between these different forms of power is vulnerable to criticism, the task of situating them within some wider social whole is more problematic still. Foucault suggests in *Discipline and Punish* that the simple efficiency and transparency of the disciplinary techniques enabled their diffusion throughout society. At one point, he comes close to suggesting a simple functionalist explanation for the success of the disciplines, pointing to the imperatives of rapid capital accumulation and population growth, the need for reformed legal systems, and the technological revolutions of the eighteenth and nineteenth centuries.[32] More generally, there is little evidence in *Discipline and Punish* of Foucault's concern with resistance and struggle. In response to criticism on this point, Foucault drew an important distinction between the idea of a 'disciplinary society' (in which programmes such as the Panopticon proliferate) and that of a completely 'disciplined society' (in which such programmes are in a sense unnecessary!).[33] Self-evidently, he argued, his concern in *Discipline and Punish* was with the former rather than the latter; there was always something to be disciplined, something beyond the Panopticon. This said, Foucault's emphasis was overwhelmingly on the disciplinary techniques themselves, rather than on the various ways in which they were actually diffused, resisted and deflected in eighteenth and nineteenth-century societies.

If the disciplines are to be located in a wider field of social relationships and resistances, then we need to know more about the actual
workings of different institutional regimes and their position in the
wider world. How were institutional programmes actually put into
effect? By what means were disciplinary practices implemented or not
implemented? To what extent was there an integrated system of
institutions?

In answering these questions, it is necessary to consider the role of
the state much more directly than Foucault does in *Discipline and
Punish*. The claim that Foucault's work betrays a 'state-centred
conception of social order'[34] seems rather odd in this context, because
the institutions of the state are conspicuous by their absence from his
account. Foucault has consistently rejected the idea that the new
regime of power was imposed 'from the top', arguing instead that the
disciplines were 'invented and organized from the starting points of
local conditions and particular needs'.[35] This position clearly reflects
Foucault's antipathy to state-centred theories of power. Yet a more
focused account of the role of the state would not necessarily undermine Foucault's account. Bentham, for example, applied his principle
of inspection to the regulation of institutions by the state as well as the
surveillance of inmates by institutional officials. More generally, the
establishment of new methods of government regulation during the
eighteenth and nineteenth centuries could also be seen in the context
of Foucault's ideas about surveillance.[36] Although Foucault was
reluctant to be drawn into an institutional analysis of this sort, he was
interested in forms of knowledge and power often associated with the
state. His work on notions of governmental power and the idea of
police inevitably raised questions about the role of the state in the
surveillance of populations. Yet it was not altogether clear how his
analysis of these forms of power might be connected with his discussions of discipline.[37]

Discipline and Punish does not offer us a self-contained history of
prisons, or anything like it. Nevertheless, it poses a number of
problems for historians as well as others to investigate; problems
about the changing nature of punishment, the diffusion of disciplinary practices, the technologies of behaviour, the government of
subjectivity. Foucault does not, of course, address these questions in
the manner of a conventional historian; at the same time, however,
he finds it worthwhile to approach them through historical work.
Indeed, *Discipline and Punish* is a book absolutely obsessed with historical details, little events and obscure figures. If anything is lacking,

it is a sense of society rather than a sense of history. What is left open by Foucault's analysis is how the exemplars of punitive regimes – the Panopticon, for example – might be located in a wider social space. If we wish to situate Foucault's account of disciplinary power in a more general context, we need to consider how various kinds of spaces and powers might be related to each other.

Foucault himself refused to outline these relationships in anything but the most schematic ways, suspicious as he was of the very idea of a theory of society.[38] He left others to ponder what might properly be described as a problem of location – how to situate the disciplines within both the broader flows of history and the complex geographies of the modern world.[39] In what follows, this issue of location is addressed in a very specific way, through a study of the diffusion of an influential disciplinary model.

THE DIFFUSION OF A DISCIPLINARY MODEL

> Were I to fix the date of completion of the carceral system, I would choose not 1810 and the penal code, nor even 1844, when the law laying down the principle of cellular internment was passed . . . The date I would choose would be 22 January 1840, the date of the official opening of Mettray.[40]

The last chapter of *Discipline and Punish* begins with a brief account of the Mettray reformatory, an agricultural colony for juvenile delinquents established in the countryside near Tours. Why Mettray? 'Because it is the disciplinary form at its most extreme, the model in which are concentrated all the coercive technologies of behaviour', argues Foucault, including those of the family, the army, the school and the factory. Mettray was a model institution in the most straightforward sense, for the colony was often to be described by contemporaries as an exemplar of the principles of reformatory discipline. For more than fifty years, Mettray exercised an extraordinary influence upon social reformers, both inside and outside France. Philanthropists and politicians flocked to its gates, eager to learn the secrets of its success; indeed, a visit to Mettray was likened to a pilgrimage to Mecca. From the late nineteenth century, however, the colony's progressive reputation began to disintegrate, and in 1939 it was finally closed. This was not the end of the story, however. For Mettray was subsequently to be resurrected in the writings of its most famous inmate, Jean Genet. In *The Miracle of the Rose*, written in 1943 from a prison cell, Genet portrays Mettray as a 'children's hell', a secret, fantastical underworld where discipline and desire seemed to feed off each other. 'I could weep with emotion', Genet writes, 'at the memory of those fifty grown-ups who guarded us, regarded us, never understanding us, for they played their role of torturer in all faith. And the three hundred kids who fooled them!'[41] Whereas Foucault offers a view of Mettray from afar, as it were, Genet writes from within, submerged in the disciplines and pleasures of its secret life in the fields and flowers of Touraine.[42]

Foucault argues that the opening of Mettray marked a new era in the techniques of modern disciplinary power. The founders of the colony aimed to reform delinquents rather than merely punish crime; their schemes of moral and industrial training were designed, above all, to instil a habitual sense of self-discipline amongst the colonists. One of the most distinctive features of the Mettray colony was its so-called 'family system', by which the boys were divided into separate 'families', lodged in separate houses. Each 'family' was placed under the charge of two 'elder brothers' and a family head, and each was given a distinctive colour and emblem. Detailed records of the progress of each colonist were maintained, and all were ranked according to the standard of their conduct in 'tables of honour', displayed for all to see. This system was intended to encourage competition between families and loyalty within them, creating a form of decentralized, mutual surveillance; as one English admirer put it, 'the eyes of the whole society [are] awake to prevent the offence from coming; the cares of the whole family [are] applied to wean the wayward from his wilfulness'.[43] Seen in the light of this and other contemporary accounts, the description of Mettray in *Discipline and Punish* as a model disciplinary institution seems to carry considerable weight. Yet Foucault's critics have paid little attention to his discussion of the colony; as if mesmerized by his coruscating account of the Panopticon, they seem almost not to have noticed it. In crudely empirical terms, however, Mettray was the more important institution. Whereas the Panopticon was dismissed in Bentham's own day as a speculative fantasy, Mettray was widely acclaimed as a working model, the original for thousands of copies. In the words of the colony's founder, Frederic Demetz: 'There are systems that never realise anything because they imagine the impossible. Mettray has defined its limit, at the proper point between utopia and real progress; this is the reason why Mettray has met with imitators.'[44]

The wide appeal of the Mettray system depended on the fact that it could be sharply distinguished from conventional penal institutions.[45] 'Our aim', declared its founders, 'was to rescue young offenders from the influence of a prison life, and to replace the walls with which they had been surrounded, by liberty and labour in the open air.'[46] By emulating the moral disciplines of family life, by exploiting the reformatory power of agricultural labour, and by designing the colony in the form of a 'well-arranged village',[47] the founders of Mettray hoped to turn the moral disciplines of nature itself into strategies of normalization. At Mettray, individual consciences were to be cultivated, characters trained, in homes, fields and workshops; in other words, through the normal routines of daily life. 'So far as any material impediments affect the matter', claimed one convert to the system, 'every inmate is free to come and free to go; the only key is . . . the key of the open fields; and the general aspect is much more that of a country watering place, than a prison'.[48] The family, labour, community; nothing, it seemed, could be further away from the closed world of the Panopticon. And yet, what was the rationale behind this liberty, these families, this 'well-arranged village'? The aim throughout was to maintain a constant regime of discipline, exercise and surveillance. Far from being an alternative to the principle of panopticism, the family system made it more effective. In the words of Demetz: 'Division by families renders the superintendence at once easier, more active and more zealous . . . and without discipline losing any of its rigour, education finds in this mutual affection a level of incalculable power.'[49]

It is clear from its reputation as the Mecca of reformatories that Mettray was a model in a way that the Panopticon was not. Although it was not the first reformatory colony of its kind, even in France,[50] it was certainly the most celebrated. Mettray won many admirers amongst reformers and policy-makers in Britain, including such influential figures as Matthew Davenport Hill, Joseph Fletcher, Mary Carpenter, Alexander Machonochie, Henry Brougham and Sydney Turner. Many of them published glowing accounts of the colony, not only in specialist reformatory journals, but also in a wide variety of popular periodicals and official reports. Mettray was never far from public attention during the well-organized campaign to secure state aid for reformatories and industrial schools, which culminated in legislation in 1854 and 1857.[51] In the words of one essayist in the *Quarterly Review*: 'There is hardly perhaps a subject, the [Crimean] war excepted, which occupies a larger share of attention at the present time than reformatory schools. To use a familiar expression, they are becoming quite the rage.'[52] Mettray was to be a popular topic of discussion at the annual conferences of the Social Science Association, not simply in the context of reformatory policy, but also in debates over Poor Law education. Mettray's reputation thus transcended the sphere of criminal policy. It was widely argued, for example, that the principles of Mettray offered a new basis for the training of pauper children. During the 1860s, the colony was identified with the 'cottage' model of pauper training, an alternative to both workhouses and large pauper schools.

In Britain, then, Mettray was less a model institution than a model anti-institution. It was offered as an alternative to large institutions, a more natural and more effective system of moral training. As far as can be judged from the vast literature on the Mettray system, there were remarkably few attempts to discredit the 'principles' on which it was based – only variations on how they were to be applied. Even the most ardent converts to the system acknowledged that some aspects of discipline at Mettray, such as its tables of honour and the relentless military-style drilling, might not easily be transplanted in British soil. Yet these were matters of practice, they argued, not principle. In England, one might have to substitute plum pudding for a badge of honour; but the moral effect would be the same. As for drill, there were some suggestions that the balance between appeals to conscience and the regimentation of inmates might have to be adapted in an English context. But the 'principle' adopted – bodily discipline as a means of moral training – was not in doubt. In 1841, James Kay and Edward Tuffnell, the leading theorists of pauper education and training in England, advocated a marching exercise in terms which were strikingly similar to those used by the advocates of the Mettray colony:

> In giving the child an erect and manly gait, a firm and regular step, precision and rapidity in his movements, promptitude in obedience to commands, and particularly neatness in his apparel and person, we are insensibly laying the foundation of moral habits most intimately connected with the personal comfort and the happiness of the future labourer's family. We are giving a practical moral lesson, perhaps more powerful than the precepts which are inculcated by words.[53]

Mettray was championed in Britain, as elsewhere, as an exemplar of a system of moral and industrial training; a system, moreover, which was designed to secure the ultimate aim of individual self-discipline. In order to understand the changing nature of its reputation in Britain, one would need to trace in more detail the ebb and flow of domestic debates over reformatory policy and pauper education than is possible here.[54] Yet in general terms it is clear that the 'principles of Mettray' had an enduring influence in Britain. And, for all their practical concerns, the English admirers of Mettray did not hesitate to describe the family system in the most abstract, generalizing terms. Florence Davenport Hill, for example, characterized it as a system in equilibrium between 'centripetal' and 'centrifugal' forces: 'mutual affection and responsibility' on the one hand, 'individualisation' on the other.[55] Others used Mettray to promote what they called 'sub-division' against association, individualization against aggregation, the family system against the mass, the cottage home against the barracks. Forces, systems, principles; these were the techniques of the new reformatory science, a science of human conduct.

CONCLUSION

What I say ought to be taken as 'propositions', 'game openings', where those who may be interested are invited to join in; they are not meant as dogmatic assertions that have to be taken or left *en bloc*.[56]

If the test of a good book lies in the stimulus it has given to further research and debate, there is no doubt that *Discipline and Punish* was one of Foucault's greatest successes. In this, as in his other writings, Foucault did not set out to write a definitive history; rather, he found historical work a useful way of posing problems about the nature of particular kinds of power. His hybrid form of analysis in fact took history very seriously; not as a set of grand continuities and totalities, but as a means of thinking about the way different forms of know-ledge and power are rooted in particular historical situations. Foucault offered his readers a kind of geopolitics of discourse, a study of the means by which subjects and objects were placed and displaced. Disciplinary power was, perhaps above all else, a colonizing form of power; it cultivated new ways of seeing, calculating and ordering.[57]

Foucault's self-confessed obsession with space and spatiality is evident throughout his work. In his genealogies, in particular, he found spatial terms and concepts useful as a way of bringing questions of power to the fore; power in terms of concrete practices rather than ideologies. Yet I have suggested at several points in this essay that Foucault does not offer much guidance for those interested in developing an account of the way spaces might be articulated with each other; in other words, he presents only one side of what I have called the problem of location. There is little sense in *Discipline and Punish*, for example, of how to place panopticism in relation to other forms of power and resistance. This is not to say that Foucault does not discuss the problem of diffusion; in fact, he places considerable emphasis on the fact that the disciplines do escape from closed institutions, taking very different spatial forms outside the prison. This is an important point, for it demonstrates that disciplinary techniques do not necessarily depend on confinement or even spatial segregation. In his account of the Mettray colony, just as in his discussion of the York Retreat in *Madness and Civilization*, Foucault stresses the way in which normalizing judgement can operate in different contexts to those of the closed institution; through the family and the community, for example.[58] What one needs to know is whether and in what ways the disciplinary techniques themselves were modified, reshaped and resisted in the very process of their 'diffusion'. This remains an open question.

NOTES

1 One critic has gone so far as to describe the influence of 'theory-mongers' (including Foucault) on historians as a 'cancerous radiation': G. R. Elton, *Return to Essentials: Some Reflections on the Present State of Historical Study*, Cambridge, Cambridge University Press, 1991, p. 41.
2 P. Dews, 'Power and subjectivity in Foucault', *New Left Review*, 144, 1984, p. 73.
3 M. Perrot (ed.), *L'impossible prison: Recherches sur le système pénitentiare au XIXe siècle*, Paris, Seuil, 1980, p. 41.
4 M. Foucault, 'The discourse of history' in S. Lotringer (ed.), *Foucault Live: Interviews 1966–1984*, New York, Semiotext(e), 1989, pp. 11–33; M. Foucault, 'The subject and power' in H. Dreyfus and P. Rabinow, *Michel Foucault: Beyond Structuralism and Hermeneutics*, Brighton, Harvester, 1982, p. 208.
5 M. Foucault, 'Nietzsche, genealogy, history' in D. Bouchard (ed.), *Language, Counter-Memory, Practice*, Ithaca, Cornell University Press, 1977, p. 153. Similar arguments will be found in both Foucault's 'archaeological' and 'genealogical' phases, suggesting that the 'break' between the two can be overdrawn.
6 M. Foucault, 'Truth and power' in *Power/Knowledge: Selected Interviews and Other Writings, 1972–1977*, Brighton, Harvester, 1980, p. 117.
7 M. Foucault, 'Space, knowledge and power', *Skyline*, March 1982, p. 18.

BODIES IN SPACE

8 G. Deleuze, 'Ecrivain non: un nouveau cartographe', *Critique*, 31, 1975, pp. 1207–27.
9 M. Foucault, *The Birth of the Clinic: An Archaeology of Medical Perception*, London, Tavistock, 1973, p. ix.
10 For comment on various aspects of Foucault's spatial obsession, see E. Soja, *Postmodern Geographies: The Reassertion of Space in Critical Social Theory*, London, Verso, 1988; M. Jay, 'In the empire of the gaze: Foucault and the denigration of vision in twentieth-century French thought' in D. C. Hoy (ed.), *Foucault: A Critical Reader*, Oxford, Blackwell, 1986, pp. 175–204; C. Philo, 'Foucault's geography', *Society and Space*, 10, 1992, pp. 136–61; R. Diprose and R. Ferrell, *Cartographies: Poststructuralism and the Mapping of Bodies and Spaces*, Sydney, Allen & Unwin, 1991.
11 M. Foucault, 'Questions on geography' in *Power/Knowledge*, p. 69.
12 Foucault, 'Space, knowledge and power', p. 20.
13 C. Lemert and G. Gillan, *Michel Foucault: Social Theory as Transgression*, New York, Columbia University Press, 1982, p. 98.
14 The key question here concerns Foucault's attitude towards humanism. The best critical account is to be found in N. Fraser, *Unruly Practices: Power, Discourse and Gender in Contemporary Social Theory*, Cambridge, Polity, 1989, chs. 1–3. See also the essays in Hoy, *Foucault: A Critical Reader*.
15 M. Foucault, 'Prison talk' in *Power/Knowldge*, pp. 53–4.
16 M. Foucault, 'The confession of the flesh' in *Power/Knowledge*, p. 199. See also M. Foucault, 'Two lectures' in *Power/Knowledge*, pp. 96–108, and *The History of Sexuality 1: An Introduction*, London, Allen Lane, 1979.
17 Cf. F. Driver, 'Geography and power: the work of Michel Foucault', reprinted in P. Burke (ed.), *Michel Foucault: Critical Essays*, Aldershot, Scolar Press, 1992, pp. 147–156.
18 Foucault, 'Two lectures', p. 100.
19 Ibid., p. 102.
20 Foucault, 'Truth and power', p. 119.
21 M. Foucault, *Discipline and Punish: The Birth of the Prison*, Harmondsworth, Penguin, 1977, pp. 141–9.
22 Foucault, *Discipline and Punish*, pp. 14–16, 139; 'The eye of power' in *Power/Knowledge*, pp. 146–65; 'La poussière et le nuage' in Perrot, *L'impossible prison*, pp. 29–39.
23 Foucault, 'La poussière et le nuage', p. 33.
24 A. Giddens, *The Constitution of Society*, Cambridge, Polity Press, 1984, pp. 153–4.
25 Foucault, *Discipline and Punish*, p. 205.
26 C. Gordon, 'Afterword', in *Power/Knowledge*, p. 246.
27 J. Bowring (ed.), *The Works of Jeremy Bentham*, London, 1843, vol. iv, p. 39.
28 A. Scull, 'Moral architecture: the Victorian lunatic asylum' in A. Scull (ed.), *Social Order/Mental Disorder: Anglo-American Psychiatry in Historical Perspective*, Berkeley, University of California Press, 1989, pp. 213–38; R. Evans, *The Fabrication of Virtue: English Prison Architecture, 1759–1840*, Cambridge, Cambridge University Press, 1982; F. Driver, 'Discipline without frontiers?', *Journal of Historical Sociology*, 3, 1990, pp. 272–93;

C. Rosenberg, 'Florence Nightingale on contagion: the hospital as moral universe' in C. Rosenberg (ed.), *Healing and History*, New York, Folkestone, Dawson, 1979, pp. 116–36; T. Markus, 'The school as machine' in T. Markus (ed.), *Order in Space and Society: Architectural Form and its Context in the Scottish Enlightenment*, Edinburgh, Edinburgh University Press, 1982, pp. 201–56. See also D. Rothman, *The Discovery of the Asylum*, Toronto, Little, Brown & Co., 1971; A. D. King, *Buildings and Society*, London, Routledge & Kegan Paul, 1980; M. Donnelly, *Managing the Mind: A Study of Medical Psychology in Early Nineteenth-Century Britain*, London, Tavistock, 1983; J. Thompson and G. Goldin, *The Hospital: A Social and Architectural History*, New Haven, Yale University Press, 1975; M. Foucault, B. Barret-Kriegel, A. Thalamy, F. Béguin and B. Fortier, *Les machines à guérir: Aux origines de l'hôpital moderne*, Brussels, Pierre Mardaga, 1976.

29 These regimes are also associated with two different kinds of subjectivity: Fraser, *Unruly Practices*, pp. 45–6.

30 Cf. M. Dean, *The Constitution of Poverty: Toward a Genealogy of Liberal Governance*, London, Routledge, 1991, pp. 216, 190–2; F. Driver, *Power and Pauperism: The Workhouse System, 1834–1884*, Cambridge, Cambridge University Press, 1993, ch. 1.

31 M. Ignatieff, 'State, civil society and total institutions', *Crime and Justice*, 3, 1981, pp. 175–6; M. Ignatieff, *A Just Measure of Pain: The Penitentiary in the Industrial Revolution, 1750–1850*, London, Macmillan, 1978, pp. 44–79.

32 Foucault, *Discipline and Punish*, pp. 218–28.

33 Foucault, 'La poussière et le nuage', p. 35.

34 Ignatieff, 'State, civil society and total institutions', p. 184.

35 Foucault, 'The eye of power', p. 159.

36 P. Corrigan and D. Sayer, *The Great Arch: State Formation as Cultural Revolution*, Oxford, Basil Blackwell, 1985; C. Dandeker, *Surveillance, Power and Modernity*, Cambridge, Polity Press, 1990; Driver, *Power and Pauperism*.

37 G. Burchell, C. Gordon and P. Miller (eds), *The Foucault Effect: Studies in Governmentality*, Hemel Hempstead, Harvester, 1992.

38 M. Foucault, 'Questions of method' in Burchell et al., *The Foucault Effect*, p. 85.

39 See also M. Donnelly, 'On Foucault's uses of the notion "biopower" ', in *Michel Foucault, Philosopher*, tr. T. Armstrong, New York, Routledge, 1992, pp. 199–203.

40 Foucault, *Discipline and Punish*, p. 293.

41 J. Genet, *The Miracle of the Rose*, Harmondsworth, Penguin, 1971, pp. 13, 173.

42 Surprisingly few critics have explored the links between Foucault and Genet; but see E. Walter, 'La prison-poème ou les disciplines perverties: jalons pour relire Jean Genet à la lumière de Michel Foucault' in A. Laurent (ed.), *Jean Genet aujourd'hui*, Maison de la Culture d'Amiens, 1976, pp. 5–33.

43 R. Hall, 'Extract from a lecture on Mettray' in J. Symons (ed.), *On the Reformation of Young Offenders*, London, 1855, p. 44.

44 F. Demetz, cited in [P. J. Murray], 'Reformatory schools in France and England', *Irish Quarterly Review*, 4, 1854, p. 740.

45 The following paragraphs draw on the account presented in Driver, 'Discipline without frontiers?'.

46 Anon., 'Mettray: its rise and progress', *Irish Quarterly Review*, 6, 1856, p. 918.

47 A. Doyle, *Proposed District School on the System of Mettray*, London, 1873, p. 7.

48 Hall, 'Extract from a lecture on Mettray', p. 37.

49 F. Demetz, *Report on Reformatory Farm Institutions*, London, 1856, pp. 26–7.

50 H. Gaillac, *Les Maisons de Correction, 1830–1941*, Paris, Cujas, 1971.

51 L. Radzinowicz and R. Hood, *A History of the English Criminal Law and its Administration from 1750*, vol. 5, London, Stevens & Sons, 1986, chs. 6–7; M. May, 'Innocence and experience: the evolution of the concept of juvenile delinquency in the mid-nineteenth century', *Victorian Studies*, 17, 1973, pp. 7–29.

52 Anon., 'Reformatory schools', *Quarterly Review*, 98, 1855, p. 32.

53 *Report from the Poor Law Commissioners on the Training of Pauper Children*, London, 1841, p. 217.

54 See Driver, 'Discipline without frontiers?'.

55 F. D. Hill, 'The family system for workhouse children', *Contemporary Review*, 15, 1870, p. 241.

56 Foucault, 'Questions of method', p. 74.

57 Recent applications of Foucault's work in the context of colonialism include T. Mitchell, *Colonising Egypt*, Cambridge, Cambridge University Press, 1989; R. Tolen, 'Colonizing and transforming the criminal tribesman: the Salvation Army in British India', *American Ethnologist*, 18, 1991, pp. 106–25.

58 M. Foucault, *Madness and Civilization: A History of Insanity in the Age of Reason*, New York, Social Science Paperbacks, 1965, pp. 243–55.

8

APPLYING FOUCAULT

Some problems encountered in the application of Foucault's methods to the history of medicine in prisons

Stephen Watson

Foucault undertook several major projects directed to the under-standing of knowledge/power relations within institutions (and by implication between institutions and the society that sanctioned them). *Madness and Civilization* examined the incarceration of the mad and the lunatic asylum; *The Birth of the Clinic* charted the rise of the modern hospital; *Discipline and Punish* examined the penitentiary. Each had its own space, its science and logic, its technologies of power. Foucault was always sensitive to the distinctions created by different discursive and physical formations; partly for this reason, he never attempted a general theory of topography and technology, the power of space. One consequence is that his major works dealing with institutions have been analysed rather separately, respectively by historians of crime, medicine and psychiatry. Stephen Watson's essay forms a pioneering attempt to break down some of these rather artificial divisions by taking the prison (as viewed by Foucault) and examining the orders of medicine and psychiatry within it. In what ways do carceral power, medical power and psychiatric power interrelate? Under what circum-stances do they clash?

This last is an important point, because, as Watson emphasizes, in a prison the medical and psychiatric services are likely to perceive them-selves as the protectors of the inmate rather than as the arm of the administration. Thus medico-psychiatric officers will at least be in an ambiguous power situation, and may even become foci of resistance.

This may point to a certain ambiguity or shortcoming in Foucault's approach. As Watson notes, unlike the class-based consciousness of Marxism, the spatial epistemologies that Foucault tended to delineate seem to afford little occasion for opposition, discord or resistance. Indeed, Foucault was to insist in his *History of Sexuality* that, in terms of sexuality, the differences between class and class, or male and female, were to be taken as counting less than the convergences. Whether or not this is an Olympian, or perhaps even a myopic, viewpoint remains a matter of debate.

There are now several works dealing with the historical development of prison psychiatry and criminology that refer directly to Foucault's *Discipline and Punish*. Most of them propose some substantial modifications to the historical chronology Foucault employs, some take issue with Foucault's methodological approach and yet all derive some inspiration from Foucault's concern to address the problem of the constitution of knowledge. Even David Garland, who offers the most substantial revision of Foucault so far, is concerned to show how the local technologies of power operating within the prison acted as a 'surface of emergence' for criminological and psychological knowledge in the nineteenth century.[1]

What I would like to do here is briefly to delineate some of the ways in which the central arguments of *Discipline and Punish* have been applied to the history of psychiatric power within the English penal system. I will then outline some of the problems that have been encountered when the methods and periodization of *Discipline and Punish* have been applied to the English prison system by looking at the work of David Garland, Joe Sim and my own work on prison medical officers. I will argue that the many problems that arise when Foucault is applied to the English experience are only different aspects of one methodological problem: Foucault's failure to show how 'power at its extremities . . . in its more regional local forms and institutions' becomes 'invested, colonized, utilized, involved, transformed, extended . . . by ever more general mechanisms and by forms of global domination'.[2] This failure to define the relationship between local technologies of power and central policy-making bodies (such as government and professional organizations) has meant that academics writing about the development of penal policy have resorted to using the more traditional concepts of class interest and professionalization as explanatory tools, thus abandoning Foucault's project of writing a history of disciplinary technologies. This essay will thus conclude with a discussion about the implications of a history of penal strategies that combines some of Foucault's insights with an interpretative framework that sees class and professional interests as factors determining the structure and content of knowledge.

The last part of Foucault's *Discipline and Punish* discusses the connection between what he calls 'the penitentiary technique' and knowledge of 'the delinquent':

> The penitentiary technique and the delinquent are in a sense twin brothers. It is not true that it was the discovery of the

delinquent through a scientific rationality that introduced into our old prisons the refinement of penitentiary techniques, nor is it true that the internal elaboration of penitentiary methods has finally brought to light the 'objective' existence of a delinquency that the abstraction and rigidity of the law were unable to perceive. They appeared together, the one extending from the other, as a technological ensemble that forms and fragments the object to which it applies its instruments.[3]

For Foucault the penitentiary technique has as one of its prime aims 'the technical transformation of individuals'. But in order that this can be achieved the prison must be able to 'rectify the penalty as it proceeds'; the retributive elements of prison life must be used freely in response to the character of the prisoner and his progress. Thus the aim of what the prison authorities called 'reformation' involved a degree of autonomy from the legal authorities who initially sentenced the criminal.[4] Thus Foucault deliberately emphasizes that the penitentiary, from its inception in the early nineteenth century, was designed to reform the criminal. This is because he wishes to argue that the discovery of 'the delinquent' was a product of the apparently humanitarian ideal of the penitentiary. For the criminal to become repentant, a certain kind of knowledge of the offender was required.

> The prison has not only to know the decision of the judges and to apply it in terms of the established regulations: it has to extract unceasingly from the inmate a body of knowledge that will make it possible to transform the penal measure into a penitentiary operation; which will make of the penalty required by the offence a modification of the inmate that will be of use to society.[5]

This knowledge Foucault calls 'biographical'. To reform an individual it becomes necessary to know not only his crime but his character as revealed in his whole life – 'psychology, social position and upbringing'. Biographical knowledge 'establishes the "criminal" as existing before the crime and even outside it'. This is where Foucault situates the rise of criminology, where 'penal discourse' and 'psychiatric discourse' cross each others' frontiers.[6]

Foucault's analysis of the development of psychiatric and criminological knowledge within the prison relies on the assumption that the production of psychological knowledge of the offender was the result of the maintenance of penal discipline aimed at the transformation of the criminal. Foucault's contention that techniques of control and psychiatric knowledge 'appeared together' as inseparable elements of a 'technological ensemble' has inspired authors such as Sim and Garland to look at the prison as a 'local surface of emergence' for psychiatric knowledge. However, Foucault assumes that the techniques used in the prison from the mid-nineteenth century were intended to modify or reform the behaviour of inmates rather than simply to punish them. Whether this applies to the English situation is open to question. Foucault also seems to assume that the local technologies he is describing are in some way connected to state policies without describing the mechanisms through which this could be possible. For example, the shift to 'panopticism' in the early nineteenth century appears to be a universal event that is illustrated by references to a variety of French and British sources. This kind of universalism has been described as 'totalitarian' by Karel Williams (who has written extensively on Poor Law reform);

> the scheme of the stages [torture, the penitentiary, modern punishment] is not a hypothesis in the empiricist sense; the scheme is a basic analytical device for constructing what happened and, as such it is immune to 'empirical' qualification and correction . . . such a framework is a grossly uninformative basis for any analysis concerned with a concrete problem such as what the poor law or the prison system was doing in the nineteenth century.[7]

Foucault's critics have thus concentrated on two problematic areas in *Discipline and Punish*: the timing of the shift towards techniques of individualization, and the relationship between disciplinary power as it operates in prisons and the functioning of the state.

THE EFFECTIVENESS OF PRISON DISCIPLINE AND ITS RELATION TO THE STATE

J. Sim's *Medical Power in Prisons* reproduces a tension inherent in Foucault's own work. On the one hand, there is the vision of a form of disciplinary/psychiatric power that is steadily infiltrating all aspects of our lives. On the other hand, as Sim notes, Foucault talks of how 'power is resisted'.[8] Sim believes that both of these elements of Foucault's perspective can be applied to the prison medical service. Thus the prison medical service is part of a 'disciplinary web which lies at the centre of penality and in which the prisoners have been positioned' and yet this web is 'fragile and brittle':

> The power of the service has never been absolute but has been constrained and contested both by prisoners on the ground and by state servants such as prison officers who have remained unconvinced that medical power, particularly in its psychiatric and psychological manifestations, possesses the key to unlocking the door of criminality.[9]

According to Sim, as 'servants of the state' prison medical officers have been involved in the disciplinary regulation of prisoners since the late eighteenth century. This has been achieved through humiliating rituals fulfilling both a hygienic and a disciplinary function (such as the shaving of heads and especially the control of diet). The prison surgeon's role in 'suspending the discipline or varying the diet of any prisoner' led to two obsessions: that of determining the 'least eligible' form of diet without weakening the prisoners so much that they succumbed to epidemics and that of distinguishing the malingerer from the truly insane prisoner. The debate over diets was conducted in the 'context of the often-reported view that prisons were more luxurious than workhouses and were therefore no deterrent to crime'.[10]

The prison medical officer's role was enhanced by increased state intervention in the prison system culminating in the centralization of control established by the 1877 Prison Act. Sim argues that 'what linked the state and the doctors were the ideologies of discipline and management', and yet there were 'contradictions and challenges'. By the 1920s there were conflicts between those who favoured a kind of Lombrosian criminology and those who professed themselves to be Freudians. A critical literature as manifested in *English Prisons Today* (1922) led to the setting up of organizations such as the Prison Medical Reform Council that drew attention to the tension between ideals of care and control within the prison medical service.[11] Nevertheless, Sim sees the history of the prison medical service as one of a continuous increase in its power and influence. After the Second World War prison doctors and psychologists were 'beneficiaries' of the ideology of social reconstruction that justified further state intervention. For example, the Criminal Justice Act of 1948 allowed for new psychiatric sentences and thus increased the demand for psychiatric reports from prison doctors. Despite criticisms from reform organizations and inquiries into whether the prison medical service should be more closely integrated with the NHS, the roles of the prison doctor and psychologist remained basically unchanged during the nineteenth and twentieth centuries. Attempts to discover the cause of criminality and to provide physical cures for this condition involved experimentation with electrocardiographs, psychotropic drugs, insulin shock therapy and leucotomies.[12]

Despite Sim's emphasis on the impact of the new Poor Law after 1834 his approach so far seems very 'Foucauldian'. It, is however, unique in that he provides a catalogue of complaints from prisoners themselves (from autobiographies, for example) and that he stresses the differences between the way male and female prisoners were treated by the prison medical service: 'the key Foucauldian concepts involving order, control, routines and timetables . . . were therefore translated into very different practices in women's prisons'.[13] Sim also takes issue with Foucault on two methodological points. Foucault argues that the power of the sovereign and the power of the state employed different technologies. The sovereign used physical means of torture and execution, the state employed 'discipline' or the regulation of the body through various regimes governing time, space and communication. Sim argues that violence has 'not disappeared but retains a central place in the repertoire of responses mobilized by the state inside prisons'. He also argues that power has not been dispersed but remains firmly within the state. While 'they may have had autonomy, medical personnel did not stand outside or above' the process through which the prison became the centre of disciplinary regulation, they were an integral part of it.[14]

To what extent, then is *Medical Power in Prisons* an application or development of Foucault's *Discipline and Punish*? It is clear that Sim endorses several of Foucault's arguments. He not only supports Foucault's contention that psychiatric knowledge of the delinquent was a product of penal discipline but, unlike other commentators (such as Garland), agrees with Foucault on the timing of this shift to the type of 'individualizing' technologies that made possible a knowledge of delinquency. As Sim points out, his book

> picks up on the original insights of both Foucault and Ignatieff. In particular, the question of discipline, regulation and exclusion which they see as integral to the genesis of medicine in institutions is traced from the late eighteenth century to the present.[15]

As we shall see, David Garland claims that the shift towards 'individualization', which Foucault claims occurs in the late eighteenth century, did not in fact occur until the 1895–1914 period. Although Garland's own analysis is not always consistent, what his book *Punishment and Welfare* does very effectively is to specify the particular form that discipline and the corresponding knowledge of delinquency took during the nineteenth and early twentieth centuries. Garland thus avoids the 'totalitarianism' that Karel Williams complains of in Foucault. The impression we gain from reading both *Discipline and Punish* and *Medical Power in Prisons* is that there is a gradual and continuous accumulation of medical/psychiatric power from the late eighteenth century onwards. Despite the fact that Sim constantly points out that medical power is resisted, it is not resisted effectively. Successive acts of parliament from the nineteenth century to the present are almost all described as resulting in a further consolidation of the power of medicine within the prison. For example, the Act of 1877, which led to the centralization of the prison system, 'further reinforced the position of the PMO'.[16] The Gladstone Commission Report of 1895 (a report that Garland sees as leading to a major change of policy) simply meant that 'reform and discipline were collapsed to mean the same thing'.[17] In the 1940s 'prison doctors and psychologists were beneficiaries' of the 'social reconstructionist ideology' as exemplified in the Criminal Justice Act of 1948 (this gave more powers to the courts to obtain medical reports on offenders and give 'psychiatric sentences').[18] The current prison programme is also looked at pessimistically: 'Discipline, individualization and normalization are cornerstones of these institutions within which the emphasis on security, order and control invariably vanquishes any notions of rehabilitation and reform.'[19]

This description of the progressive accumulation and consolidation of medical/psychiatric power in prisons is contested both by Garland and by my own work on the prison medical officers' concern with 'moral imbecility' in the 1920s. The virtue of an approach that attempts to follow some of Foucault's 'methodological precautions' (if not Foucault himself) is that it avoids replacing the rhetoric of continuous humanitarian progress with the rhetoric of the continuous expansion and infiltration of state/medical/psychiatric power.[20] It is clear through my own work that what Sim calls the 'ideology of reconstruction' that took the hospital as the model of medical care in the forties and fifties created problems for prison medical officers who knew that their expertise was based on their position within the prison and yet wished to retain credibility as clinical experts. As Garland has also noted, from the 1920s there is a split between those (such as

Hamblin Smith) who took the hospital as the model of care for the mentally abnormal prisoner and those (such as Norwood East) who argued that the prison was an ideal place for the study of 'mentally inefficient' classes such as subnormals and psychopaths.[21] Clearly, the movement towards a more integrated mental health system that was apparent from the 1930 Mental Treatment Act was seen by many in the prison medical service as a threat to their expertise and professional status. Such differences and contradictions should not be glossed over by referring vaguely to ways in which certain 'ideologies' were 'beneficial' to medical power.[22]

The problem that Sim faces in describing a form of medical power that is both effective and entrenched within the prison system and yet resisted and suffering from internal contradictions reflects a tension in Foucault's own work between the 'totalitarian' tendencies Williams describes and Foucault's own advice to study in detail the way in which power and knowledge operate simultaneously on the local level in the forms of regulations, codes and knowledges. We thus move back to the central theme of this chapter: the fact that Foucault fails to show how the knowledge encoded in local institutional practice is taken up, acted upon or even imposed by central organizations through agencies of the state. The value of Sim's work lies in the way in which he integrates debates over the new Poor Law (post-1834) and prison dietaries with the role of the PMO as an arbitrator of discipline. What Sim does not address is the way in which particular forms of medical power are specific to particular institutional and political goals. Medical power as Sim describes it has been more or less homogeneous since the late eighteenth century. Garland on the other hand argues that it is necessary to specify exactly when the techniques of 'individualization' Foucault describes were implemented in England and that Foucault's own account of the origin of these techniques is fundamentally flawed.

INDIVIDUALIZATION AND 'MODULATION OF THE PENALTY': A QUARREL OVER TIMING

David Garland's *Punishment and Welfare* aims at a substantial revision of Foucault's thesis. Garland does not deny Foucault's assertion that there was a definite link between techniques of individualization (such as classification and segregation) and psychological knowledge of the criminal. But his account differs from Foucault's in two important ways: in his periodization of the history of penal practice and the amount of emphasis he places on official representations of policy as opposed to the practice in prisons at a local level.

Garland locates the formation of the modern penal system in the brief period between the Gladstone Committee Report of 1895 and the start of the First World War in 1914. Although many of the new institutions such as probation, borstal and preventive detention had 'obvious precursors and parallels in the previous period', the 'pattern of penal sanctioning which was established in this period, with its new agencies, techniques, knowledges and institutions, amounted to a new structure of penality'. Garland maintains that the technologies of 'individualization' (that is the provision of separate regimes according to individual character differences) which Foucault claims were inherent in the ideal of the penitentiary simply did not operate until 1895.[23]

If a difference in periodization were all that distinguished Garland's account from Foucault's it would be relatively easy to determine the value of their respective characterizations through empirical research; but the differences in periodization described above are the result of fundamentally different ways of describing the relationship between power and knowledge. Garland definitely wishes to assign economic forces a causal role in the constitution of modern penality. According to his account, the period of transition in terms of penal policy, 1895–1914, was also a period of economic crisis:

> The crisis centred around two related issues: the proper role and function of the state in relation to the economic and social spheres, and the condition and regulation of the lower classes. The penal complex, being a series of agencies dealing over-whelmingly with the poor, was clearly implicated in this crisis – its ideological foundations and strategic position being under-mined by the breakdown of market society and its political balances.[24]

Foucault's analysis of the growth of psychiatric knowledge uses an 'ascending' model of power relations, in which techniques introduced at a local level become codified, extended and applied to other institutional contexts, whereas Garland's study of penal policy implies a descending model. Although Garland is careful not to see penal strategies as the 'battle plan of an omniscient ruling bloc', throughout his book penal practice is always subservient to the prevailing ideology. Thus the period of change between 1895 and 1914 is the result of 'a breakdown of the free-market of social organization and its corresponding disciplinary apparatus'.[25] Because Garland is tied to the metaphors of base and superstructure, and of reflection and correspondence implied by his analysis of psychiatric/criminological knowledge as an ideology, he does not consider the possibility that techniques developed in the prison may have altered the way in which power was conceived and operated. Garland also needs to stress discontinuity in order to make the relation between economic crises, ideologies and penal practice convincing.

In order to choose between these two accounts it is necessary to consider whether by 1900 the effect of penal policy had been to modify the penalty according to the character of the inmate and, if so, whether this result was a continuation of existing practices or the result of a sudden change in policy in response to a social crisis. More fundamentally perhaps, it is also necessary to consider the extent to which a descending analysis of power relations can provide a sufficient explanation for the form that psychiatric/criminological knowledge took in the nineteenth century.

Official policy: punishment or reform?

Several commentators on the history of the penal system have attempted to establish when reform of the prisoner became the primary aim of the prison authorities. Gunn et al., for example, suggest that reform became official policy after 1898,[26] while according to Garland reform, which before 1895 had been a 'subsidiary or secondary aim', had, by the time of the Gladstone Commission (1895), 'moved from being a subsidiary term in a series of aims to become the central and predominant signifier in the new penal discourse'.[27] Garland chooses his words carefully here, for although reform may have become a 'predominant signifier' in many official reports, this does not necessarily imply that any new policies aimed at the reformation of the criminal were implemented.

It is also possible to find plenty of official publications that demote reform to a subsidiary aim even after 1895. For example, in their report for 1911–12 the commissioners of prisons stated:

> Our constant effort is to hold the balance between what is necessary as punishment and for the due execution of the sentence from a penal and deterrent point of view, and what can be conceded, consistently with this, in the way of humanising and reforming influences.[28]

Subsequent prison commissioners' reports confirm the impression that retributory punishment and deterrence rather than reformation were perceived to be the primary aims of imprisonment.[29] The Gladstone Committee of 1895 insisted that reformation should be the main task of the prison system but, as J. E. Thomas in *The English Prison Officer since 1850* comments, this merely 'introduced confusion' into the prison system by forcing it to pursue incompatible goals.[30]

Not only is the evidence of official reports inconclusive, it can also be misleading. If we are to test Foucault's hypothesis on the relation between penal practice and psychological knowledge, we must be careful not to confuse official ideals of what constituted reform with what Foucault calls the 'technical transformation of individuals', which he claims was the result of prison practice from the early nineteenth century. It was the principles of segregation, classification, and observation, introduced with the penitentiary in the early nineteenth century that in Foucault's interpretation constituted the technologies aimed at the reform of the criminal.[31] These principles were not necessarily described as reformative in official reports, although some commentators did notice a 'reformative element' in them. As *English Prisons Today* noted:

> Certain of these component parts of the discipline are regarded as having something also of the 'reformative' element [for example] the denial . . . to all prisoners of the right of open communication one with another by word or hand is considered as being not only punitive but reformative in a negative sort of way, as it is intended . . . to prevent the moral contamination of the less corrupt by the more corrupt.[32]

It was through the extension and refinement of principles of segregation and classification to prevent 'moral contamination' that the prison began to usurp some of the traditional functions of the judiciary. Despite changes in official representations of the aims of imprisonment, segregation and a system of privileges were employed in the prison throughout the nineteenth century, and it was in carrying out his administrative duties relating to the maintenance of segregation and discipline within the prison, that the prison medical officer began to acquire a knowledge of mental disease amongst criminals.

Segregation and classification according to character

Foucault's account of prison practice begins with the French penal codes of 1808 and 1810, which established that penal imprisonment would cover 'both the deprivation of liberty and the technical transformation of individuals'. Foucault isolates three principles governing the regulation of prisons from this time: isolation, work, and the 'modulation of the penalty'.[33] Before looking in detail at the relations between the discipline of the penal regime and psychiatric/criminological knowledge, it is worth considering the extent to which the prison authorities in England were able to achieve this 'modulation of the penalty'.

According to Ignatieff's detailed account of early prison reform movements in England, the acceptance of the principle that imprisonment was to be the punishment for every major crime except murder was not established in England until the 1850s, when transportation was no longer viable and the building of the penitentiary of Pentonville in 1842 had established a model for subsequent prisons. From its inception Pentonville operated a system of 'micro-punishments' in which penalties such as the stopping of letters or visits and reductions in diet could be imposed for minor misdemeanours such as nodding or winking. A strict system of separation involving long periods of solitude was upheld to force the inmates to reflect upon themselves, with the intention of both encouraging the growth of a conscience and preventing moral contamination. It was not long before attempts at reformation led to the discovery of the unreformable and sections of the prison became a penal quarantine.[34]

As Garland states, the prison had 'always offered a potential space for reform and transformative practices',[35] but it was only after a long process of negotiation between the prison authorities and the judiciary that the prison established a degree of legally recognized autonomy in its ability to modify the quality of penal discipline in accordance with the character of the offender. The centralization of the prison system in 1877 and the subsequent drive for uniformity characteristic of Sir Edmund Du Cane's chairmanship of the Prison Commission (which ended in 1895),[36] meant that the ideals of moral segregation implicit in the earlier penitentiaries were not developed into a formal recognition of what Foucault terms 'carceral autonomy'. As Ignatieff comments,

> the penitentiary, which had been introduced in the 1840s as an instrument for remaking human character, survived into the

late nineteenth century by virtue of its penal features. Solitary confinement, initiated as an instrument of reform, was retained as an instrument of punishment.[37]

By 1900 the prison authorities did have a degree of autonomy from the judiciary with regard to the classification of prisoners, but this was not the result of a concerted campaign by the prison authorities but rather a response to the failure of magistrates to utilize the powers granted them in sentencing prisoners. In the 1898 Prison Act an attempt was made to place the responsibility for classifying prisoners in the hands of the magistrates, who were able to direct that prisoners should be placed in either of two 'divisions'. The first division was intended for non-recidivists such as debtors, while the second could be used where there was evidence that 'exceptional temptation or special provocation has led to a merely temporary deviation from the paths of honesty'.[38] The result was only further confusion.

> The judges and magistrates not only made very little use of their new powers; when they did take advantage of them they placed many men in the second division who would not have been considered fit to belong to the Stars. Consequently the Star class was continued among third division prisoners, in addition to the second and first division classification.[39]

The classification employed in the prison in the early twentieth century was a mixture of classifications introduced on internal initiative and through parliamentary enactment. By the 1920s there were three classes, the 'star' class (those who had not been previously convicted of cime), the 'intermediate' class, and the 'recidivists' (those who made crime a profession).[40] This situation was, in the view of the prison authorities, a result of the failure of magistrates to act on the authority granted to them.[41] Despite attempts by the prison authorities to formalize their de facto control over classification, the 1914 Criminal Jurisdiction Act gave visiting magistrates the power to place prisoners in the second division, but again little advantage was taken of this provision.[42]

When we look at the history of the use of techniques of segregation in prison we can find no evidence of a continuous and progressive extension of legally recognized carceral autonomy. Not only did the centralization of the prisons in 1877 prevent the development of techniques of segregation employed in the early penitentiaries, but the later use of classifications within the prison was a result of compromise and negotiation. This is where the subtleties of Garland's account can help us to avoid the mistake of applying the periodization of Foucault's *Discipline and Punish* directly to the English system.

However, Garland's characterization is itself misleading. The fact that he begins his study in 1877 leads him to undervalue those elements of the Victorian penal system that were continuous with the post-1895 system, and some of these elements were indeed intended to 'rectify the penalty as it proceeds' in Foucault's terms. The system of 'progressive stages' used since the mid-nineteenth century in convict prisons is a good example. Sir Edmund Du Cane (under whose regime it was introduced) describes the system thus:

> The principle on which this system is founded is that of setting before prisoners the advantages of good conduct and industry, by enabling them to gain certain privileges or modifications of the penal character of the sentence by the exertion of these qualities. Commencing with severe penal labour – hard fare and a hard bed – the prisoner can gradually advance to more interesting employment, somewhat more material comfort . . . His daily progress towards these objects is recorded by the award of marks, and any failure in industry or conduct is in the same way visited on him by forfeiture of marks, and consequent postponement or diminution of the prescribed privileges.[43]

By the early twentieth century the system of progressive stages was incorporated into the classification system both in convict and local prisons, so that different classes of prisoner received different privileges.[44] The system of progressive stages effectively meant that the prison formed an enclosed regime enforcing its own rewards and punishments according to the behaviour of the inmate. Some of the prisoners who did not respond to such a system were labelled 'unfit for discipline' and came under the scrutiny of the prison medical officer. It is therefore suprising that in such an exhaustive study, Garland only mentions progressive stages in two footnotes.[45]

This failure to give prominence to the system of progressive stages is symptomatic of Garland's desire to discover discontinuities in the history of the penal system. This is not to undervalue Garland's analysis; indeed, on the level of the history of official policy, we would find it difficult to challenge Garland's broad outline of the foundation of the modern 'penal complex', but there are other possible levels of analysis open to the historian of penal techniques. In my own work I have demonstrated that there was a continuity between what Garland calls the 'Victorian' and 'modern' penal complex, by examining an area that receives little attention in Garland's study – the development of a distinctly medical knowledge of 'the delinquent' from the first half of the nineteenth century. This development took place on a local level within the prison as an almost imperceptible extension of the duties of the prison medical officer. The fact that this process was only recognized retrospectively by the prison authorities should not prevent us from realizing its importance. By the turn of the century, the prison operated separate regimes for the 'weak-minded', and its medical officers were recognized by the judiciary as able to pronounce on the mental soundness of many categories of deviant. This growth of carceral independence in the form of a claim to a special psychological knowledge of criminal deviance occurred by stealth, as an extension of practices that were peculiar to the prison: techniques of surveillance (involving observation and identification) and the maintenance of penal discipline.

I have discussed in detail elsewhere[46] how the techniques of observation and surveillance contributed to a knowledge of the mentally abnormal offender; what I would like to do here is briefly outline how one of the PMO's duties – that of reporting to the governor 'when discipline or treatment appeared to be injuriously affecting a prisoner's mind or body' – led to a concern with the 'weak-minded' criminal. This duty was established by the 1843 Regulations for Local Gaols[47] and was considered to be of the utmost importance by prison medical officers well into the twentieth century. Earl Russell, in a talk delivered to the Medico-Legal Society in 1912, stated that 'the chief function of a [prison] doctor in earlier days was to say how far a prisoner could safely suffer his punishment, and that is still one of his most important functions'.[48] The prison medical officer was required to fill in a form that read as follows:

I hereby certify that I have this day examined convict (Reg. No. . . . . .) (Name) and find him capable of undergoing the several descriptons of Punishments as specified below: [confinement in separate cells, corporal punishment, scales of diet] also that he is . . . (here insert 'fit' or 'unfit') for restraint of Handcuffs, Leg Chains or Cross Irons, Body Belt, and Canvas Dress.[49]

The prison medical officer's function to report to the governor when it seemed that a prisoner might be 'injuriously' affected by punishment was a direct example of one of the ways in which the prison was able to 'modulate the penalty' imposed by the court in the light of the 'character' of the prisoner and had several important results. Those prisoners who were not certifiably insane but were in the opinion of the prison medical officer 'unfit for punishment' came to be labelled 'weak-minded' – a term that later came to be synonymous with 'feeble-mindedness' or 'mental deficiency'. Thus this function led to the recognition of new categories of delinquent defined by their inability to respond to punishment. This duty also meant that the prison medical officers became involved in judgements about whether the prisoner was 'of a mental capacity to be responsible for the misconduct he has committed'.[50] The PMO thus became involved in the judicial role of determining criminal responsibility. Lastly, the duty of the PMO to 'do all things necessary to maintain the health of the prisoner' had by the 1850s led to the creation of specialized subregimes within prisons such as Dartmoor for those classified as 'weak-minded'. These special regimes were maintained despite the drive for uniformity after 1877.[51]

This is only one example of the way in which official regulations governing the day-to-day operation of the prison led to what Foucault has termed 'modulation of the penalty' and 'carceral autonomy'. Although the impetus for the expansion of the prison medical officers' functions came from an innocuous standing order it is clear that the prison medical officers' interpretation of their functions under that standing order must be considered in any account of the growth of medical power within prisons. If we only look at the level of 'official discourses' we can miss the kinds of detail that indicate the extent to which official codes could be interpreted through, and provide space for, the development of professional expertise. J. Sim's *Medical Power in Prisons* provides another example of the way in which the ability to modify the penal regime for special cases led to enhanced status for the prison medical officer. The prison medical officer's view became critical after 1834 in the context of debates over prison dietaries and the principle of less eligibility enshrined in the 1834 Poor Law Amendment Act. Prison doctors such as Dr Guy became embroiled in debates over whether the prison diet was too luxurious:

under the banner of medical science then, the quantification of punishment via experimentation in dietary provision and workload allowed doctors to articulate their views and make interventions into the increasingly intense debate about the nature of the prison regime.[52]

Whether the official policy was for deterrence, retribution or reform, during the nineteenth century the expertise of the prison medical officer had become established through those aspects of standing orders governing prisons that allowed him to modify or adapt the normal penal regime for special cases. This process of what Sim terms the 'consolidation' of medical power in prisons was continuous (up until the 1920s at least) and does not fit neatly into the periodization Garland adopts. However, while one must reject Garland's assertion that it was an economic crisis that led to the large-scale deployment of techniques of individualization, it would not be true to say that the consolidation of medical power was a process that was not affected, for example, by wider debates about 'national efficiency' in the late nineteenth and early twentieth centuries. Concerns with 'national efficiency' both employed evidence already produced by prison medical officers and encouraged further investigations into mentally deficient criminals, but they did not initiate the discovery of new forms of criminal delinquency or determine the form that criminological knowledge took in the early twentieth century. In order to understand the subtleties in the relationship between national concerns, central policy-making bodies and local technologies of power we need a form of analysis that can incorporate an awareness of the importance of the role of national policy-making bodies without automatically giving them the determining role that is implied by the kind of analysis which sees state policy as a reaction to economic crises.

I believe that such an analysis is possible if we bear in mind the following points. First of all, we must acknowledge that there were 'multiple surfaces of emergence'[53] for psychiatric knowledge. Attempts to see either the asylum, the school, the prison or the workhouse as the source and locus of the human sciences are inevitably one-sided. What is needed is an approach that compares the different classifications used in different institutional contexts and specifies exactly how knowledge between these areas was transmitted. Second, we should remember that the purpose of such an approach would not be to locate the 'origin' of a particular category of mental illness in one particular institutional context. Clearly, during the nineteenth century there were similarities in terms of the regulations and codes that governed institutions such as the prison, workhouse and asylum that would lead to parallels in the types of classification used. But there would also be differences resulting from the particular aims of the institution involved, the different professional status of the doctors in these institutions and the way in which knowledge produced

148

in these institutions could be subsumed within wider political debates.

As to the problem of how to account for the role of government in implementing shifts in social policy, several things need to be considered if we are to avoid some of the problems inherent in *Discipline and Punish*. First, we must note the mediating effect that concerns with professional status within the medical profession had on the way in which psychiatric knowledge was presented to official policy-making bodies. It is not enough to simply regard prison medical officers as 'servants of the state', nor should we see the desire for professional status as a given somehow existing outside of the institutional situations in which doctors worked. Medical perceptions of what professional status involved were influenced by the particular opportunities that existed within institutions for the development of specialist knowledge and expertise. Second, we must look at what kind of knowledge formed the preconditions for national debates such as, for example, that fuelled by the eugenics lobby in the early twentieth century. Clearly, the Poor Law, prison and education systems were vital sites for the production of a knowledge of the 'imbecile', the 'weak-minded' criminal and the 'feeble-minded' child, and it was the existence of these categories that played an important role in fuelling the panic on racial decline and national inefficiency. While, as Garland points out, the Liberal welfare reforms included measures that led to a greater differentiation of types of criminality within the prison system, these reforms were not a direct reaction to an economic crisis. The perceived effects and causes of the 'crisis' Garland describes were themselves mediated through already established administrative procedures which drew attention to problem categories that did not fit neatly into the classifications of pauper, prisoner or schoolchild.

NOTES

1 D. Garland, 'British criminology before 1935', *The British Journal of Criminology*, 28, 1988, p. 1. D. Garland, *Punishment and Welfare: A History of Penal Strategies*, Aldershot, Gower, 1985.
2 M. Foucault, 'Lecture given on 14th January 1976' in M. Foucault, *Power/Knowledge: Selected Interviews and Other Writings, 1972–1977*, ed. C. Gordon, Brighton, Harvester, 1981, pp. 96, 99.
3 M. Foucault, *Discipline and Punish: The Birth of the Prison*, tr. A. Sheridan, Harmondsworth, Penguin, 1979, p. 255.
4 Ibid., p. 246.
5 Ibid., pp. 250–1.

6 Ibid., p. 252.
7 K. Williams, *From Pauperism to Poverty*, London, Routledge & Kegan Paul, 1981, pp. 141–2.
8 J. Sim, *Medical Power in Prisons: The Prison Medical Service in England 1774–1989*, Milton Keynes, Open University Press, 1990.
9 Ibid., pp. 10, 7.
10 Ibid., pp. 14–16, 27.
11 Ibid., p. 70.
12 Ibid., pp. 86–9.
13 Ibid., p. 178.
14 Ibid., p. 179.
15 Ibid., p. 5.
16 Ibid., p. 53–4.
17 Ibid., p. 62.
18 Ibid., pp. 77, 72.
19 Ibid., p. 128.
20 As described in Foucault, 'Lecture'.
21 N. East, 'The incidence of crime and mental defect', *British Medical Journal*, 11 August 1923, p. 228; N. East, *Society and the Criminal*, London, HMSO, 1949, p. 129. See S. Watson, 'The moral imbecile: a study of the relations between penal practice and psychiatric knowledge of the habitual offender', unpublished Ph.D. thesis, University of Lancaster, 1988, ch. 6.
22 Sim, *Medical Power*, p. 72.
23 Garland, *Punishment and Welfare*, p. 5.
24 Ibid., p. 11.
25 Ibid., p. 5.
26 S. Dell, J. Gunn, G. Robertson and C. Way, *Psychiatric Aspects of Imprisonment*, London, Academic Press, 1978, p. 15.
27 Garland, *Punishment and Welfare*, p. 15.
28 *Report of the Commissioners of Prisons for 1911–1912*, London, HMSO, 1912–13, Cd 6406, 6407, xliii, 345, p. 27.
29 S. Hobhouse and F. Brockway (eds), *English Prisons Today, Being the Report of the Prison System Enquiry Committee*, special edn for subscribers, London, 1922, p. 76, from *Report of the Commissioners of Prisons 1912–1913*, pp. 22–33.
30 J. E. Thomas, *The English Prison Officer since 1850: A Study in Conflict*, London, Routledge & Kegan Paul, 1972, p. 117.
31 Foucault, *Discipline and Punish*, p. 233.
32 Hobhouse and Brockway, *English Prisons Today*, p. 78.
33 Foucault, *Discipline and Punish*, pp. 233–6.
34 M. Ignatieff, *A Just Measure of Pain*, London, Macmillan, 1978, pp. 198–204.
35 Garland, *Punishment and Welfare*, pp. 31–2.
36 Hobhouse and Brockway, *English Prisons Today*, pp. 73–4; S. Dell et al., 1978, p. 10.
37 Ignatieff, *A Just Measure of Pain*, p. 204.
38 Hobhouse and Brockway, *English Prisons Today*, p. 215.
39 Ibid., p. 215. See *Report of the Commissioners of Prisons 1903–1904*,

London, HMSO, 1905, Cd 2273, xxxvii, 1, p. 25, and *Report of the Commissioners of Prisons for 1911–1912*, p. 23, for reactions to the 1898 Act.

40 Hobhouse and Brockway, *English Prisons Today*, p. 317.

41 *Report of the Commissioners of Prisons 1906–1907*, London, HMSO, 1908, Cd 3738, lii, 1, p. 12.

42 Garland, *Punishment and Welfare*, p. 36.

43 Hobhouse and Brockway, *English Prisons Today*, p. 103. From Sir Edmund Du Cane, *Punishment and Prevention of Crime*, 1885, p. 77.

44 The system was a complex one. In local prisons there were First Division, Second Division, and Star Class (Garland, *Punishment and Welfare*, pp. 218–24). In the convict prisons inmates were labelled Star Class, Intermediate and Recidivist (this last class created in 1903–1904) (ibid., p. 317).

45 Ibid., p. 34.

46 Watson, 'The moral imbecile', ch. 3; see also S. Watson, 'Malingerers, the "weakminded" criminal and the "moral imbecile": how the prison medical officer became an expert in mental deficiency, 1890–1930' in M. J. Clark and C. Crawford (eds), *Legal Medicine in History*, Cambridge, Cambridge University Press, 1944, pp. 223–41.

47 1843 Regulations for Local Gaols, quoted in N. Walker and S. McCabe, *Crime and Insanity in England 2*, Edinburgh University Press, 1973, p. 50.

48 *Transactions of the Medico-Legal Society*, 10, 1912–13, p. 4.

49 Public Record Office, Home Office, 170/A43422, 1897, 'Mathew Sampson, Weakminded Prisoner'.

50 Walker and McCabe, *Crime and Insanity*, p. 50.

51 Ibid., p. 39; this was begun in 1852. See also *Report of the Departmental Commission on Criminal Lunacy*, London, HMSO, 1882, Cd 3418, xxxii, 789, p. 841; and E. Ruggles-Brise, *The English Prison System*, London, Macmillan, 1921, p. 42. The provisions included the concentration of the 'weak-minded' at Millbank after 1863 (Walker, p. 39), and at Woking Invalid Wing in the 1860s (J. Campbell, *Thirty Years Experience as a Medical Officer in the English Convict Service*, London, T. Nelson, 1884, p. 79). The 1879 Penal Servitude Commission recommended that 'weak-minded convicts should be concentrated in special prisons and placed in the charge of specially selected officers' (Ruggles-Brise, *The English Prison System*, p. 41).

52 Sim, *Medical Power*, p. 29.

53 P. Miller, 'Critiques of psychiatry and critical sociologies of madness', in P. Miller and N. Rose (eds), *The Power of Psychiatry*, Cambridge, Polity Press, 1986, pp. 29–30.

9

FOUCAULT'S THEORY OF DISCOURSE AND HUMAN AGENCY

Dieter Freundlieb

Foucault grew increasingly antagonistic towards Marxism, but his writings have been the object of censure for the same reason that Marxist thinking has been widely denounced: his apparent denial of human agency, both as a reality in its own right and as an explanatory force in historical accounts. Indeed, Foucault may be read as being far more rigorous (or, if one prefers, doctrinaire) on this score. Partly because of Marx's insistence upon the dialectical, it has been possible for various Marxist theorists and historians, notably in recent years E. P. Thompson, to retrieve the historical role of human choice, experience and activity. But it is hard to imagine any such 'humanist' leanings in Foucault himself, or a plausible humanist reading of his works. Foucault resolutely insisted upon the 'death of the author' – texts were to be analysed as texts, not as the outpourings of individuals, and texts in turn were determined by wider discourses; he saw 'humanism' not as a truth but as a framework of thought that rose and fell between Renaissance and Romanticism', and he regarded Marxist thinking itself as a late specimen of such an 'anthropology'.

Foucault's stance on such matters, and particularly the notion of 'discursive formation' most clearly set out in *The Archaeology of Knowledge*, has been variously read: as an uncompromising version of the structuralist and deconstructionist doctrine that there is no life beyond the text; as a negation of political activism; as a rather Nietzschian style of pessimism; or as a profound and consistent recognition of the never-ceasing and all-powerful constraints operating within society. Dieter Freundlieb here examines the philosophical roots of Foucault's position and its practical implications. While laying bare the dilemmas in traditional historical thinking that the notion of discursive structures was intended to settle, Freundlieb contends that Foucault's formulation itself created more problems than it resolved and radically begged the question of the ontological status of discourse. It might be said that Foucault manoeuvred himself into the unusual corner of being both an idealist and a determinist or, as some would say, a reviver of the exploded notion of the *Zeitgeist* or *Weltanschauung*.

It is a peculiar fact in the history of thought that every now and again a major writer succeeds, whether intentionally or not, in establishing a new theoretical concept that proves to be almost irresistible even in contexts and disciplines where its use is inappropriate. Thomas Kuhn's notion of a scientific paradigm and, more recently, Jacques Derrida's concept of deconstruction are cases in point. Such concepts turn out to be attractive to the community of scholars (and subsequently even to journalists), it seems, not because of their semantic precision and fruitfulness within a particular theory, but precisely because of their general vagueness. This makes them almost infinitely adaptable. Their advantage, from the point of view of those who deploy them, is that they seem to lend some of the prestige they enjoyed in their original context of use to new fields of application. Kuhn's concept of paradigm, whose well-known vagueness was noted and commented on fairly early,[1] and Derrida's notion of deconstruction, which according to Derrida is not even a concept, have been and continue to be, highly successful outside their original contexts if success is measured by frequency of use. Almost anyone dissatisfied with a dominant mode of theorizing has called for a 'paradigm change', and one is likely to get away, today, with calling almost any kind of critical analysis a deconstruction. It needs to be remembered, of course, that both Derrida's and Kuhn's concept owe their popularity not *just* to their adaptability, but also to the fact that they were part of a genuinely innovative theoretical project.

Anyone familiar with contemporary debates about post-modern theory will have noticed that the concept of discourse is yet another case of such an irresistible notion. While the term 'discourse' has, of course, a long and venerable history as well as a quite specific use in areas such as modern linguistics and cognitive psychology,[2] no one has perhaps done more to re-establish it as a key term in post-modern philosophy, and the various disciplines drawing on post-modern thought, than Michel Foucault. It is on Foucault's theory of discourse (or discursive formations) that this essay will focus.[3] My discussion will be partly expository and partly critical, because Foucault's work on discourse analysis is neither lucid nor uncontroversial. In fact, one of the consequences that could be drawn from my critique is that the current inflationary use of the term 'discourse' is unhelpful, to say the least; for the question needs to be raised whether the term 'discourse', though undeniably part of Foucault's generally innovative work, designates a well-defined theoretical object.

First of all, then I would like to demonstrate that discourses or discursive formations, as described by Foucault, do not constitute a uniformly theorizable domain of objects or events. I will be arguing, in other words, that the notion of a discursive formation is a theoretical fiction. The set of empirically identifiable phenomena referred to by Foucault in the context of his programme of an archaeology of knowledge is too heterogeneous to be open to a unified explanatory theory that would adequately account for these phenomena.[4] In particular, Foucault's attempt to theorize this domain of objects within a largely structuralist framework is unworkable. Second, I want to argue that the epistemological role that the theoretical concept of a discourse as a historical a priori plays in Foucault is incoherent because it implies an untenable ontology and leads, if interpreted in a way Foucault himself encourages, to a self-destructive relativism. Third, I want to show that a major reason for the failure of Foucault's theory of discourse, either as an independent enterprise or as part of a genealogy of the human sciences, is his refusal to provide adequate space, within his theory, for human agency. As is well known, in putting forward his project of an archaeology of knowledge, Foucault's aim was precisely to 'define a method of analysis purged of all anthropologism'.[5] But it turns out that an analysis that deliberately ignores the intentions of historical agents within the process of the production of knowledge (savoir), even if these intentions are always only a part of what drives the history of the sciences, is not feasible. None the less, the present essay is not meant to be a wholesale rejection of Foucault's ideas on discourse. We owe to Foucault a number of important insights into phenomena of the social use of language that need to be disentangled from the failed project of a theory of discursive formations. However, such a salvaging operation will not be attempted here.

I

Foucault develops his theory of discourses (or discursive formations) mainly in his book *The Archaeology of Knowledge*, originally published in 1969, which will therefore be our main point of focus. And while Foucault is often said to begin a new phase in his intellectual career from the mid-1970s when he published *Discipline and Punish*, it is important to realize that his turn to a genealogical analysis of what he called regimes of power/knowledge by no means meant an abandonment of the notion of an archaeological analysis of discourses. Discourse analysis from now on focuses on how discourses function within such regimes, but Foucault always argued that archaeology and genealogy are both necessary and complementary to each other. It could be said, in fact that even in his late work on so-called 'technologies of the self' the notions of discourse and of archaeological analysis are still present as methodological tools.[6] So what precisely is an archaeological analysis of discourses and why is it a theoretical failure? In order to answer this question, two things are necessary: a brief general comment on how Foucault's archaeological analysis fits in with other forms of understanding the human sciences and a detailed investigation of key chapters and passages in *The Archaeology of Knowledge*.

Dreyfus and Rabinow, in their *Michel Foucault: Beyond Structuralism and Hermeneutics*, see Foucault's archaeology as an (ultimately unsuccessful) attempt to overcome the problems Foucault had identified in what he called the 'analytic of finitude', that is the project of providing a philosophical foundation for knowledge in the face of the recognition of the finitude of human beings, a finitude which was recognized not only by Kant but by both Husserl's phenomenological programme and Heidegger's hermeneutical project of a fundamental ontology. Foucault believed that the aporias of trying to get to know what makes knowledge possible, to turn our own cognitive limitations and our ultimately unknowable origin into the basis for the possibility of objective knowledge, could only be overcome if we abandon totally what he regards as the underlying anthropologism of this figure of thought. This made him reject both Husserl's attempt to turn the practices of social life that form the background of meaning into sets of propositional beliefs that can be objectified and analysed, as well as the hermeneutic project of a never-ending interpretation of the historically shifting situations we find ourselves in. In this context, structuralism, because of its rejection of humanism, must have seemed to Foucault more attractive than any of the other alternatives to a study of the human sciences. And in spite of Foucault's objections to being associated too closely with structuralist thought, his archaeology, as we will see shortly, is very much informed by a structuralist mode of analysis.[7]

Early on in his discussion of how what he calls archaeology differs from more traditional forms of historical analysis, Foucault compares his project with that of a structuralist analysis of language and makes the following claim: language, understood as *langue*, is 'a finite body of rules that authorizes an infinite number of performances' (27). This principle of generative grammar – and we may ignore here the fact that what is generated in such a grammar is not performances but abstract objects called grammatical sentences – does not operate, according to Foucault, in the archaeological analysis of discourses as a finite set of statements considered as 'events':

> The question posed by language analysis of some discursive fact or other is always: according to what rules has a particular state-ment been made, and consequently according to what rules could other similar statements be made? The description of the events of discourse poses a quite different question: how is it that one particular statement appeared rather than another?
>
> (ibid.)

On the one hand, Foucault's project claims to be a '*pure description of discursive events*' (ibid., Foucault's emphasis) so as to make possible an entirely new way of setting up and grouping discursive unities, independent of all the old and in Foucault's view only seemingly self-evident unities such as the book and the *œuvre*.[8] On the other hand, his project of a discursive analysis turns out to be an extremely ambitious endeavour since it tries to explain why certain statements appeared (or at least give an analysis of a number of necessary con-ditions for statements *qua* events to be possible), what the relations are between statements and whole groups of statements, and how what governs such relations changes historically.

Foucault further clarifies the aims of his project when he argues that an archaeological analysis differs from the traditional history in so far as it is not concerned with any interpretation of a hidden mean-ing, that is, the unsaid of a text. Rather, he argues that

> we must grasp the statement in the exact specificity of its occur-rence; determine its conditions of existence, fix at least its limits, establish its correlations with other statements that may be connected with it, and show what other forms of statement it excludes . . . We must show why it could not be other than it was, in what respect it is exclusive of any other, how it assumes, in the midst of others and in relation to them, a place that no other could occupy.
>
> (28)

In Chapter 2, entitled 'Discursive formations', Foucault looks at four potential ways of describing relations between statements within groups of statements that have been formed, provisionally, on the basis of more traditional classifications such as medicine, grammar and political economy. Each of the four hypotheses as he calls them is then rejected and replaced by a different set of hypotheses, each of which he addresses in much more detail in the four subsequent chapters of Part II called 'The formation of objects' (ch. 3), 'The formation of enunciative modalities' (ch. 4), 'The formation of concepts' (ch. 5) and 'The formation of strategies' (ch. 6).

The first hypothesis that needs to be replaced concerns the idea that discursive formations may be held together by a common set of objects of reference. This is obviously an important question because of its epistemological implications. So on what grounds is this hypothesis rejected? The example Foucault uses is madness as the object of the discipline of psychopathology, but he claims that he 'soon realized that the unity of the object "madness" does not enable one to individualize a group of statements, and to establish between them a relation that is both constant and describable' (32). Abandoning the approach he took in his earlier book on madness,[9] Foucault no longer seems to believe in the real and independent existence of a genuine but pre-discursive experience of madness and a 'being of madness itself', which are subsequently falsified and misconceived by the discourse of psychiatry. Instead, he argues that

> mental illness was constituted by all that was said in all the statements that named it, divided it up, described it, explained it, traced its developments, indicated its various correlations, judged it, and possibly gave it speech by articulating, in its name, discourses that were taken to be its own.
>
> (32)

The example of madness is, of course, a complex and potentially controversial one because even from a realist rather than Foucault's nominalist perspective, madness is not considered a natural kind, as it were, but a family of illnesses that often manifest themselves in quite different forms, depending at least in part on their cultural context. Also, the history of the acquisition of knowledge about madness, unlike the history of our knowledge of physical objects and their behaviour, is a chequered one, so that it may not always be clear how to determine the referential meanings of key concepts about madness that were developed over a period of time. In spite of these inherent uncertainties, it is clear that Foucault takes a radically anti-realist line with regard to the object 'madness'. Thus he claims that even if we look at specific kinds of mental illness such as neuroses, we will find that the object of the discourses on neurosis is as much constituted and historically variable as that of madness in general. Any discourse-independent identity of the object of the discourses on madness is expressly and repeatedly denied (32–3). So what *is* it that gives the discourses on madness their unity? As usual, Foucault's answer is far from straightforward. This is what he says:

> The unity of discourses on madness would not be based upon the existence of the object 'madness', or the constitution of a single horizon of objectivity; it would be the interplay of the rules that make possible the appearance of objects during a given period of time; objects that are shaped by measures of discrimination and repression, objects that are differentiated in daily practice, in law, in religious casuistry, in medical diagnosis, objects that are manifested in pathological descriptions, objects that are circumscribed by medical codes, practices, treatment, and care. Moreover, the unity of the discourses on madness would be the interplay of the rules that define the transformations of these different objects, their non-identity through time, the break produced in them, the internal discontinuity that suspends their permanence. Paradoxically, to define a group of statements in terms of its individuality would be to define the dispersion of these objects, to grasp all the interstices that separate them, to measure the distances that reign between them – in other words, to formulate their law of division.
>
> (33)

A number of things need to be noted here. First of all, we must be aware that Foucault postulates two kinds of rules: those whose interaction produces new objects and those whose interaction brings about transformations of these objects, though these two types of rule interaction need not be very dissimilar. Second, and more importantly, Foucault's insistence on the *constitutive* role of discursive rules associates his project with a form of epistemological idealism that is difficult to make sense of, unless residual forms of realism are admitted through the back door, as it were. For if different discourses on madness produce their own discourse-specific objects rather than discover and refer to discourse-independent entities, it is not at all clear how a set of rules that makes the appearance and modification of quite different objects possible can provide a criterion for the individualization of a group of statements. If madness is a motley of different discourse-specific objects, it seems impossible to say what the boundaries of such a set of objects could be. In other words, it seems that we would never be able to say where madness ends and something else begins.

A further complication arises when we apply Foucault's idea of the object-constitutive role of discursive rules to his own endeavour. If the discourse from within which Foucault is speaking is likewise governed by rules that make the appearance of certain objects possible, that is if it is not a discourse that has the power to refer to objects independent of the discourse in which they are discussed, then Foucault has not discovered anything about past discourses and the way they function, but has simply brought yet another set of discourse-specific objects into existence that have no identity over time. This would be a disastrous conseqence of his project, because its effectiveness depends on the non-local validity of its truth claims. In the dialogue with his imaginary opponent that forms the conclusion to *The Archaeology of Knowledge* Foucault seems to be aware, at least to some extent, of the problem that arises if the validity of his own discourse is questioned. But his answer is evasive and in the end unsatisfactory, for the problem of the object-constitutive character of discourses is never squarely addressed. Instead of confronting the epistemological challenge, he launches a psychological counter-attack.

Third, we need to be aware of the fact that so far the ontological status of what Foucault calls rules for the appearance and transformation of objects is very much in the dark. In fact, it would follow from the last point I just made that these rules, too, are objects constituted by (rather than discovered through) Foucault's own discourse. But this is clearly not what he means to say. Rather, he makes the claim that his way of individualizing groups of statements that make up a discourse is superior, in some *objective* way, to more traditional accounts of the history of knowledge and that his whole project is meant to *discover* new kinds of objects.[10] Where and how, then, do the rules that allegedly govern discourses exist? If they have a real existence and real effects on a discursive practice but are not conceived of as located in the minds of subjects who have the competence to make use of these rules, their ontological status is rather obscure.

The second hypothesis concerning the possible unity of a discourse which Foucault says he had to abandon fairly early on is described somewhat vaguely as a certain 'style' or a 'way of looking at things', for example in nineteenth-century medical discourse. This characterization of medical discourse as a series of descriptive statements of a certain type is said to be unsuitable because the medical discourse was not just such a series of statements but 'a group of hypotheses about life and death, of ethical choices, of therapeutic decisions, of institutional regulations, [and] of teaching models' (33). And again Foucault argues that because all these things change considerably throughout the nineteenth century, there is no obvious unity at the level of statements themselves but a unity at the deeper level of the rules which make possible the statements and all the other elements he has listed, including their historical changes:

> If there is a unity, its principle is not therefore a determined form of statements; is it not rather the group of rules, which, simultaneously or in turn, have made possible purely perceptual descriptions, together with observations mediated through instruments, the procedures used in laboratory experiments, statistical calculations, epidemiological or demographic observations, institutional regulations, and therapeutic practice? What one must theorize and individualize is the coexistence of these dispersed and heterogeneous statements; the system that governs their division, the degree to which they depend upon one another, the way in which they interlock or exclude one another, the transformation that they undergo, and the play of their location, arrangement, and replacement.
>
> (34)

As in the case of the first hypothesis and its subsequent rejection, Foucault claims that there are 'rules' and a 'system' that govern a heterogeneous body of statements produced by what he calls medical discourse, but which in fact comprises practices that are by no means purely discursive. This time, however, the rules do not 'constitute' objects but are said to 'make possible' the various statements and other practices characteristic of a discourse. What exactly is meant by the phrase 'make possible' is difficult to determine, but a clarification of what Foucault has in mind here is crucial if we want to understand his whole project of an archaeology of knowledge. First of all, however, we should note that the idea that all the various activities that according to Foucault make up the medical discourse are governed by a set of 'rules' or a 'system' is highly unlikely and counter-intuitive; second, while it is perfectly obvious that anything that happens must have been 'made possible' by a set of necessary conditions, either in a causal or a logical sense, it is again extremely unlikely that these conditions (whether conceived of as rules or something else) somehow form a unity, given the heterogeneous nature of the discursive (and at least partly non-discursive) practices enumerated by Foucault. Finally, it seems that Foucault confounds the possible with the actual. If the 'rules' he postulates are conceived of as conditions of *existence* rather than conditions of *possibility* as in the case of grammatical rules, then whatever a historical a priori allowed to happen or allowed to be thought and said is identical with what in fact happened or was thought and said. The problem with this is that it leaves unexplained the *changes* that occurred. The fact that changes *did* occur needs to be theorized in terms of conditions of possibility rather than conditions of existence, and while it is safe to say that certain theoretical innovations are inconceivable at a certain point in the evolution of a body of knowledge – Einsteinian physics surely could not have been developed a hundred years earlier than it actually was – the actual never exhausts the (logically and empirically) possible at any point in time. Applied to processes of cognitive problem-solving this means that individual imagination, creativity and reasoning cannot be excluded from an understanding of how the acquisition of knowledge develops. In order to give this crucial point some more argumentative substance, a brief look at an example from the history of medicine might be helpful.

A classic case in point is the discovery by John Snow (1813–1858) that Asiatic cholera is a communicable disease spread by contaminated water, described in his monograph *On the Mode of Communication of Cholera*.[11] At the time Snow formed his hypotheses concerning the nature of cholera, a number of competing theories were available to the medical profession, and it was not until much later that the bacteria that cause cholera could actually be observed microscopically and identified as the causative agent. None the less, it was Snow's careful observation of various regularities accompanying outbreaks of the cholera, guided by hypotheses and relying on important data provided by 'natural' experimental situations,[12] that led him to the conviction that cholera is a communicable disease and that the organism causing it must be carried, largely, in the water supply used by its victims. While details of Snow's theory can be seen to be faulty in a number of respects today, the scientific rationality behind his reasoning, for example in the way he dealt with competing theories, is open to logical reconstruction, and it was the compelling force of Snow's reasoning which contributed crucially to the adoption of hygienic measures that saved many lives. Now this is precisely the kind of 'Whiggish' history Foucault wishes to overcome, but the point is that while there is always another, less glorious, story to be told, the history of medical science would be incomprehensible without the reconstruction of the reasoning of its practitioners.

Foucault's third hypothesis, which, again, he only introduces in order to dismiss it in favour of his project of an archaeological analysis, is that groups of statements might be held together by a system of permanent and coherent *concepts*. He rejects this by arguing that the example of what he calls classical grammar shows that the concepts that emerged within this field over time are too heterogeneous and in some cases even incompatible to form a unity. Instead, he suggests that 'one might discover a discursive unity if one sought it not in the coherence of concepts, but in their simultaneous or successive emergence, in the distance that separates them and even in their incompatibility' (35). From a more traditional point of view, which may well turn out to be superior, one would argue that, just as history itself is not governed by any specific laws of development, the development of a discipline is in principle unpredictable and not amenable to any precise analysis in terms of rules, systems or laws. What is possible is a reconstruction in terms of a history of scientific problem-solving and a situational logic, particularly if this is combined with an underlying conception of what the general aims of science were at a given point in time. Foucault's suggestion that one can find a system of rules that determines which concepts were able to emerge and which ones were not is therefore extremely unlikely.

The last hypothesis for unifying groups of statements is 'the identity and persistence of themes'. Like the previous three, this hypothesis is replaced by the proposal of a unifying criterion at a more submerged level. What Foucault believes might form a principle of the individualization of a discourse is 'the dispersion of the points of choice that the discourse leaves free' (36) and the way in which a discourse defines 'a field of strategic possibilities' (37). We will discuss this proposal when we look more closely at Chapter 6 of Part II.

Finally, and on the basis of the four hypotheses that are meant to replace more traditional principles of individualization and which are nearly all concerned with rules governing dispersion rather than unity, Foucault provides the following definition of a discursive formation:

Whenever one can describe, between a number of statements, such a system of dispersion, whenever, between objects, types of statement, concepts or thematic choices, one can define a regularity (an order, correlations, positions and functionings, transformations), will say, for the sake of convenience, that we are dealing with a *discursive formation*.

(38)

As far as the underlying rules of a discursive formation are concerned, Foucault makes the following statement:

> The conditions to which the elements of this division [i.e. the discursive formation] (objects, modes of statement, concepts, thematic choices) are subjected we shall call the *rules of formation*. The rules of formation are conditions of existence (but also of coexistence, maintenance, modification, and disappearance) in a given discursive division.
>
> (ibid.)

II

Chapter 3 of Part II of *The Archaeology of Knowledge* takes up the first principle of individuation, that is the formation of objects, and it does so in relation to 'the discourse of psychopathology from the nineteenth century onwards' (40). In order to determine the formation of objects in this discourse, Foucault distinguishes between what he calls (a) surfaces of emergence, (b) authorities of delimitation, and (c) grids of specification. Surfaces of emergence, with regard to the discourse of psychopathology are: the family, the immediate social group, the work situation, the religious community, but also a range of newly established ones such as art and penality. Under the heading of 'authorities of delimitation' Foucault lists: medicine, the law, the religious authority and literary art and criticism. Finally, the grid of specification, that is the system of classification used to subdivide mental illnesses, characteristic of psychopathological discourse, is said to comprise the soul, the body, the life and history of individuals, and the interplay of neuropsychological correlations.

While all these are seen as responsible, to some extent, for the formation of objects, the analysis of the formation of psychopathological concepts also, and most importantly, needs to take into account that the psychologization and pathologization of the delinquent, which is a key feature of this discourse, was made possible by a whole set of relations; for example, the relation between the authority of medical decision and the authority of judicial decision and the relation between therapeutic confinement in hospital and punitive confinement in prison. Foucault claims that 'these are the relations that, operating in psychiatric discourse, have made possible the formation of a whole group of various objects' (44). A more general result that is said to follow from these examples is the fact that a discursive formation is defined, in terms of the formation of its objects, 'if one can show how any particular object of discourse finds in it its place and law of emergence' (ibid.).

Now, in spite of the often infuriatingly vague notions Foucault has invented to describe what one is looking for when one engages in an archaeological analysis focused on the formation of objects, it seems that what he is describing here are both conceptual and social or institutional conditions that must be fulfilled for certain kinds of investigations focusing on certain kinds of objects to be possible. But it seems inconceivable that the particular constellations of conceptual, social and institutional changes that make possible certain kinds of investigations (such as investigations into the psychological make-up of delinquents) emerge in a way that is governed by specifiable rules or laws. In many cases these constellations will no doubt come about entirely coincidentally and should be conceived of as unintended consequences of sets of more or less intended historical actions. If it is a 'complex group of relations' (45) between institutional bodies that is responsible for the emergence of certain kinds of investigations, then it seems impossible to argue that their emergence is the result of rules. Rules, as something one follows or does not follow in the performance of an action, just are not the kinds of entities that determine relations between institutions if intentional actions between members of institutions are systematically ruled out as objects of study. It seems therefore that Foucault forces the structuralist idea of a rule-governed system of elements, underlying the formation of grammatical sentences, upon a domain of elements that has nothing in common with a linguistic system. Even less plausible is it to argue that not only are there specifiable laws or rules – which for reasons that are now becoming obvious Foucault hardly ever actually formulates – but that they are object-constitutive rather than making something visible that was already there beforehand. Yet this is precisely what Foucault claims when he says that the object 'does not pre-exist itself, held back by some obstacle at the first edges of light' (ibid.). So what is extremely implausible even under a realist interpretation, namely the idea that the historical emergence of new forms of investigation is governed by rules or laws, becomes even less plausible if postulated from within Foucault's anti-realism. In fact, as I argued above, since Foucault cannot exempt his own investigation from being another example of a discourse in operation, the objects allegedly emerging in other discourses must now be seen as brought into existence, together with their associated discourses, by Foucault's own discourse. Discourses, as described by Foucault, are therefore fictions in a double sense. They are fictions since even within a realist interpretation they are too heterogeneous to be amenable to systematic theorization in terms of rules or laws, and they are fictions because if they are object-constitutive, then the discourses Foucault talks about, that is the discourses that are the object of Foucault's own discourse, do not pre-exist the discourse Foucault himself is engaged in.

On the last few pages of Chapter 3 it appears that the relations between various institutions that Foucault claims operate in the production of discursive objects are not the kind of relations historians would normally assume to exist. Rather, these relations are given a special status that is meant to explain their object-constitutive function. The relations Foucault has in mind 'must be distinguished first from what we might call "primary" relations, and which, independently of all discourse or all object of discourse, may be described between institutions, techniques, social forms etc.' (45). But there are also 'secondary' relations which appear within discourses, for example when nineteenth-century psychiatrists themselves talk about relations between the family and criminality. These are considered to be surface phenomena, however, which cannot be taken at face value. The relations Foucault is really interested in are said to be *discursive* rather than either primary or secondary. They are not internal to the discourse, but form the rules which govern the discourse as a practice. Here, as in so many instances in *The Archaeology of Knowledge*, entities are defined by Foucault very much in terms of what they are not – which means that it is very difficult to understand what exactly Foucault is saying. To define, or redefine, relations between institutions as practices is hardly very precise and illuminating.

At the end of the chapter, Foucault reiterates his anti-realist stance and argues that a discursive analysis of the formation of objects is neither about language or words nor about things, but about 'the regular formation of objects that emerge only in discourse' (47). These objects must be related 'to the body of rules that enable them to form as objects of a discourse and thus constitute the conditions of their historical appearance' (48). A discourse 'is not a slender surface of contact, or confrontation, between a reality and a language (*langue*), the intrication of a lexicon and an experience' (ibid.).

Archaeological analysis is therefore not about 'words and things', but an investigation that treats discourses 'as practices that systematically form the objects of which they speak' (49).

Chapter 4, entitled 'The formation of enunciative modalities', addresses the question of how the unity of a group of very heterogeneous kinds of statements within nineteenth-century medical discourse can be determined from yet another angle. Foucault lists such areas as 'qualitative descriptions, biographical accounts, the location, interpretation, and cross-checking of signs, reasonings by analogy, deduction, statistical calculation, [and] experimental verifications' (50). Assuming, against all normal expectations, that one can discover 'the law operating behind all these diverse statements' (ibid.), Foucault sets himself three tasks in order to determine this 'law'. First of all, he wants to find out who has the authority to produce medical statements and what the criteria are by which the competence of the individuals is determined who are allowed to assume the role of authoritative speakers in matters medical. As in all the other cases, this question is given a historical dimension as well, since the right to make medical statements did not remain unchanged in the period under consideration. Yet it seems obvious, again, that far from being explicable in terms of any one 'law', the answer to this historical and sociological question can only be given through detailed empirical analyses, within a historical sociology of knowledge, which would have to identify many different causal mechanisms.

The second task Foucault thinks it is necessary to undertake is the specification of the various institutional sites from which the medical discourse emanates. He identifies four such sites: the hospital, the private practice, the laboratory, and the library or documentary field, all of which, again, undergo a process of modification during the nineteenth century. This is obviously an interesting field of investigation, but the suggestion that the social norms and mechanisms governing the institutional sites and the causes that bring about historical changes in their constitution form a 'system', a set of 'rules' or a 'law', which in turn make statements possible and provide 'positions' that speaking subjects can occupy, seems extremely implausible. Of course it is possible, in principle, to write a history of the institutional sites related to the medical profession and their historical changes over a specific period of time and in a certain geographical location; but one could hardly expect to find some determinate set of rules or a law that would account for the functioning and transformation of the sites and the statements that are disseminated from them. Again it seems that Foucault's structuralist leanings in the late 1960s led him to postulate language-like rule systems in an area where they simply do not exist.

Foucault's strongly anti-anthropological and anti-humanist stance manifests itself in the third question concerning the role of the subject within the institutional context of a discourse. The intentions of thinking subjects and their perception of medical problems and their possible solutions are completely ignored in favour of the idea that it is the discourse itself that provides a limited set of positions for the subject to occupy. Thus, at the end of the chapter, he says:

> Thus conceived, discourse is not the majestically unfolding manifestation of a thinking, knowing, speaking subject, but, on the contrary, a totality, in which the dispersion of the subject and his discontinuity with himself may be determined . . . it must now be recognized that it is neither by recourse to a transcendental subject nor by recourse to a psychological subjectivity that the regulation of its enunciations should be defined.
>
> (55)

Positions that can be taken up by a subject endowed with the requisite authority are, for example, 'the questioning subject', 'the listening subject', 'the seeing subject', and 'the observing subject' (52). Each of these subject positions is determined by pregiven structures of one kind or another. Largely, these structures are conceived of as relations between elements, but the causality underlying all the discursive practices remains unclear. In fact, there seems to be a circularity involved in Foucault's account. The various relations between elements, such as the relation between immediate observations and acquired information, for example, are conceived of as both what makes clinical discourse possible and as what is effected by this discourse. For Foucault argues, on the one hand, that if, in clinical discourse,

> the doctor is in turn the sovereign, direct questioner, the observing eye, the touching finger, the organ that deciphers signs, the point at which previously formulated descriptions are integrated, the laboratory technician, *it is because a whole group of relations is involved*.
>
> (53; my emphasis)

On the other hand, and at the same time, Foucault claims that these relations are the result of the discursive practice itself (53–4). It appears that Foucault is driven to this kind of circular argument precisely because his virtually complete neglect of human agency and of processes of reasoning does not allow him to account for historical change and innovation within a discipline other than in terms of the 'agency' of a system of anonymous rules and elements. Foucault may have rejected the idea that his project was a structuralist one, but there is ample evidence that he in fact tried to impose a structuralist way of thinking on historical processes centrally involving reasoning subjects and historically contingent causalities, neither of which can be accounted for in terms of relations between elements in the way grammatical systems might be.[13]

Chapter 5 on the formation of concepts proceeds in a fashion similar to the previous two. The organization of a field of statements is said to involve three elements that are described in a characteristically vague way:

1 forms of *succession*, including such things as the 'order of inferences, successive implications, and demonstrative reasonings' as well as 'the order of descriptions' and 'the schemata of generalization' (56);
2 forms of *coexistence*, comprising a 'field of presence', a 'field of concomitance', and a 'field of memory'; and lastly
3 *procedures of intervention* such as techniques of rewriting, modes of transcribing, modes of translating and some others we need not list here.

Foucault admits that these are very heterogeneous phenomena, but he claims that

> what properly belongs to a discursive formation and what makes it possible to delimit the group of concepts, disparate as they may be, that are specific to it, is the way in which these different elements are related to one another . . . It is this group of relations that constitutes a system of conceptual formation.
>
> (59–60)

Again, we can see that Foucault, whether he is aware of this move or not, treats an extremely variegated and not very precisely defined field of phenomena as if it were, in strict accordance with structuralist principles, a 'system' whose behaviour is governed by 'relations' between its 'elements'. He is not concerned with the actual theoretical concepts used in a discipline, but with some allegedly underlying set of schemata: 'These schemata make it possible to describe – not the laws of the internal construction of concepts, not their progressive and individual genesis in the mind of man – but their anonymous dispersion through texts, books, and *œuvres*' (60). Even when he acknowledges that concepts are indeed formed in the consciousness of subjects, he makes it quite clear that individual subjects themselves cannot take any real credit for this:

> In the analysis proposed here, the rules of formation operate not only in the mind or consciousness of individuals, but in discourse itself; they operate, therefore, according to a set of uniform anonymity, on all individuals who undertake to speak in this discursive field.
>
> (63)

Finally, in Chapter 6, Foucault looks at what he calls the 'formation of strategies', by which he means the choices that were made, in the evolution of discourses, for or against certain large-scale theories and themes. Not surprisingly, such 'choices' are not attributed to individuals but are seen as the result of non-subjective mechanisms or processes of 'derivation'.[14] Thus he says:

> A discursive formation will be individualized if one can define the system of formation of the different strategies that are deployed in it; in other words, if one can show how they all derive (in spite of their sometimes extreme diversity, and in spite of their dispersion in time) from the same set of relations.
>
> (68)

Important relations, in the case of the formation of strategies, are said to be relations to other discourses as well as to non-discursive practices, and these relations function very much like higher-order rules that restrict the generative power of theory choice at a lower level. Foucault therefore refers to the restrictive function that surrounding discourses and non-discursive practices have on a given discourse as 'authorities'. Each discourse is placed within an 'economy of discursive constellation' (66) that determines which aspects of its total potential for theory formation are realized:

> This whole group of relations forms a principle of determination that permits or excludes, within a given discourse, a certain number of statements: these are conceptual systematizations,

enunciative series, groups and organizations of objects that might have been possible (and of which nothing can justify the absence at the level of their own rules of formation), but which are excluded by a discursive constellation at a higher level and in a broader space. A discursive formation does not occupy therefore all the possible volume that is opened up to it of right by the systems of formation of its objects, its enunciations, and its concepts; it is essentially incomplete, owing to the system of formation of its strategic choices.

(67)

The analogies with structuralist conceptions of grammar, in spite of Foucault's objections to being labelled a structuralist, are again obvious. Discourses are attributed a generative power to produce statements which is restricted by higher-level rules belonging to an external system operating on the discourse. But since the phenomena Foucault is addressing are not really like grammatical rule systems at all but historical contingencies, he constantly wavers between a structuralist vocabulary and a vocabulary taken from the realm of action description. Hence his use of terms such as 'choice' and 'strategy' which are unintelligible outside the framework of human agency and reasoning, a framework whose role Foucault wants to minimize.

In the final chapter of Part II Foucault elaborates and qualifies some of the results of the previous four chapters, all of which were concerned with a four-fold 'system of formation': the formation of objects, the formation of enunciative modalities, the formation of concepts, and the formation of strategies. He makes the point, for example, that the four macro-elements of discourses he has isolated form another system of relations that can vary considerably from one discourse to another and over time. The production of statements is partly determined by the (often hierarchical) relations between the four systems of formation, but the dependence of statements and the system of formation can also work bottom-up rather than top-down. In an archaeological analysis, what he calls the system of formation is also to be investigated in its historical transformation. Unlike Saussure, who (wisely) argued that diachronic changes of the system are usually caused by highly contingent factors and therefore not amenable to a systematic analysis in terms of rules, Foucault is arguably more wedded to a structuralist mode of thinking by claiming that the historical changes occurring in discursive formations are also governed by rules. As said before, this is extremely unlikely. And yet, the system of formation, Foucault maintains, outlines

> the system of rules that must be put into operation if such and such an object is to be transformed, such and such a new enumeration appear, such and such a concept be developed, whether metamorphosed or imported, and such and such a strategy be modified – without ever ceasing to belong to this same discourse; and what it also outlines is the system of rules that has to be put into operation if a change in other discourses (in other practices, in institutions, in social relations, and in economic processes) is to be transcribed within a given discourse, thus constituting a new object, giving rise to a new strategy, giving place to new enunciations or new concepts. A discursive formation, then, does not play the role of a figure that arrests time and freezes it for decades or centuries; it determines a regularity proper to temporal processes.

(74)

Forcing quite heterogeneous and contingent historical processes into the mould of a rule-governed system is, of course, theoretically fruitless to say the least. As a consequence, all the examples Foucault provides of changes in discursive formations simply name singular historical events. In other words, each so-called 'rule' he postulates only applies once, thus emptying the notion of a rule of all content. The only other cases of discourses or elements of discourses affecting other discourses or elements of discourses seem to be restraints based on logical implications and conceptual dependencies between sets of beliefs. Beliefs and the use of certain concepts always commit those who operate with them to certain other beliefs and concepts. In that sense, beliefs are mechanisms for inclusion and exclusion. It seems that Foucault often looks at propositional implications and conceptual hierarchies within systems of beliefs as discursive 'rules' of inclusion and exclusion, but while this makes at least *some* sense at a synchronic level, it is disastrous if one's aim is to analyse historical changes in the production of knowledge, since all such implications and dependencies are at best purely deductive and truth-preserving. The reasons and causes behind the continuing *change* and *innovation* in scientific and other beliefs is precisely what *cannot* be accounted for on the basis of implications. Foucault contrasts 'the density of systematicities' underlying discursive formations with what he variously calls 'the silent work of thought', 'the "living" disorder of attempts, trials,

171

errors, and new beginnings' (75), or 'the bubbling source of life itself', all of which are unacceptable to him because of their humanist connotations. But whatever the problems might be of more traditional approaches to the history of the human sciences, Foucault's case for an archaeology of knowledge that operates exclusively at the level of discourses and their allegedly anonymous systems of rules remains unconvincing.

III

Foucault's analysis of the smallest element of a discursive formation, which he calls the statement, is notorious for its unclarity, due to Foucault's characterization of statements in terms of what they are not, rather than what they are. Dreyfus and Rabinow have argued that Foucault's notion of 'statement' is best understood as a serious speech act, and in support of their interpretation they can even point to Foucault's own admission that he was wrong when he said that statements are not speech acts.[15] In his letter to Searle, in which he made this admission and from which Dreyfus and Rabinow quote, Foucault added, however, that he looked at speech acts from a different angle. This is a crucial point, of course. Foucault is not concerned with the reconstruction of a universal communicative competence to produce well-formed kinds of speech acts, but, unlike Austin and Searle, he claims to be able to determine general conditions for the possibility or even the existence of the particular propositional content of speech acts since this content is seen as made possible by a system of rules functioning as a historical a priori. Foucault's focus on the content of speech acts rather than their formal pragmatic properties means that he needs to say something about the meaning and the intelligibility of statements. He quite rightly points out that the meaning and the intelligibility of a statement depend on what he calls a 'referential' or an 'associated field'. As a result, the same sequence of signifiers can constitute two different statements just as two different sequences of signs can form the same statement, depending on which referential they are associated with.[16] But his claim that there are specific rules that can explain the very existence of statements is rather implausible, as we have seen above.

While Foucault's meaning holism with regard to statements is relatively uncontroversial, at least in the sense that it is generally recognized that concepts come in clusters, his account of the relation between the speaking/writing subject and the statement is very questionable. One of the key characteristics of constative speech acts, particularly within a Habermasian interpretation of speech act theory, is that they are used to make a number of validity claims. According to Habermas, they claim to be true in relation to an external world of facts, they express a genuine belief of the speaker who takes responsibility for this claim, and they claim to be socially acceptable in the communicative context in which they are performed. Foucault, for obvious reasons, ignores these issues and argues instead that statements define positions which, in principle (though not necessarily in fact), any subject can take up. He maintains that

> the subject of the statement should not be regarded as identical with the author of the formulation – either in substance, or in function. He is not in fact the cause, origin, or starting-point of the phenomenon of the written or spoken articulation of a sentence . . . If a position, a sentence, a group of signs can be called 'statement', it is not therefore because, one day, someone happened to speak them or put them into some concrete form of writing; it is because the position of the subject can be assigned. To describe a formulation *qua* statement does not consist in analysing the relations between the author and what he says (or wanted to say, or said without wanting to); but in determining what position can and must be occupied by any individual if he is to be the subject of it.
>
> (95–6)

This passage makes it perfectly clear that Foucault wishes to abstract from everything to do with human agency in the performance of serious speech acts. Statements are conceived of as providing positions that can be occupied by subjects, and the reasoning processes and validity claims that underlie statements are systematically excluded from consideration. Foucault is neither interested in the objective validity of a statement nor the individual motives behind its utterance. What he calls the 'psychological halo' of the formulation of a statement 'is controlled from afar by the arrangement of the enunciative field' (98). The 'referential', which is in fact very similar to the discursive formation or the enunciative field itself, is seen as 'the place, the condition, the field of emergence, the authority to differentiate between individuals or objects, states of things and relations that are brought into play by the statement itself' (90). As a result, even the verification of a statement is explicitly excluded from archaeological analysis (92). Yet procedures of verification, in fact, the whole realm of methodological norms of a discipline, is something that can never be determined completely on the basis of an already existing system of anonymous rules nor by some algorithm for the transformation of rule systems. While the practice of science does operate, in part, in terms of rules and customs, that is a body of tacit knowledge that may not be entirely representable propositionally, this happens largely during periods of 'normal' science in Kuhn's sense. In revolutionary periods, or in the case of pre-paradigmatic and therefore highly contested disciplines like the ones Foucault is particularly concerned with, questions of verification are very prominent. Changes in what is considered acceptable practice and what is considered true, or at least a superior explanation, do not come about without a process of communal reasoning and negotiation in which 'subject positions' are, if anything, newly created rather than simply available for occupation. Yet for Foucault the direction of causality always seems to operate from the system to the subject, never the other way round. Subjects only have the amount of freedom that the system of rules makes available. Thus he argues that 'the enunciative domain' must be described as 'an anonymous field whose configuration defines the possible position of speaking subjects' and that statements 'should no longer be situated in relation to a sovereign subjectivity, but recognize in the different forms of the speaking subjectivity effects proper to the enunciative field' (122). Foucault's reply, therefore, in the concluding chapter of his book, to the objection of his imaginary opponent that he allows himself all the freedom that his theory of discourse denies those who occupy positions made available to them – this reply is clearly unsatisfactory. He argues that the 'positivities' he has identified 'must not be understood as a set of determinations imposed from the outside on the thought of individuals, or inhabiting it from the inside, in advance as it were', but it is difficult to see, from what he adds, what else they could be: 'they constitute rather [sic] the set of conditions in accordance with which a practice is exercised' (208). While rules of grammar can indeed be seen as enabling conditions rather than restrictions, particularly if subjects are accorded (as in Chomsky's model of language) not only a rule-following but a rule-changing and a rule-creative power, rules that are said to be conditions of *existence* rather than conditions of *possibility* are restrictive by definition. They determine what statements can or cannot be made, and the freedom they leave is a freedom provided by the system, not a space for innovation on the basis of reasons open to public scrutiny.

Of course, an analysis of the history of a discipline must be aware of the fact that it is indeed very difficult, as Foucault insists, to say something new. There is clearly something like a 'law of rarity' in the sense that practices, beliefs, and systems of propositional and conceptual dependences can usually only be altered slowly and against the conservative pull of established customs and modes of thought. Conceptual innovation, in whatever field, is difficult to accomplish. But we cannot begin to understand the history of the production of knowledge unless we recognize the role of the ability of human beings to engage in individual and collective forms of solving cognitive problems. This form of human agency is crucial, and while Foucault tries very hard to eliminate it from his archaeological project, it keeps resurfacing in his vocabulary and through his habit of metaphorically attributing agency to systems of rules which in themselves cannot perform acts but rely, to a large extent, on human beings who can *apply* and, if necessary, modify or abandon those rules. On numerous occasions in *The Archaeology of Knowledge* Foucault says that discourses 'put into operation' sets of rules. However, it remains unclear just how anonymous systems of rules can have such a power to act. In other places Foucault claims that it is groups of statements that put rules into operation (147), but since statements are not regarded as the result of intentional acts, the question of what exactly causes rules to become operative remains unresolved.

Foucault's tendency to see the functioning of discourses as largely autonomous also leads to problems when it comes to explicating the relation between discursive and non-discursive practices and when he considers historical changes or what he prefers to call 'transformations'. What he deliberately ignores here is both human agency and ordinary forms of social causality. Archaeology is neither interested in isolating causal mechanisms between the discursive and the non-discursive nor in what might have 'motivated' what Foucault calls 'enunciative facts' (162). As a result, Foucault produces what is ultimately an unintelligible account of the relation between discourses and non-discursive practices and institutions. He says, for example, that medical discourse is 'articulated on practices that are external to it' (164), but it is impossible to say what exactly is meant by 'articulated on'.

In Chapter 5 of Part IV Foucault objects to a number of traditional ways of conceiving historical change and argues instead that archaeological analysis understands change as a transformation of elements within the system of discourses or as the transformation of entire discourses themselves. But since he tries to avoid both ordinary causality and the individual or collective motivation and intention of historical agents, his archaeological account of transformations is restricted to a purely descriptive level. Since pure description is an illusion, however, a description of how various elements, and the rules which allegedly govern them, are transformed would simply disguise the explanatory model it relies on. The following example concerning the discourse of clinical medicine exemplifies this point. Referring to the necessary description of 'how the different elements of a system of formation were transformed', Foucault claims that one must look at 'what, for example, were the variations in the rate of unemployment and labour needs, what were the political decisions concerning the guilds and the universities, what were the new needs and possibilities of public assistance at the end of the eighteenth century', since all these are said to be 'elements in the system of formation of clinical medicine' (172). Now it is obvious from this list of 'elements' that a mere description of them would not shed any light on the discourse of clinical medicine unless they were situated in a network of cause-and-effect relationships. It seems therefore that whatever plausibility Foucault's characterization of an archaeological analysis of historical transformations of discourses may have relies largely on a hidden model of historical sociology. While such a model would not be likely to operate within an explanatory framework of individual human agency, it would certainly not be able to exclude human agency altogether.

When Foucault changed his focus from a structuralist analysis of discourses, conceived as systems of elements governed by anonymous sets of rules, to a genealogical history of the formation of subjectivities within regimes of power/knowledge, he did not completely abandon his earlier project of a theory of discourses, but neither did he revise or develop it to any great extent. This is why there is no need, in the context of this essay, to pursue the relation between discourse and human agency any further. Suffice it to say then, in conclusion, that since Foucault conceived of power not as the power individuals have over one another, human agency does not play a significant role in his later genealogical phase, at least not at an explicit theoretical level. The will to knowledge and power is not investigated by Foucault in its individual manifestations. Human agency only comes to the fore again in his late project of an aesthetics and ethics of existence concerned with 'technologies of the self'. How autonomous the subject capable of shaping his or her life was considered to be by Foucault remains to be determined. There are clear indications that even in his late work, in spite of its focus on individual self-fashioning, Foucault was very reluctant to grant the subject any real self-determination.

NOTES

1 See the article by Margaret Masterman, 'The nature of a paradigm' in *Criticism and the Growth of Knowledge*, ed. I. Lakatos and A. Musgrave, Cambridge, Cambridge University Press, 1970, pp. 58–59.

2 See for example the work published in journals such as *Discourse Processes* and *Text*.

3 I am not the first to complain about both the inflationary use and the looseness of the term 'discourse'. Manfred Frank makes a very similar point in his essay 'On Foucault's concept of discourse' in *Michel Foucault: Philosopher*, ed. F. Ewald, tr. T. J. Armstrong, New York, Harvester, 1992.

4 Though criticizing Foucault from a different and, in general, more sympathetic perspective, B. Brown and M. Cousins also come to the conclusion that Foucault fails to demonstrate the unity of discursive formations he postulates and that he runs together, in the term 'condition of existence', a range of quite heterogeneous phenomena. See their essay 'The linguistic fault: the case of Foucault's archaeology', *Economy and Society*, 9, 1980, pp. 251–78.

5 M. Foucault, *The Archaeology of Knowledge*, London, Tavistock, 1972, p. 16. All references in parentheses are to this edition. For a trenchant critique of Foucault's interpretation of all Kantian and post-Kantian philosophy as forms of anthropologism see H. Schnädelbach, 'The face in the sand: Foucault and the anthropological slumber' in *Philosophical Interventions in the Unfinished Project of Enlightenment*, ed. A. Honneth, T. McCarthy, C. Offe and A. Wellmer, Cambridge, Mass., MIT Press, 1992, pp. 311–40. Foucault's critique, however, is not just directed at philosophy but at the French *sciences de l'homme*.

6 We should note here, however, that Mark Poster has claimed that while Foucault successfully uses an archaeological method in *The Use of Pleasure*, in *The Care of the Self* Foucault abandons this method in favour of a traditional history of ideas type interpretation of his sources – much to the detriment of his analyses. See M. Poster, 'Foucault and the tyranny of Greece' in *Foucault: A Critical Reader*, ed. D. C. Hoy, Oxford, Basil Blackwell, 1986, p. 217. Hubert L. Dreyfus and Paul Rabinow, in their *Michel Foucault: Beyond Structuralism and Hermeneutics*, Chicago, The University of Chicago Press, 1982, argue that Foucault retains an archaeological method in his later work but abandons the idea of discourse as an autonomous rule-governed entity.

7 Dreyfus and Rabinow, as the title of their book indicates, argue that Foucault's work is situated 'beyond structuralism and hermeneutics', and they maintain that Foucault's archaeology differs from structuralism in its interest in history and historical changes, but this is not convincing. Arguably, the fact that Foucault tries to account for historical changes in discursive formations in terms of systems of rules makes his project more rather than less structuralist in orientation.

8 Foucault appears to ignore here the well-established fact that a pure description, uninformed by any prior theory and allegedly opening up 'an entire field' (26), is impossible.

9 M. Foucault, *Folie et déraison: Histoire de la folie à l'âge classique*, second edn, Paris, Gallimard, 1972; *Madness and Civilization: A History of Insanity in the Age of Reason*, tr. R. Howard, London, Tavistock, 1977.

10 This is obvious, for example, when Foucault says that he hopes to 'discover' a 'new domain' of objects, 'hitherto obscure or implicit relations', and 'transformations that have hitherto remained outside the reach of historians' (71). He thus endows his own discourse with the power to make genuine discoveries while simultaneously denying this power to the discourses he investigates. *These* discourses are not concerned, according to Foucault, with pre-existing objects, waiting to be discovered. This unequal treatment is entirely unjustified.

11 Republished in *Snow on Cholera*, New York, The Commonwealth Fund, 1936. The history and logic of Snow's discovery is discussed in detail in M. Goldstein and I. F. Goldstein, *How We Know: An Exploration of the Scientific Process*, New York and London, Plenum Press, 1978, ch. 3.

12 Since controlled human experiments were out of the question for ethical reasons, Snow had to rely on data gained in other ways. The most important source was made available by the fact that a large number of houses in certain areas of London were supplied by two different water companies, one of which delivered highly contaminated river water from the Thames while the other used (relatively) uncontaminated water from much further upstream. The fatalities in houses supplied with contaminated water were found to be 8 or 9 times higher than those supplied with cleaner water (Snow, p. 86).

13 The similarities between structuralism and Foucault's project of an archaeology of knowledge are discussed in some detail by Dreyfus and Rabinow in their *Michel Foucault: Beyond Structuralism and Hermeneutics*. The authors distinguish between an atomistic and a holistic structuralism, linking Foucault's archaeology with the latter. Although they, too, are critical of Foucault's structuralist analysis, they are far more sympathetic to his work than this essay. Dreyfus and Rabinow also deal with what appears to be a circularity in his account of the relations between discursive and non-discursive practices. Since Foucault, on the whole, rejects a causal analysis and insists on the autonomy of discursive practices as linguistic phenomena, he wants to argue that discursive practices are not causally dependent on non-discursive ones. But it remains unclear how, precisely, the relations between the two can be described and explained. Dreyfus and Rabinow's example of the functioning of the university (p. 66), which is meant to elucidate Foucault's somewhat obscure claims, is not entirely convincing. They argue that 'the idea of a university' is conditioned by something else that 'cannot be described in objective nor in mentalistic terms'. Rather, it is said to be 'a currently acceptable way of talking (describing, discussing, demanding, announcing) which is taken seriously in a domain called higher education'. While the authors admit that this type of discourse is 'related to what administrators, professors, and students think about university education', they maintain that 'these

ways of *thinking* no more organize all the factors that make up the university system than do the various social and economic forces'. They conclude therefore that 'what organizes the institutional relations and the thinking is finally the system of rules which govern what sort of *talk* about education (and which talkers) can, in a given period, be taken seriously. It is these rules "governing" what can be seriously said that, counter-intuitive as it may first seem, ultimately "effect" or "establish" university life as we know it'. It is not quite clear what 'organizes' means here. The authors are clearly aware that this account 'does not preclude questions about the way the discourse and its rules are dependent upon the social and economic practices they unify . . . The current institutions and practices must somehow sustain the discourse' (66). But they none the less contend, with Foucault, that 'organizing' and 'unifying' functions of discursive rules are relatively autonomous.

In any case, two things need to be said here. First, it is difficult to conceive of rules governing serious talk about higher education other than in mentalistic terms, bearing in mind that a mentalistic account does not necessarily imply *conscious* thought. Second, to characterize the discourse about higher education, in the sense of what can be said if one wants to be taken seriously, as governed by 'rules' is in itself of doubtful validity. If one equates statements with serious speech acts, as Dreyfus and Rabinow do, one is dealing with validity claims (in Habermas's sense) rather than with mere (claims to) rule conformity. Reasons and rules are different entities, and the seriousness of statements cannot be reduced to rule conformity, just as rationality cannot be reduced to rule conformity (though this is the only account of rationality Foucault can offer within an archaeological framework). Particularly if one adds a temporal dimension to one's analysis one is confronted with the question of *why*, that is on the basis of what *reasons*, rules of discourse were changed. To postulate rules for how rules can be changed would lead to an infinite regress. Of course, good reasons for theory change may not always be immediately recognized, and this was the case in Foucault's own example (mentioned in his *L'ordre du discours*, Paris, Gallimard, 1971) of Gregor Mendel who 'spoke the truth' but whose statements were not '*dans le vrai*'; but a history of discursive changes that refuses to look at the reasoning processes of scientists as one of its crucial components will not be very enlightening. Foucault's project, in its attempt to isolate a relatively autonomous linguistic realm of discursive practices, is situated somewhere between a Lakatosian 'internal history' and a purely causalist 'external' history. But instead of mediating between the two, it is in danger, by postulating a mysterious efficacy of the discursive, of not being able to explain any historical change.

14 A characteristic consequence of Foucault's refusal to consider human agency here is that he frequently uses the terminology of human agency but imposes it, at the same time, on elements that have no such intrinsic capacities.

15 See their *Michel Foucault*, p. 46, n. 1. Whether Foucault's admission is appropriate is another question. Some of the examples of statements Foucault gives (such as graphs or an age pyramid) are clearly not speech

acts in Searle's sense, and his definition of a statement in ch. 3 does not fit speech act theory either.

16 If this is the case, then Foucault should have abandoned his strictly anti-interpretative attitude towards language. If the meaning of a statement depends on its associated field, then its meaning is never immediately readable but a matter of interpretation and negotiation as hermeneutic philosophy claims. Yet Foucault claims that the analysis of statements 'is a historical analysis, but one that avoids all interpretation' (109).

10

THE RECEPTION OF MICHEL FOUCAULT'S IDEAS ON SOCIAL DISCIPLINE, MENTAL ASYLUMS, HOSPITALS AND THE MEDICAL PROFESSION IN GERMAN HISTORIOGRAPHY[1]

Martin Dinges

The impact of Foucault's writings within the historical profession has been highly varied. Different specialisms have reacted differently. Historians of science in France trained on Bachelard and Canguilhem, for example, have found it less difficult to embrace his work than those grounded in a more conventional political or social-history approaches. Despite the respect which Foucault envinced for the famous *Annales* School in France, his feelings were never fully reciprocated, and the major figures of the school (Braudel, Le Roy Ladurie, Le Goff, and others) kept their distance from a figure often seen as a historical maverick. The difficulties derive in part from Foucault's ideas and methods, but in part also from his cavalier disregard for many of the protocols of historical scholarship (scrupulous footnoting, thorough immersion in, and scrutiny of, secondary literature, etc.). There have consequently been those who have doubted Foucault's credentials as a historian altogether. (Those who make this claim can never have strayed into the thicket of minor scientific and administrative works on which he developed his theories and which are listed in the bibliographies of *The Birth of the Clinic* and *Histoire de la folie*, and over which he held an astonishing mastery.)

Different patterns of reception are detectable in different countries as well as in different subdisciplines of history. As Martin Dinges shows, Foucault's reception in Germany has been highly diverse, and characterized by as much hostility, indifference and incomprehension as acceptance and utilization. Cosmetic uses of Foucault's name have often been more evident than a skilful deployment of his ideas. His association with the idea of medicalization has been most willingly accepted in the German historical school, for example, only at the price of deformation: for most German historians, the medicalization process

181

requires historical agency (whether through the state, the ruling class, or whoever) and social as well as, or instead of, discursive practices. It would be challenging to extend this overview of German scholarship – which covers an enormous amount of material most of which is scarcely known outside Germany – to other national schools. One suspects that a systematic comparative review of his reception would reveal a Foucault impossible to pin down definitively. From this, we can be sure, Foucault – ever anxious in his lifetime to throw his critics off his tracks – would have taken ironic satisfaction.

INTRODUCTION

The name of Foucault has become synonymous with the history of discipline, of prisons, asylums and hospitals and of medical perception. These topics have become more central than they were ten or twenty years ago, though they are still less discussed in the German-speaking than in the Anglo-American or French worlds. As Foucault is the author whose work has done much to foster interest in these topics, it seems worthwhile to examine the reception of Foucault by German historians. This approach might illuminate not only these particular subjects but also some of the fundamental assumptions of German historiography.

I will present the analysis in three stages. First, I will compare the German with the international attention paid to Foucault's writings, and describe the part that historians have played in it. Second, I will analyse the arguments historians put forward in reviews of Foucault's books, focusing on the history of criminal justice and discipline and on mental asylums and hospitals in the early modern and contemporary periods. Third, I will present examples of how German historians have appropriated and used Foucault in their own work. This will provide us with a complex view of the uses German historians have made and continue to make of Foucault's writings. I will restrict my analysis mainly to the three works *Madness and Civilization*, *The Birth of the Clinic* and *Discipline and Punish*, with less systematic reference to the first volume of *The History of Sexuality*. Later works of Foucault's have been excluded from the analysis because historians have not incorporated them into the debate on our topics. I do not intend to present the content of Foucault's work, which is widely known (cf. Clark 1983, Guédon 1977, Fink-Eitel 1989). The historians I will cite publish in German and include general and social historians, historians of medicine and psychiatry and to a certain extent those working on pedagogy, literature and law.[2]

THE RECEPTION OF FOUCAULT IN GERMANY

German translations came out at the same time as English and Spanish ones and were reviewed in the important journals.[3] Articles concerning Foucault listed in the *International Bibliography of Periodical Literature* (*IBPL*) provide a good indicator of the attention Foucault's work received in international comparison (see Table 2).

Table 2 The reception of Foucault: an international comparison

	1964–9	1970–4	1975–9	1980–4	1985–9	1990
Articles in *IBPL*						
French	9	5	4	3	6	0
English	0	4	3	8	44	7
German	2	4	2	5	4	0
Dutch	0	0	1	0	3	1
Spanish	0	0	1	1	1	0

Two German articles in the 1960s preceded the first English articles in the early 1970s. Only in the second half of the 1980s did English reception peak, while the number of German articles remained constant. That the debate on Foucault was being increasingly internationalized is corroborated by the growth of Dutch and Spanish interest in the 1980s. Although German participation in the debate on Foucault started early, it remained rather moderate and diminished in the 1980s. More attention to Foucault was shown in the fields of philosophy (8 articles), social sciences (4), political science (2) and literature (2) than history: only one article in the *IBPL* listing was written by a (medical) historian. That the German debate on Foucault started almost without historians is confirmed by the *German Dissertation Index*. Since 1970 there have been four philosophical dissertations on Foucault and one in medical history. The first historical dissertation will be presented in Bochum in 1993.

One would expect the leading scholarly journals to have had a natural interest in Foucault's work. Here, however, the picture is equally disappointing. There was only one review each in *Sudhoffs Archiv* and the *Zeitschrift für Rechtsgeschichte*, and none in the *Historische Zeitschrift*, except for a general review article on criminal history referring in passing on one page to *Discipline and Punish*. General historians did not take note of the three important historical studies by Foucault, let alone his general theories of knowledge. Given this lack of interest, we may wonder whether the reviews tell us something about the reasons why historians abstained from the discussion on Foucault.

EXPLICIT RECEPTION OF FOUCAULT'S IDEAS

The few historians who received Foucault's work considered him strange, very interesting and a challenge to historical research.[4] In his initial enthusiasm Blasius even found that *Madness and Civilization* contained 'questions and methods which might show new approaches for a critical history of society' (Blasius 1986 [1970], p. 17). The focus on the analysis of the administration of society, rather than on politics in a traditional sense, was one of Foucault's merits. His work, for Blasius, provided new insights into complex historical contexts. It was seen as a history of institutions in the manner of *Ideengeschichte* (the hermeneutic history of ideas) or as a history of different stages of social control.

Despite the positive note sounded in that review (partly based, moreover, on a misperception of Foucault's work as a history of ideas), other reviews engaged in a general critique. Reviewers reproached Foucault for using history for non-historical (political, present-day) purposes, while some held that his works were 'anti-Enlightenment' (*Gegenaufklärung*) and resolved the 'dialectic of the Enlightenment' in a negative sense.[5] Foucault's critique of the idea of progress was the element of his work with which historians had most difficulty. Even if they conceded that Foucault sensitized historians to the negative effects of progress, they did not wish to accept his questioning of progress as a historiographical principle. As this point is sacrosanct to German-speaking historians, they criticized Foucault for his political stance, too: 'Foucault presents the *ancien régime* too positively; he has no utopia of his own' (Saurer 1978, p. 354). In sum, historians manifested great ambivalence towards Foucault: while acknowledging him to be an innovative and challenging thinker, they also represented his approach as an exemple of *Ideengeschichte*, and they rejected his attitude to progress.

In this general critique, reservations concerning Foucault's basic concepts or his methodological approach did not play an important role. Foucault's idea that power is at the same time productive and disciplining was not commented upon (cf. Raulf 1977). Historians rejected his concept of the ubiquity of power, preferring to assume a clearly defined centre of power in society. They did not discuss Foucault's point that knowledge always produces power and that power always produces knowledge. They held that the panopticon, so to speak, 'floats in the air' – by which they meant Foucault's failure to situate power socially. Apart from some references to Foucault's use of language, they did not address Foucault's idea that the individual constitutes a sum of interrelated influences of power and knowledge.[6] Nor did they comment on the chronological propositions regarding the epistemological development of early modern Europe.

An exception to this general picture is the literary historian Osinski who, in her book *Über Vernunft und Wahnsinn* (1983), attempted a historical reconstruction of the problem of reason in literature, considering fiction and non-fiction texts. Starting from the view that all scientific results must be presented in a way which makes it possible for other scholars to reproduce them, Osinski reproaches Foucault for placing himself, with *Madness and Civilization*, outside the discourse of the scientific community. In this work, she states, Foucault claims that all modern reason is only a limited form of reason, since in a historical process of growing domination it has been separated from the other half of reason: madness. Osinski objects to this on the grounds that this concept of an original separation, offering the vague hope of a reunion of reason and unreason, stands in the tradition of the 'aesthetic reason of romanticism' (ibid., p. 42; cf. pp. 56–7). It is incompatible with empiricism as a historical method and, more fundamentally, it makes it impossible to falsify Foucault's theories on the basis of empirical findings.

In general, however, the criticism from historians has been limited to more specific points. They have maintained, for example, that Foucault misleadingly isolates fields of knowledge such as criminal law from their context. Their fundamental problem, however, has been with Foucault's concept of reality.[7] For Foucault, they claim, reality is based exclusively on language (Altwegg and Schmidt 1987). Thus the humanities become prisoners of language games (*Sprachspiele*). In his debates with historians, Foucault underlined the two central points of his idea of discourse: discourse creates reality by stating the existence of an object and by then claiming the truth of the message. Historians reject this concept of reality, without any discussion of the philosophical background to Foucault's assumptions. At best, they claim, the discourse presented by Foucault illuminates the utopian ideals of contemporaries (of the nineteenth century). But for historians – for whom historical reality consists of both discourse and social practices

– his method bypasses the reality of the period.[8] Foucault himself conceded that his analysis of discourse describes only a segment of history, and that his generalizations invite misunderstandings. Indeed the relation between discourse and non-discursive practices is an open question in the thinking of Foucault, so that historians have been quite right to identify this as a weak point. But rather than discussing it systematically, they present elements of 'historical reality' – such as the continuing resistance of people against criminal justice or medicalization – and elevate them to the status of 'proof' against Foucault's presumptions about 'historical reality'. Thus historians reject Foucault's universal explanations based on a certain philosophy of language and advocate a different concept of reality. In so doing, they lose sight of the challenge Foucault makes to the sociology of knowledge.

Historians muster the sharpest arguments at their disposal against Foucault's view of modern history as marked by the development of a disciplinary universe penetrating the most remote corners of bourgeois society: instead of a history of social control, they argue, Foucault presents an 'ontology of discipline'; his thinking replaces the myth of Enlightenment with just another myth – that of discipline – but the macro-structures of discipline remain obscure. These charges – mythological thinking, philosophy of history and ahistorical methods – are so strong that Foucault must have struck a sensitive nerve among German historians.

Foucault's philosophical background is considered to be a key to understanding his work. Foucault is perceived as a follower of Nietzsche – since 1945 the philosopher most hated by Germans. The French philosopher is viewed as part of a tradition of bourgeois critiques of modern civilization exemplified by such as Jacob Burckhardt and Oswald Spengler.[9] As Blasius (1983, p. 74) states: 'Foucault's destruction of the idea of "reasonable" progress in modernity, his destruction of the idea that bourgeois modernization offers itself to a rational [social] order is the political essence of his philosophy of history'.

Against Foucault's philosophical approach, German historians explicitly use elements of philosophical and sociological theories which better serve their concept of progress. I will enumerate them so as to make clear how their approaches differ from Foucault's. The most influential of thinkers fielded against Foucault is Max Weber, who as early as the 1920s had stated that modernization was inevitable and necessary and that the imposition of discipline lay in the hands of individuals such as absolutist kings or corporate managers who alone had the necessary material means (Weber, 1980). Later on, Theodor W. Adorno and Max Horkheimer's concept of the 'dialectic of Enlightenment' (Horkheimer and Adorno 1975) played an important role. Begun as a movement which continues the process of rationalization, Enlightenment tends to be reversed and undone by the very means invented to emancipate human beings. It is in these two traditions that Jürgen Habermas, who stresses the negative effects of modernization, can be situated. For him, modernization is a means of colonizing the 'life world', thereby destroying the basic resources of civilization – such as nature, communicative competence and so on (Habermas 1985; cf. Gumbrecht 1992). He proposes to solve these problems by communication beyond domination as a regulative idea (cf. Honneth 1985). Historians prefer these conceptions of the dialectics of rationalization as better able to express the ambivalence of tendencies in modern history.

German historians can also identify with the concept of social discipline advocated by the historian Gerhard Oestreich (1968). He saw modern history as a process in which the absolutist monarch, inspired by neostoicism, disciplined society. Rulers introduced discipline first in the army, the bureaucracy and the priesthood, and then in the rest of the population. In an initial phase of fundamental 'social regulation' from 1450 to 1650 the cities produced laws and institutions experimenting with the potential of social discipline. In a second phase, from 1650 onwards, territorial states took over this legislative work and enforced its implementation. The process had ups and downs but continued into the twentieth century. This idea is more acceptable to German historians because it retains a historical subject, a sense of history, a sociology of power and an idea of progress.

In general, all these 'theories' of modernity or rationalization subscribe to a belief in progress, even if they acknowledge its ambivalence. They characterize very well the limits of German historians' understanding of Foucault: historiography has to be oriented towards a standard of progress which gives history meaning. Similarly, history is unimaginable without a historical subject which may be defined within the tradition of the sociology of power.

Once this background is understood, it becomes easier to understand the German discussion of Foucault's ideas on the role of the total institution in history. Historians agree with Foucault that the analysis of institutions tells us a lot about societies and that the historical tendency towards discipline accelerated in the eighteenth century. They disagree, however, on just about everything else. Foucault does not present a 'genealogy' – understood as chronologically oriented historiography – of the prison, it is claimed, because he does not sufficiently connect the development of asylums for the mentally ill in the seventeenth century with the rise of the prisons of the nineteenth.[10] Furthermore, the links between general forms of social domination and the discipline in institutions like prisons are called into question: is discipline as a general historical movement an abstraction of correctional institutions? If so, these should present specific elements of discipline, and the diffusion of discipline in society should be charted, if the entire 'form of social reproduction' is to be characterized as a disciplinarian society. Alternatively, if it is claimed that discipline resides only in institutions without an acting subject, then the notion of power loses its significance. Historians remark that discipline is much less mystical than Foucault believes and point to the absolute monarch as a historical agent capable of exercising power. They insist on the need for an acting subject or at least a centre of power, and reject the idea of power being diffuse. Finally, they disagree about institutions' ability to normalize, and consider the 'carceral system' much less effective in disciplining people, who are quite capable of thinking for themselves. But they agree that domination is broader than coercion and find this an idea to be kept in mind.

USE OF FOUCAULT'S WORK BY HISTORIANS

In what follows, I will discuss the major forms in which historians have appropriated and used Foucault's ideas. This broadens our overview of the reception of Foucault's work to include other fields.

Marxist rejection

In 1977, the historian E. Köhler published *Arme und Irre: Die liberale Fürsorgepolitik des Bürgertums*. His book provides a good example of the Marxist reception of Foucault's ideas in Germany, which began, compared with other historiographical tendencies, quite early – certainly by the second half of the 1970s. Köhler either rejects Foucault's concepts outright as representing a bourgeois historiography of ideas or attempts to integrate his ideas into the framework of theories of modern capitalism as a history of growing repression. In Köhler's view, class struggle causes unbridgeable cleavages in society, with which social policy cannot cope, and his main objective is to unmask this as the character of bourgeois welfare policy in the nineteenth century. As long as Foucault is useful for this purpose, Köhler cites him extensively (1977, pp. 124, 127). He praises the French philosopher's work as the 'best of this kind of sociologically aware historiography of ideas'.[11] However, Köhler criticizes Foucault for remaining 'on the level of social perception', even if he 'shows very well certain aspects of the confinement of non-reason' (ibid., p. 151). Foucault is characterized as 'writing not in the tradition of revolutionary Marxism, but in one of bourgeois Enlightenment and humanism'. According to Köhler, Foucault was idealistic, and over-estimated the marginal effect of the total institutions on the initial accumulation of capital. There was no general policy of putting all deviant persons into asylums. The asylums were limited to the cities and Köhler agrees with Foucault that the reform impulses of the early nineteenth century were realized only in a minority of asylums and then only after 1860. 'Foucault was too interested in the unmasking of scientistic positivism to notice the meagre effects of these debates on the real life of asylums.' 'It was not the absolutist but only the later bourgeois state which really put these people [the poor, the deviant and the mad] *en masse* (though not in their entirety) into total institutions' (ibid., pp. 151–3). As for the implementation of the new ideas and the chronology of the introduction of total institutions, Köhler denies that Enlightenment thinking could have caused these changes. His argument is that they only occured after 1860, which makes a direct temporal link between them impossible. 'New buildings were not constructed according to the counsels of science but rather in the functional interest of imprisoning the highest number of the mad at the lowest possible cost' (ibid., p. 155). Overcrowding and chaos were common in the asylums. Rather than viewing Enlightenment thinking – 'the sense of order of the bourgeois class or its specific moral aggressiveness' – as the historical agent, Köhler prefers to see the 'state as agent of the historical needs of capital' (ibid., pp. 153, 154). The state only reluctantly accepted a minimum number of new asylums.

At the same time, Köhler also criticizes Foucault as an author who, while claiming to provide 'the whole story', presents only a history of social perception. The criticism regarding 'the whole story' seems wide of the mark, in that Foucault does include factors such as the construction of buildings, etc., which are beyond social perception.

But the specific Marxist problem with Foucault is the fact that the French philosopher denies a historical subject even so reified as class struggle or the requirements of capital.

This is a point taken up by Ingersleben in a rather aggressive review of *Madness and Civilization* published in the most influential periodical of the Marxist left, *Das Argument*. Rehearsing the eternal truths and the methodological essentials of Marxist historiography, Ingersleben criticizes Foucault's 'lack of method', his 'avalanche of facts ordered arbitrarily' and his 'expressionist, free-associationist way of thinking' (Ingersleben 1981, pp. 196–8). Foucault's 'hedonist thinking refuses logical discipline . . . [and] . . . travesties arbitrarily chosen details of unusual aspects of reality in a way comparable to satire and caricature' (ibid., p. 198). Against Foucault's 'anti-Enlightenment phenomenology', Ingersleben offers the virtues of progress, plus some details on the history of natural and medical science – and a good deal of irony. Foucault is considered blind to 'the connection between science and anti-feudal opposition as a movement of bourgeois emancipation (in Germany) and as resistance against imperial restoration (in France)' (ibid.).

Inspiration

The following examples show how some German scholars have been inspired by Foucault to reconsider various fields of research. The sociologists Treiber and Steinert published *Die Fabrikation des zuverlässigen Menschen* in 1980.[12] Their subject is the historical roots of disciplinary society, on which Foucault did not elaborate. They take the idea of the ubiquity of power seriously and present the medieval monastery and the factory as strategic institutions in the development of discipline. In them, inmates learnt a disciplined 'habitus' which slowly became an unspecific disposition of Western individuals and has since been useful for very different purposes.

Foucault's work on medicalization has also had an impact on German historiography. In its most basic form, it has been well received by sociologists and historians working either on discourses about health or on the professionalization of doctors.[13] The social historian Brügelmann, for instance, used the concept of the 'medical gaze' as a new paradigm for medical history (1983, p. 66). He analysed public health reports of physicians in the first half of the nineteenth century and stressed the role of social interaction in emerging medical perception. He characterizes physicians' changing perception of illness as a succession of different medical discourses. As innovators favouring smallpox vaccination, doctors had to take into account the resistance of the population, who had a different perception of life from their own. In this case, the analysis of discourse in Foucault's manner is integrated with the processes of social interaction and professionalization.

In his analysis of discourse on health 'in the bourgeois world', the sociologist Göckenjan suggests that it always represents a discourse about the 'social obsessions of the bourgeoisie' (1985, p. 15). He argues that this discourse denotes more than simply social discipline. It allows questions to be posed systematically about the objects of discipline and the succession of historical subjects advocating discipline, as well as about the changing intentions and targets of hygienic discourse. Göckenjan shows, for example – I can only present some of his conclusions here – the forms and conditions of discipline in hospitals to be a consequence of the hospital's roots in poor relief. This suggests a 'genealogy of the clinic' which Foucault did not provide. In hospitals, physicians could develop a superiority over patients which they later transferred to their bourgeois clientele as well.

Göckenjan thus follows Foucault quite closely and refines the concept of discourse for social history. Similarly, the sociologist Barthel takes on board the general idea of medicalization proposed by Foucault in applying his methods to the analysis of medical discourse and the hospital, and he shows – albeit only on the basis of limited source material – that biopolitics worked in Germany as it did in France: the alliance of an enlightened state bureaucracy with physicians led to the progressive medicalization of the population. Barthel stresses the importance of bourgeois demand for medical services as a third factor in the medicalization process, and one underestimated by Foucault. He argues that medical enlightenment had a paradoxical effect: instead of encouraging medical self-reliance, it led to people becoming more sensitive: medical enlightenment thus led to an avalanche of discourses on new symptoms, illnesses and sensibilities (Barthel 1989, p. 146). Barthel also underlines popular resistance to medicalization (ibid., p. 173ff.). This historical study also leads Barthel to stress the contemporary relevance of the Foucauldian thesis concerning the present-day trend in the social politics of medicine towards disciplining patients through medicalization.

The historian Frevert re-evaluates the meaning of the term 'medicalization' in the context of nineteenth-century Germany. She interprets medicalization as an attempt both to integrate the poor into the medical system and to discipline them. The social security system finally gave them the possibility of expressing conformity with the expectations of the medical system (Frevert 1984, pp. 15, 85, 334ff.). She agrees with Foucault's evaluation of the role of the hospital in the development of medical perception. Working mainly on source material of organizations for social security and company assurance, she claims to concur with Foucault's alleged view of medicalization as a process initiated from above and effectively covering the entire population. Yet, in fact, she writes solely about organized labour, so this claim must remain unproven.

The historian of pedagogy Pongratz, who tried to apply the concepts Foucault developed in the *Archeology of the Human Sciences* and *Discipline and Punish* to the history of pedagogy provides an example of a quite different kind (Pongratz 1988, 1989, 1990). He notes similar epistemological changes in pedagogic thinking beginning in the sixteenth century, and goes on to view the school as another apparatus (*dispositif*) of power in which social practices of space and time and the production of knowledge are intimately connected within one institution. Thus he traces a development from repressive strategies to integration and then on to panoptic strategies. He observes them operating within the school as an institution and also in knowledge about education.

These examples show how Foucault's thought can be – and has been – developed in a creative manner.[14] The choice of examples, along with some studies of asylums, reflects quite well the reception of Foucault by German historians. But it is certainly no mere chance that no general historian and only two social historians figure in this list. On the contrary, four sociologists with historical research interests and one historian of pedagogy are those who seem to have profited from Foucault in a fundamental way.

Corresponding counter-schemes

The uses made of Foucault by the psychiatrist Dörner and the general historian Blasius are rather different. In *Madmen and the Bourgeoisie: A Social History of Insanity and Psychiatry* (1984), Dörner presents a comparison between several countries. This distinguishes him from Foucault who deliberately limited himself to France, which is certainly too narrow a base for the kind of generalizations to which he is inclined. Dörner differentiates between internal and external coercion and focuses on the effects of changing knowledge and institutions on the situation of inmates in hospitals for the mentally ill. The claims and intentions of Enlightenment philosophy form the basis for his research on the changing forms and methods of social control.[15] Thus he explicitly rejects as overly reductionist Foucault's view of society as subject to ever-growing disciplinarian pressures. Instead, he stresses the ambivalent effects of psychiatric knowledge: at the level of intentions, the Enlightenment was emancipatory, while in terms of performance, it was repressive.

The German historian who has published most about Foucault is Blasius. In his *Der verwaltete Wahnsinn: Eine Sozialgeschichte des Irrenhauses* (1980), Blasius argues that it is symptomatic of the problems facing the historiography of psychiatry in general and Foucault in particular that even in 1980 not a single real biography of a mentally ill person had been written. Blasius criticized current historiography for not considering the mentally ill as subjects in their own right but only as objects of bureaucratic arbitrariness. He stresses this point by examining, for example, the family networks of the mentally ill and their system of values, which differ from those of bureaucratic rationality. He demonstrates a continuity between the old poor-relief hospitals and state hospitals as instruments of effective discipline oriented to the lower classes and underlines their repressive character. His chronology therefore differs from Foucault's. He centres his research on the political debate about these institutions and stresses the functionality of asylums for political domination in the modernization process, showing how useful they were in intimidating undisciplined workers. At the same time, he considers the mentally ill as subjects with their own interests and strategies even inside the bureaucratic system of discipline. And he is in agreement with Foucault in seeing the institutions as having a disciplining effect on society as a whole, through conditioning the inmates and intimidating persons outside.

Explicit application of Foucault's method of analysis

Stekl's unjustly neglected *Österreichs Zucht- und Arbeitshäuser 1671–1920* (1978) provides a more detailed insight into the debate in German historiography about the relationship between total institutions and the wider society. One year after the translation of *Discipline and Punish*, Stekl cites Foucault in support of his thesis that the ruling class deliberately used workhouses and prisons as a means of disciplining the lower classes. This happened 'under the new [capitalist] mode of production (Stekl 1978, p. 14). His application of Foucault's ideas is limited to an analysis of the mechanisms employed by institutions created to enforce discipline. The calculated use of sanctions to drill the inmates into disciplined behaviour, which Foucault considers so typical of the classical age, existed in Austrian workhouses, too. But negative sanctions predominated. They formed the basis for new patterns of behaviour which, later on, became useful when applied to workers in the factory and citizens in the bourgeois state (ibid., p. 216). Stekl remains sceptical about the real effects of these behavioural changes, but does not go so far as to reconsider Foucault's generalizations concerning the ontology of discipline. Perhaps Stekl is a little too credulous in accepting the prestige of the French philosopher as an authority, and he blends Foucault with various ingredients of Marxist philosophy of history in a way which leads him to disregard his own empirical results.

Pilgram (1979) subsequently criticized Stekl for underestimating the relationship between asylums and the wider society, and in particular the symbolic value of the asylums. By 1986, Stekl, taking up Pilgram's idea, wrote that 'the importance of the asylums lay less in the effecting of their programmes than in the ideology of normality they represented' (Stekl 1986, p. 119). He went on to evoke the techniques of normalization within the institution, thus supporting Foucault's arguments that institutions are particularly useful for collecting knowledge about inmates, and that architecture is a specific means of doing this. But he holds that in the seventeenth and eighteenth centuries these aspects played a minor role. In order to discipline inmates, it was more important to deprive them of their freedom and to use forced labour and religious indoctrination (ibid., p. 125). Stekl stresses the scope for inmate resistance and argues that inmates' system of values differed completely from the ideas of reformers. Though he underlines the importance of the new norms being internalized, he follows Foucault's method of citing prescriptive texts, so that he is not able to show the effects of these projects on inmate behaviour.

In summary, Stekl's reception of Foucault reminds one of the uses of knowledge which Levi-Strauss (1968) defined as *la pensée sauvage*. Stekl agrees with elements of Foucault's work on an abstract level only by dint of misconceiving him as a theorist of the Left, as so many German scholars have done. He assumes that Foucault believes in an intentionally acting ruling class using discipline according to their class interests in the period of the developing capitalist mode of production. He applies Foucault's method of analysis empirically, refining the chronology and the character of the internalization of discipline. He does not, however, use his own empirical results to call Foucault's generalizations into question.

Application of Foucault's method of analysis to other fields

In 1986, Jütte used Foucault's analysis of disciplining techniques as a guideline for research on poor relief in the sixteenth and seventeenth centuries. Jütte argues that Foucault's only error was to start his history of discipline with examples from the eighteenth century (Jütte 1986, p. 101). Jütte explicitly uses Oestreich's concept of social discipline as his theoretical framework, thus distancing himself from Foucault; but he presents historical evidence, which matches Foucault's methodological approach. The spatial dimension of discipline is visible in the spatial exclusion of the poor, in their categorization (*parcellation*) and in the major distinction made between local beggars and outsiders. Hierarchical classification is evident in the creation of different groups of indigents, while disciplinarian techniques are used by the police and the administration. Systematic techniques inquiring into the life of the poor are thus not new in the 'age of reason': they were habitual even in sixteenth-century alms distribution. Normalizing sanctions existed earlier, too, in the form of punishment and forced labour (ibid., pp. 105–10).

Onset of a systematic debate on Foucault

In 1991, I discussed Jütte's application of Foucault and the idea of the disciplinarian society in an article which appeared in the journal *Geschichte und Gesellschaft* (Dinges 1991).[16] Based on empirical research on sixteenth- and seventeenth-century Bordeaux, the article concluded that the ruling classes had strong disciplining intentions but lacked an effective police force, money and educational concepts to carry them through. Laws were hardly enforced at all, and strangers and beggars were seldom prosecuted and practically never punished as prescribed in the city statutes. I widened my critique of the disciplining thesis at three levels. First, I argued that the clear inability of the state to enforce its policies must be considered as a fundamental structure of early modern Europe. In particular, the possibility of the poor helping themselves had to be seen as an important limiting factor on all disciplining projects.[17] Second, on a methodological level, I argued that historians of discipline have been wrong to base their evidence mainly on normative sources which bypass 'historical reality' (including acts of resistance and deviant behaviour). Third, I made the theoretical point that the concept of a disciplinarian society implied a teleological view of history, with the past being viewed as an ever-developing process of disciplination. Within this schema, opposing tendencies are interpreted only as 'reverses', thus demonstrating the ideological character of the concept.[18] The idea of a disciplinarian society contains both a description of reality and a normative evaluation of it. The relation between disciplining institutions and the general form of domination is not clear. Finally, the concept tends towards the reification of discipline.

Since this article appeared, Jütte has accepted some of the criticisms – for example, the difference between intentions and achievement. Though he agrees about the danger of reifying discipline, he sees this as a problem only with Foucault's work, and not with that of Oestreich (cf. Peukert 1991, p. 330). Jütte wants to hold on to the discipline paradigm as a means of describing the politics of the ruling classes (*Obrigkeit*) and of conceptualizing history as an oriented process (Jütte 1991, p. 101). His remarks manifest a certain conceptual distance from Foucault: Jütte retains the *Obrigkeit* as historical subject, concedes that there is an active dialectic between their acts and the dominated, and views history as an oriented process. His arguments illustrate very well the limits of German historians' acceptance of Foucault: against Foucault's 'ontology of power', they counterpose the idea of a historical transformation with a subject qualified in terms of the sociology of power.

The most serious discussion of Foucault's concept of medicalization is Loetz's recent Ph.D. thesis on 'Medicine, political programmes for health care and social reality in Germany' (Loetz 1993). Loetz's case-study of the processes of medicalization in Baden between 1750 and 1850 underlines how the German reception of Foucault's work has led to an accentuation of certain aspects of his concepts. The process of professionalization has the effect of displacing 'fringe' medicine, while the provision of modern health care has an important political impact on the long-term process of disciplining the population.[19] Loetz gives a differentiated analysis of the various uses made of the medicalization concept. Criticizing the reception of Foucault in Germany, she notes 'a general tendency to apply directly those (hypo)theses developed in the analysis of discourse to reality, thus underlining the well-known problem of a concept seducing historians into overestimating discourse and neglecting everyday realities' (ibid., p. 25). The main point of criticism concerns the concept of medicalization. Loetz argues that Foucault represents medicalization as a one-sided process in which the state and doctors act while the people only receive and react. Basing her arguments on the approaches of Oestreich and, in particular, Max Weber, Loetz stresses that domination has two sides: the behaviour of the dominated has to be taken into account (cf. Barthel 1989, pp. 35ff, 173ff). Medicalization can only be understood if the aspirations of the population to health and health care are properly taken into account. For this reason Loetz wants to do away with the notion of medicalization and to replace it with the concept of medical socialization (*medizinische Vergesellschaftung*). To do so, she argues, would have the effect of viewing the sick as historical agents in their own right.

Loetz's empirical findings buttress her criticism of Foucault. For example, in Baden, she finds, there was no alliance between doctors and the state fostering health care since doctors had not organized themselves; when the state administration acted on professional regulation and fringe medicine, it did so pragmatically and without implementing the wishes of certain radical doctors. There was, Loetz continues, no 'medical desert' to medicalize, because the population was quite well served with medical services at the very beginning of the period of so-called medicalization, and the sick chose indiscriminately between all sorts of healers. Furthermore, there was no superseding of fringe medicine but rather interaction between 'official' and lay healers and therapeutics. Loetz suggests that the main wave of 'medical socialization' has to be seen in the context of cholera and chronic pauperism, both of which led to the emergence of new levels of medical demand from below. On this point, she is in agreement with other critics of Foucault working on the history of asylums and prisons, who have also pointed to the second half of the nineteenth century as a period when many of the changes Foucault placed earlier in time were finally achieved.[20]

A psychiatrist's view

In 1973, in his account of psychiatric ideas between 1789 and 1848, Schrenk stressed the differences between, and the influences on, English, French and German concepts of mental illness. 'Umgang mit dem Geisteskranken' (the art of treating the insane) – basically the relationship between doctor and patient – constitutes the organizing concept of his work and is seen against a background of Enlightenment, philanthropic and pedogogical ideas. He presents the history of psychiatry as part of the broader history of the ongoing Enlightenment, a humanist view which he occasionally buttresses with citations from Kant. In two small sections on Foucault, based largely on *Madness and Civilization*, Schrenk argues that 'Foucault presented facts and phenomena which – taken as images, figures and structures – give a vivid picture of the history of madness' (Schrenk 1973). He itemizes two particular ideas of Foucault's. First, he accepts that madness is always a mirror of reason. Second, he agrees with Foucault's view that the end of leprosy in the fifteenth century left an empty space in European society. In the subsequent search for new rituals of purgation, madness took the place of leprosy, with leper houses being transformed into workhouses in the seventeenth and eighteenth century (ibid., p. 17).

Schrenk criticizes Foucault's stress on 'sociological, historical, ideological structures', which omits, he argues, structures important to the history of medicine. The history of medicine cannot be understood without a profound understanding of contemporary medical and natural science. 'We agree with Foucault that the history of psychiatry canot sufficiently be explained from the history of medicine. But against Foucault . . . we consider that the history of psychiatry will be biased if classical texts are cited only fragmentarily. . . .' It would appear that Schrenk finds *Madness and Civilization* an interesting book, especially because it confirms his own professional aspirations to establish a history of psychiatry independent of the history of medicine. For this purpose Foucault is a useful tool.[21] This comes out clearly in the second section, where Schrenk deals with Foucault's ideas. Schrenk returns to the idea of the empty space left by leprosy. He criticizes the Foucauldian idea of a direct development from leperhouses to workhouses as being too linear. But Schrenk's intention is merely to underline 'how important it is to use guidelines coming from the history of psychiatry and not to confine oneself to guidelines derived from the history of medicine; better still, how indispensable it is to see medical history and especially the history of psychiatry as part of the history of ideas or the history of culture – and even of political and social history'. The underlying aim of Schrenk's work – to establish an independent history of psychiatry – thus makes it possible for him to present on two further pages the main ideas of *Madness and Civilization* without any commentary or impact on his overall thesis. There is nothing resembling open reception of Foucault's ideas in all this, but rather a certain use of the French philosopher for the vested interests of the history of psychiatry.

Pseudoreception, partial reception and implicit reception

By the mid-1980s, Foucault had entered the German list of theorists who are rarely read but often cited. There were many occasions when Foucault was cited alongside Weber and Oestreich without any distinction as just another theorist of discipline and as a critic of the modern world. Among such cases of 'pseudo-reception', one can instance Peukert's work on social discipline. Peukert attacks modernization theories as one-sided, because they omit the 'life world' – everyday experiences in social context – and the sufferings of people during the modernization process.[22] Because it only alludes to Foucault without discussing his work, and concentrates on German theorists, Peukert's book cannot be considered as authentic reception.

Another form of reception is limited to very specific concepts or details of Foucault's works, which are either only mentioned in passing or specifically rejected. I myself, for example, rejected Foucault's evaluation of seventeenth-century workhouses (*hôpitaux généraux*) as an effective means of disciplining the entire poor population, while Finzsch, for his part, showed that the asylums of eighteenth-century Rhineland did not develop according to Foucault's ideas (Dinges 1988, Finzsch 1990).

Finally, Foucault's concepts have had an immense implicit influence. A vague idea of the disciplinarian society seems to inspire many scholars. The growing interest in the hidden effects of institutions, such as asylums or prisons, on society as a whole and the interest in educational 'discourse' may be seen as exemplifying another form of the impact of Foucault on German historians.[23] But this reception of Foucault's ideas is too vague to be presented here.

Underlying lack of interest in key areas of historiography

It is worth noting how Foucault is perceived in the standard German work on the history of asylums in Europe, published by the Wissenschaftliche Buchgesellschaft. In 1981, the most widely published author on hospitals and asylums in Germany, the medical historian Jetter, published his *Grundzüge der Geschichte des Irrenhauses* (Jetter

1981). Foucault's *Madness and Civilization* and *Discipline and Punish* – but *not Birth of the Clinic*! – are listed in the bibliography, but there is no direct influence of his ideas in the text. Jetter implicitly tries to refute Foucauldian ideas. Without naming the French philosopher, he states that 'recently it has been claimed that the art of isolating undesirable minorities from society and thereby making them invisible was an irruption into history caused by French absolutism and *raison d'état*' (ibid., p. 20). Jetter shows that this practice was a basic way of coping with the mad as early as late medieval times. He cites the example of noblemen and kings who often put members of their family who were causing them difficulties into monasteries as gardeners or bell-ringers thus removing them from view. This is Jetter's way of invalidating the Foucauldian chronology of isolation. However, this example shows that Jetter simply fails to distinguish between, on one hand, individual and collective social practices of certain social strata, and, on the other, Foucault's project of conceiving the role of madness during modernity in an epistemological way. Jetter continues an apologetic historiography of the asylum as the triumph of Enlightenment: he sees the reason behind Germany's first modern asylum (in 1805 in Bayreuth), for example, as the 'enlightened humanity of an efficient administrator'. Continuing the pro-Prussian historiography of the nineteenth century, he underlines the fact that the Protestant north – not the Catholic south – was the first to invent the institution, under the guidance of Prussia (ibid., p. 34).[24]

In his chapter on France, Jetter devotes a lot of time to historicizing and demythologizing Pinel. He regards it as an open question whether the chains of the mad were taken off in 1789 or in 1792 (ibid., p. 127). But there is absolutely no hint of acknowledging the fundamental reinterpretation of Pinel proposed by Foucault. For Jetter, the humanization of psychiatry could only spring from an enlightened advocate such as Pinel, whose only problem was to impose his views outside Bicêtre, where he worked.

This example is symptomatic of the attitude of a large part of the history of medicine towards Foucault.[25] Fourteen years after the German translation of *Madness and Civilization*, it is still common not even to cite the French philosopher. This is made apparent in two doctoral theses which were presented in 1985 at the University of Aachen's *Lehrstuhl* for medical history, which specializes in the history of hospitals. One thesis concerns the psychiatric asylum in Düren between 1878 and 1934, the other the development of psychiatric measures in the Netherlands during the nineteenth century (Hertling 1985, Schmidt 1985). None of Foucault's works is even mentioned in either bibliography.

Ignorance is not, however, the exclusive privilege of medical history. At the beginning of the 1990s it was still possible to list a work of Foucault's in the bibliography of a German doctoral thesis in general history, defended at the famous Bielefeld faculty and write as if Foucault had never existed. An example is the Ph.D. of B. Wischhöfer on 'Illness, health and society in the Enlightenment: The example of Lippe county 1750–1830' (1991). Wischhöfer provides us with a valuable analysis of regional source material on historical demography, the medical system, medical everyday life and medical Enlightenment (*Medizinische Volksaufklärung*), but there is no reference at all to the French philosopher in the text.

CONCLUSIONS: PAST AND FUTURE

In the light of this discussion of how historians have appropriated and used Foucault's writings and concepts, it is helpful to consider the context of the German intellectual climate and the state of the scholarly disciplines. These constitute important preconditions for the reception of an author's views.

I would first like to suggest that strict boundaries between scholarly disciplines represent a strong barrier against a positive reception of Foucault's ideas in Germany. This problem is particularly acute as regards the relationship between philosophy and history. Since the dominance of historicism was established in German historiography, the discipline has always cultivated antagonistic attitudes towards the philosophy of history. Historians tend to stress their methodological achievements in utilizing sources and reject any explicit concept of the philosophy of history in their work. This gulf between a methodological self-image and the explicit rejection of philosophy is particularily striking in social history, which normally deals with the subjects on which Foucault wrote. Social history had laboriously emancipated itself from general history which, in the 1960s, was still essentially political history and history of ideas. It replaced the weak links with philosophy with an openness to American sociological approaches and a faithful reading of Max Weber and Karl Marx. But this sociological bent made it difficult to detect an implicit philosophical tendency towards the myth of progress inherent in modernization theory. There is also in Germany a much greater distance between history and linguistics than is the case elsewhere. In Germany, only Koselleck has worked on *Begriffsgeschichte*, which is a hermeneutic project aimed at reconstructing the historical meanings of central concepts (Brunner et al. 1972, cf. Koselleck 1979). The acceptance of linguistics in historiography is just in its beginnings in Germany (cf. Reichardt 1985; Jütte 1990, 1992; Dinges 1994). Discourse analysis has remained a foreign concept for most historians.

Different intellectual fashions between countries have posed another barrier to the reception of Foucault. Nietzsche – who is important for Foucault – has been an intellectual taboo in Germany since 1945, because of the Nazis' use of the philosopher. Late bourgeois critique of civilization in the style of Burckhardt and Spengler was also out of fashion in the optimistic 1960s and 1970s. Foucault's fascination with madness was not generally acceptable in a country where social historians were trying to overcome the madness of Germany's own history with the well-channelled, tranquillizing rationality of modernization theories.

Native theoretical orientations also constituted a powerful barrier against the reception of Foucault's idea of a disciplinarian society. The works of Weber, Horkheimer, Adorno, Elias, Habermas and Oestreich stand for the solid German tradition concerning the 'dialectic of Enlightenment' and the ambivalence of domination and discipline. This theoretical bastion has proved more than sufficient to reject Foucault's scandalous critique of the Enlightenment. As all these theories more or less maintain the idea of progress, Foucault's critique of the one-sidedness of Western rationality could not really penetrate the faithful traditional belief of German historians in the meaning of history and in progress (Rüsen 1988). When this belief went out of fashion, historians could turn to two other native alternative theories of modernity nearer to their own intellectual traditions, namely those of Blumenberg and Luhmann (1982).[26] The debate about post-modernism – linked to Kamper and Marquardt – has not yet reached historians, except for one author who rejects it in the name of the well-known optimism of the Bielefeld School of modernization theory.[27] Only the younger generation, which does not necesarily share the belief in progress and is open to new approaches, might be more disposed to accept the challenge of Foucault.

Crucial for understanding the lack of interest in Foucault has been the state of the historical disciplines in Germany. As we have seen, general and social historians had idiosyncratic reasons for resistance to Foucault's ideas, and few historians of psychiatry have been open to them (cf. Ester 1994; Osinski 1983, pp. 17–27). Foucault's work on insanity highlighted one of the fundamental debates in current psychiatry, namely the question of the discipline's role in society as an instrument of repression or emancipation. In such situations, history is always useful as an argument for contemporary reformatory preoccupations. At the same time, the public debate about psychiatry in the 1980s – linked to the euthanasia question – touched the very centre of German historians' identity. It was implicitly a discourse about the role of the state, the limits of state intervention and the rights of the individual in the face of 'total institutions'. Foucault was welcome: he might even have been used more.

What of medical and legal history? Medical history in Germany is institutionalized within the medical faculties and is still largely dedicated to a very conservative historiography of ideas, 'great' physicians, institutions and therapies, serving – with very few exceptions – the ideological needs of the medical profession. The social history of medicine is only beginning to develop; the history of hospitals is still only at the stage of a history of architecture and medical progress.[28] Given the state of the discipline, there is evidently little interest in Foucault among medical historians. The social history of criminal justice started in Germany – with one exception – only in the mid 1980s.[29] The traditional history of law was institutionalized within the law faculties and mostly focused on the systematic reconstruction of legal systems, applying the model of modern codifications to societies of the *ancien régime* (Dinges 1992). In the 1970s, the discipline began to work on legal facts (*Rechtstatsachen*), but its interest in the function or reality of prisons was limited to highlighting the humanizing effects of modernity.

The future of the reception of Foucault's work in Germany seems to depend on a number of factors. First, the intrinsic problems with Foucault's approach will continue to be a barrier to reception. The relationship between 'total' institutions and the 'general mode of domination' is an open question. The production of power from below and its relation to the disciplinarian tendencies in history is another important problem which Foucault does not resolve. In the latter case, the internal development of Foucault's *œuvre* presents major contradictions, which might come to constitute a serious barrier for the acceptance of his ideas. The relationship between language and reality, the transformation of discursive formations, the validity of discourse beyond domination and the normative effects of discourse are other important problems at the heart of Foucault's work. To pick out only one of these points, it could be argued, for example, that social practices as well as discourses imply normative claims which create reality. This view might be integrated into Foucault's framework, though preferably not in a way which used the notion of social practice to deny the importance of discourse.

The account I have presented of Foucault's reception in Germany highlights the many interesting new questions and concepts which Foucault's work opens up. The inspirational effect of the *œuvre* is evident in a wide variety of historical fields including the history of psychiatry, criminal justice, social control and medicalization. Certainly, chronological errors of the French philosopher must be rectified and biased perceptions of historical tendencies based on too limited source material criticized. Different national historiographical traditions provide a wider variety of historical evidence, suggesting ways in which Foucault's generalizations based on France can be relativized. Nevertheless Foucault's ideas are challenging. Only a more interdisciplinary approach to historical problems can open up the different historical disciplines to accepting the challenge. This would include a deeper understanding of linguistics.[30] At present, these conditions are not yet fulfilled. However, new research orientations are – even if with some difficulty – emerging among younger historians.

The enormous gulf which has separated German historians from Foucault becomes even more evident when we consider Foucault's most radical propositions.[31] The thesis that history has no meaning, for example, would spell the end to the hermeneutic approach; to state that there is no aim or direction in history – neither emancipation nor decadence – would mean the end of the belief in progress, which has been the implicit philosophy underpinning the approach of German historians; to view power as ubiquitous leads to the end of a subject of history represented in terms of the sociology of domination; to focus on the importance of everyday practices in institutions leads on to recognizing the end of predominance of high politics approaches; while to consider language as the only reality provokes systematic reflection on historical source material and on the reconstruction of reality in historiography. To sum up, Foucault proposes a new paradigm for a scientific revolution which calls into question the entire credo of German historiography and proposes the basis for a post-modern historiography (cf. Peukert 1991, p. 323). This is the challenge. German historians will respond to it only if they become more open-minded. If they fail to do so, they risk losing the entire field to sociologists, philosophers and journalists with ever-growing historical interests.

NOTES

1 An earlier version of this paper was presented at the conference on 'The Prerogative of Confinement' in Washington D.C. in June 1992. I want to thank all the participants of this conference and especially H. Talkenberger (Stade), R. Jütte (Stuttgart), O. Marx (W. Chesterfield, N.H.) and T. Schlich (Stuttgart) for their suggestions and useful advice. For bibliographical aid I would like to thank H. P. Schmiedebach (Berlin), C. Vanja (Kassel) and U. Brieler (Bochum).

2 Not considered here (though listed in the bibliography at the end of this chapter) are works in the fields of philosophy: Raulf (1977), Jara-Garcia (1977), Feige (1978), Sloterdijk (1972), Seitter (1980), Schneider (1988); sociology: Breuer (1983, 1987), Gerstenberger and Voigt (1979); psychology: Reinke-Köberer (1979); art criticism: Fleck (1988); linguistics and literature: Behler (1989), Frank (1988), Kallweit (1988); political science: Bambach (1984); nor articles translated into German: for example White (1986).

3 *Histoire de la folie* (1961): English 1965, German 1969, Spanish 1967; *Naissance de la clinique* (1963): E. 1973, G. 1973, S. 1973; *Surveiller et punir* (1975): E. 1977, G. 1976, S. 1976. At the beginning of the Foucault cycle, the German translation is four years behind the English one. Later, the international market of ideas becomes more homogeneous.

4 My observations are based on Blasius (1981, 1983, 1986 [1970], 1988), Leibbrand (1964), Saurer (1978), Steinert (1978), Thom (1972). All translations from German texts are my own.

5 The term is from Horkheimer and Adorno (1975). It has become quite common in German literature to designate the ambivalence of progress.

6 This idea of the individual might be interpreted differently in the light of the late Foucault whom, as pointed out above, I have deliberately left out of consideration here.

7 German historians formulate it as well as their French colleagues; cf. Perrot (1980).

8 Cf. for the sociological critique Breuer (1983), p. 261; Bambach (1984); p. 124; Gerstenberger and Voigt (1979), p. 228.

9 I present here the arguments of Blasius (1983).

10 I present here mainly the arguments of Steinert (1978).

11 'das beste dieser Art . . . soziologisierender Geistesgeschichte', Köhler (1977), p. 152, n. 5.

12 They criticize Foucault's work for not being based on a sociology of power (Treiber and Steinert 1980, pp. 77ff.).

13 Besides the authors cited in the following paragraph, cf. Huerkamp (1985), Sander (1989), Stolberg (1985), Drees (1988), Labisch (1992).

14 Other examples are Lüsebrink (1983) and Dülmen (1988).

15 Dörner bases his argument explicitly on the dialectic of Enlightenment.

16 Cf. Dinges (1988). For a systematic debate on Foucault see Peukert (1991).
17 On self-help see Dinges (1993a).
18 Habermas calls this implicit annihilation of opposite evidence 'strategies of immunization' (*Immunisierungsstrategien*).
19 The French insisted more on cultural conflict; cf. pp. 48, 36.
20 See Köhler and Blasius for asylums, Stekl for prisons.
21 Schrenk criticizes the German translation of Foucault, false citations Foucault himself made from Pinel, and Foucault's method of shortening cited sentences. According to Schrenk, 'Foucault thus deformed the original author's intention' (Schrenk 1973, p. 19). Schrenk's detailed critique of Foucault's errors is especially amusing when compared with Schrenk's own confusion of leprosy and plague (ibid., p. 137). In this way, the historian of psychiatry seems to claim that the plague vanished from Europe at the end of the fifteenth century.
22 See Peukert's rejection of Foucault's essayistic and philosophical method (1986, p. 23). Peukert (1991) discusses Foucault systematically.
23 Cf. Dreßen (1982), to say nothing of the inflationary use of the term discourse.
24 Pro-Prussian historiography supported enthusiasm for Prussia's historical mission – especially in Germany – during the nineteenth century.
25 But see as a counter-example Labisch (1992), p. 295ff.
26 Both works are important and almost ignored by historians. See as exceptions Walz (1989) using Luhmann (1982).
27 Cf. Niethammer (1989), who presents the historical root of the debate and considers it a problem of bourgeois intellectuals recognizing their waning influence on society.
28 Cf. for example Jetter (1986). Murken (1988) and Braum (1986) make no mention of Foucault in their bibliographies.
29 The exception is the work of Blasius who was for a long time the only general historian interested in Foucault (see above). For the state of the historiography of criminal justice in Germany see the excellent introduction in Schwerhoff (1991).
30 On historians and theory cf. Baecker (1992).
31 On problems in the English reception of Foucault, cf. Guédon (1977), pp. 245ff.

BIBLIOGRAPHY

Altwegg, J. and A. Schmidt (1973) *Französische Denker der Gegenwart*, Munich, 1987.
Améry, J., 'Wider den Strukturalismus: Das Beispiel des Michel Foucault', *Merkur*, pp. 468–82.
Baecker, D. (1992) 'Anfang und Ende in der Geschichtsschreibung' in B. J. Dotzler (ed.), *Technopathologien*, Munich, pp. 59–86.
Bambach, R. (1984) 'Ein "glücklicher" Positivist: Bemerkungen zu Michel Foucault's "Erneuerung" der Theoriengeschichte' in U. Bernbach (ed.), *Politische Theoriengeschichte*, Opladen, pp. 194–222.

Barthel, C. (1989) *Medizinische Policey und medizinische Aufklärung*, Frankfurt a. M.

Behler, C. (1989) 'Humboldt's "radikale Reflexion über die Sprache" im Lichte der Foucault'schen Diskursanalyse', *Deutsche Vierteljahresschrift für Literaturwissenschaft und Geistesgeschichte*, 63, pp. 1–24.

Blasius, D. (1978) *Kriminalität und Alltag: Zur Konfliktgeschichte des Alltagslebens im 19. Jahrhundert*, Göttingen.

Blasius, D. (1980) *Der verwaltete Wahnsinn: Eine Sozialgeschichte des Irrenhauses*, Frankfurt a. M.

Blasius, D. (1981) 'Kriminologie und Geschichtswissenschaft: Perspektiven der neueren Forschung', *Historische Zeitschrift*, 233, pp. 615–26.

Blasius, D. (1983) 'Michel Foucault's "denkende" Betrachtung der Geschichte', *Kriminalsoziologische Bibliographie*, 10, pp. 69–83.

Blasius, D. ([1970] 1986) 'Pathologie der Gesellschaft als historisches Problem: Die Anfänge der modernen Psychiatrie im Spiegel der Bücher von Michel Foucault und Klaus Dörner' in D. Blasius, *Der Umgang mit Unheilbarem*, Bonn.

Blasius, D. (1988) 'Kriminologie und Geschichtswissenschaft: Bilanz und Perspektiven interdisziplinärer Forschung', *Geschichte und Gesellschaft*, 14, pp. 136–49.

Bloch, M., F. Braudel et al. (1977) *Schrift und Materie der Geschichte: Vorschläge zur systematischen Aneignung historischer Prozesse*, ed. C. Honegger, Frankfurt a. M.

Braum, D. (1986) *Vom Tollhaus zum Kastenhospital: Ein Beitrag zur Geschichte der Psychiatrie in Frankfurt a. M.*, Hildesheim.

Breuer, S. (1983) 'Die Formierung der Disziplinargesellschaft: Michel Foucault und die Probleme einer Theorie der Sozialdisziplinierung', *Sozialwissenschaftliche Informationen für Unterricht und Studium*, 12, pp. 257–64.

Breuer, S. (1986) 'Sozialdisziplinierung: Probleme und Problemverlagerungen eines Konzepts bei Max Weber, Gerhard Oestreich und Michel Foucault' in C. Sachße and F. Tennstedt (eds), *Soziale Sicherheit und soziale Disziplinierung*, Frankfurt a. M.

Breuer, S. (1987) 'Foucaults Theorie der Disziplinargesellschaft: Eine Zwischenbilanz', *Leviathan*, 15, pp. 319–37.

Brieler, U. (1991) 'Die Anonymität als Existenzform: Die erste Biographie über den französischen Philosophen und Historiker', *Kommune*, 11, pp. 36–41.

Brügelmann, J. (1982) 'Der Blick des Arztes auf die Krankheit im Alltag, 17. Jahrhundert – 1850: Medizinische Topographien als Quelle für die Sozialgeschichte des Gesundheitswesens', diss. phil., Freie Universität, Berlin.

Brügelmann, J. (1983) 'Medikalisierung von Säuglings- und Erwachsenenalter in Deutschland zu Beginn des 19. Jahrhunderts aufgrund von medizinischen Topographien' in A. E. Imhof (ed.), *Leib und Leben in der Geschichte der Neuzeit: L'homme et son corps dans l'histoire moderne*, Berlin, pp. 177–92.

Brunner, O., W. Conze and R. Koselleck (eds) (1972 ff.) *Geschichtliche Grundbegriffe*, 5 vols., Stuttgart.

Clark, M. (1983) *Michel Foucault: An annotated bibliography*, New York and London.

Dinges, M. (1987) 'L'hôpital Saint André de Bordeaux: objectifs et réalisations de l'assistance municipale au XVIIe siècle', *Annales du Midi*, 99, pp. 303–30.

Dinges, M. (1988) *Stadtarmut in Bordeaux (1525–1675): Alltag, Politik, Mentalitäten*, Bonn.

Dinges, M. (1991) 'Frühneuzeitliche Armenfürsorge als Sozialdisziplinierung? Probleme mit einen Konzept', *Geschichte und Gesellschaft*, 17, pp. 5–29.

Dinges, M. (1992) 'Frühneuzeitliche Justiz: Justizphantasien als Justiznutzung am Beispiel von Klagen bei der Pariser Polizei im 18. Jahrhundert' in H. Mohnhaupt and D. Simon (eds), *Vorträge zur Justizforschung: Theorie und Geschichte*, Frankfurt a. M., pp. 269–92.

Dinges, M. (1993a) 'Michel Foucault's impact on German historiography of criminal justice, social discipline and medicalization' in N. Finzsch and R. Jütte (eds), *The Prerogative of Confinement: Social, Cultural, Political and Administrative Aspects of the History of Hospitals and Carceral and Penal Institutions in Western Europe and North America 1500–1900*, New York.

Dinges, M. (1993b) 'Self help, assistance and the poor in early modern France', *Proceedings of the Conference on International Perspectives in Self Help, Lancaster 1991*, London.

Dinges, M. (1993c) 'Michel Foucault, Justizphantasien und die Macht' in A. Blauert and G. Schwerhoff (eds), *Mit den Waffen der Justiz*, Frankfurt a. M., pp. 189–212.

Dinges, M. (1993d) 'Self help and reciprocity in the parish relief system' in R. Smith (ed.), *Communities, Caring and Institutions*, London.

Dinges, M. (1994) *Der Maurermeister und der Finanzrichter: Ehre, Geld und soziale Kontrolle im Paris des 18. Jahrhunderts*, Göttingen.

Dörner, K. (1969) *Bürger und Irre: Zur Sozialgeschichte und Wissenschaftssoziologie der Psychiatrie*, Frankfurt a. M. (*Madmen and the Bourgeoisie: A Social History of Insanity and Psychiatry*, Cambridge, 1984).

Drees, A. (1988) *Die Ärzte auf dem Weg zu Prestige und Wohlstand: Sozialgeschichte der württembergischen Ärzte im 19. Jahrhundert*, Cologne.

Dreßen, W. (1982) *Die pädagogische Maschine: Zur Geschichte des industrialisierten Bewußtseins in Preußen/Deutschland*, Frankfurt a. M. and Berlin.

Dülmen, R. van (1988) *Theater des Schreckens: Gerichtspraxis und Strafrituale in der Frühen Neuzeit*, Munich.

Eribon, D. (1991) *Michel Foucault: Eine Biographie*, Frankfurt a. M.

Ester, M. (1994) 'Psychiatrie und Geschichtswissenschaft: Einige Anmerkungen zu aktuellen Trends in der Medizingeschichtsschreibung der Psychiatrie', *Medizin, Gesellschaft und Geschichte*, 12.

Feige, M. (1978) 'Geschichtliche Struktur und Subjektivität: Eine transzendental-phänomenologische Kritik an Michel Foucault's Archäologie des Wissens', diss. phil., Cologne.

Fink-Eitel, H. (1989) *Foucault zur Einführung*, Hamburg.

Finzsch, N. (1990) *Obrigkeit und Unterschichten: Zur Geschichte der rheinischen Unterschichten gegen Ende des 18. und zu Beginn des 19. Jahrhunderts*, Stuttgart.

Fleck, R. (1990) 'Das Nichtverhältnis von Sprache und Bild: Michel Foucault', *Parnass*, 6, pp. 8–10.

Foucault, M. (1965) *Madness and Civilization: A History of Insanity in the Age of Reason*, New York.

Foucault, M. (1973) *The Birth of the Clinic: An Archeology of Medical Perception*, New York.

Foucault, M. (1977) *Discipline and Punish: The Birth of the Prison*, London.

Foucault, M., B. Barret-Kriegel, A. Thalamy, F. Begvin and B. Fortier (1976) *Les machines à guérir: Aux origines de l'hôpital moderne*, Brussels.

Foucault, M. (1978ff.) *The History of Sexuality*, 3 vols., New York.

Frank, M. (1988) 'Zum Diskursbegriff bei Foucault' in H. Müller (ed.), *Diskurstheorien und Literaturwissenschaft*, Frankfurt a. M.

Frevert, U. (1984) *Krankheit als politisches Problem, 1770–1880*, Göttingen.

Gerstenberger, H. and B. Voigt (1979) 'Macht und Dissens: Anmerkungen zu den Arbeiten von Michel Foucault', *Leviathan*, 7, pp. 227–41.

Göckenjan, G. (1985) *Kurieren und Staat machen: Gesundheit und Medizin in der bürgerlichen Welt*, Frankfurt a. M.

Guédon, J. (1977) 'Michel Foucault: the knowledge of power and the power of knowledge', *Bulletin of the History of Medicine*, 51, pp. 245–77.

Gumbrecht, H. (forthcoming)) ' "Everyday-world" and "life-world" as philosophical concepts: a genealogical approach' in M. E. Blanchard (ed.), *The Problematics of Daily Life*, Baltimore.

Habermas, J. (1981) *Theorie des kommunikativen Handelns*, 2 vols., Frankfurt a. M. (*The Theory of Communicative Action*, 2 vols., Boston 1985, 1989).

Habermas, J. (1985) *Der philosophische Diskurs der Moderne*, Frankfurt a. M. (*The Philosophical Discourse of Modernity: Twelve Lectures*, Cambridge, Mass., 1987).

Hertling, M. (1985) 'Die Provinzial-Heil- und Pflegeanstalt Düren: Die Entwicklung einer großen psychiatrischen Anstalt der Rheinprovinz von ihrer Gründung 1878 bis 1934', Herzogenrath.

Honegger, C. (1980) 'Überlegungen zu Michel Foucaults Entwurf einer Geschichte der Sexualität', diss. phil., Bremen.

Honegger, C. (1982) 'Michel Foucault und die serielle Geschichte: Über die Archäologie des Wissens', *Leviathan*, 16, pp. 500–23.

Honneth, A. (1985) *Kritik der Macht*, Frankfurt a. M.

Horkheimer, M. and Th. W. Adorno (1975) *Dialectic of Enlightenment*, New York.

Huerkamp, C. (1985) *Der Aufstieg der Ärzte im 19. Jahrhundert: Vom gelehrten Stand zum professionellen Experten: Das Beispiel Preußens*, Göttingen.

Ingersleben, S. von (1981) 'Foucaults Ansichten einer leichen-zentrierten Medizin: Anmerkungen zu Michel Foucaults *Die Geburt der Klinik: Eine Archäologie des ärztlichen Blicks*', *Argument*, 73, special issue on 'Organisierung der Gesundheit', pp. 195–200.

International Bibliography of Periodical Literature (1965ff.) ed. O. and W. Zeller, Osnabrück.

Jara-Garcia, J. (1977) 'Die Archäologie des Wissens: Zu Michel Foucaults Theorie der Wissensbildung', diss. phil., Munich.

Jetter, D. (1981) *Grundzüge der Geschichte des Irrenhauses*, Darmstadt.

Jetter, D. (1986) *Das europäische Hospital: Von der Spätantike bis 1800*, Cologne.

Jütte, R. (1986) 'Disziplinierungsmechanismen in der städtischen Armenfürsorge der Frühneuzeit' in C. Sachße und F. Tennstedt (eds), *Soziale Sicherheit und soziale Disziplinierung*, Frankfurt a. M.

Jütte, R. (1990) 'Moderne Linguistik und "Nouvelle histoire" ', *Geschichte und Gesellschaft*, 16, pp. 104–20.

Jütte, R. (1991) ' "Disziplin predigen ist eine Sache, sich ihr zu unterwerfen eine andere" (Cervantes): Prolegomena zu einer Sozialgeschichte der Armenfürsorge diesseits und jenseits des Fortschritts', *Geschichte und Gesellschaft*, 17, pp. 92–101.

Kallweit, H. (1988) 'Archäologie des historischen Wissens: Zur Geschichtsschreibung Michel Foucaults' in C. Meier and J. Rüsen (eds), *Historische Methode*, Munich, pp. 267–99.

Köhler, E. (1977) *Arme und Irre: Die liberale Fürsorgepolitik des Bürgertums*, Berlin.

Koselleck, R. (1979) *Vergangene Zukunft*, Frankfurt a. M.

Labisch, A. (1986) ' "Hygiene ist Moral – Moral ist Hygiene": Soziale Disziplinierung durch Ärzte und Medizin' in C. Sachße and F. Tennstedt (eds), *Soziale Sicherheit und soziale Disziplinierung*, Frankfurt a. M.

Labisch, A. (1992) *Homo hygienicus: Gesundheit und Medizin in der Neuzeit*, Frankfurt a. M.

Leibbrand, W. (1964) 'Das Geschichtswerk Michel Foucaults', *Sudhoffs Archiv für Geschichte der Medizin und der Naturwissenschaften*, 48, pp. 352–9.

Lévi-Strauss, C. (1968) *Savage mind*, Chicago.

Loetz, F. (1993) 'Der Prozeß der Medikalisierung: Heilkunde, gesundheitspolitische Programme und soziale Wirklichkeit in Deutschland. Das Beispiel Baden 1750–1850', Stuttgart.

Lüsebrink, H. (1983) *Kriminalität und Literatur im Frankreich des 18. Jahrhunderts*, Munich.

Lüsebrink, H. and R. Reichardt (1990) *Die 'Bastille': Zur Symbolgeschichte von Herrschaft und Freiheit*, Frankfurt a. M.

Luhmann, N. (1982) *The Differentiation of Society*, Edmonds.

Lukes, S. (1983) 'Macht und Herrschaft bei Weber, Marx, Foucault' in J. Matthes (ed.), *Krise der Arbeitsgesellschaft? Verhandlungen des 21. Deutschen Soziologentages in Bamberg 1982*, Frankfurt a. M., pp. 106–19.

Megill, A. (1987) 'The reception of Foucault by historians', *Journal of the History of Ideas*, 48, pp. 117–41.

Murken, A. (1988) *Vom Armenhospital zum Großklinikum: Die Geschichte des Krankenhauses vom 18. Jahrhundert bis zur Gegenwart*, Cologne.

Murken, A. (1989) *Die bauliche Entwicklung des deutschen Allgemeinen Krankenhauses im 19. Jahrhundert*, Göttingen.

Niethammer, L. (1989) *Posthistorie: Ist die Geschichte zu Ende?* Reinbek.

Oestreich, G. (1968) 'Strukturprobleme des europäischen Absolutismus', *Vierteljahresschrift für Sozial- und Wirtschaftsgeschichte*, 55, pp. 329–47.

Osinski, J. (1983) *Über Vernunft und Wahnsinn: Studien zur literarischen Aufklärung in der Gegenwart und im 18. Jahrhundert*, Bonn.

Perrot, M. (ed.) (1980) *L'impossible prison: Recherches sur le système pénitentiaire au XIXe siècle*, Paris.

Peukert, D. (1986) *Grenzen der Sozialdisziplinierung: Aufstieg und Krise der Deutschen Jugendfürsorge von 1878–1932*, Cologne.

Peukert, D. (1991) 'Die Unordnung der Dinge: Michel Foucault und die deutsche Geschichtswissenschaft' in F. Ewald and B. Waldenfels (eds),

Spiele der Wahrheit: Michel Foucaults Denken, Frankfurt a. M., pp. 320–33.

Pilgram, A. (1979) '(Review of) Hans Stekl, *Österreichs Zucht- und Arbeitshäuser 1671–1920*', *Kriminalsoziologische Bibliographie*, 6, pp. 71–4.

Ploetz, K. von (1980) 'Ideologische Aspekte in der Auffassung des Wahnsinns bei Michel Foucault', diss. med., Heidelberg.

Pongratz, L. (1988) 'Michel Foucault: Seine Bedeutung für die historische Bildungsforschung', *Informationen zur erziehungs- und bildungshistorischen Forschung*, 32, pp. 155–68.

Pongratz, L. (1989) *Pädagogik im Prozeß der Moderne: Studien zur Social- und Theoriegeschichte der Schule*, Weinheim.

Pongratz, L. (1990) 'Schule als Dispositiv der Macht: pädagogische Reflexionen im Anschluß an Michel Foucault', *Vierteljahresschrift für wissenschaftliche Pädagogik*, 66, pp. 298–308.

Raulf, U. (1977) 'Das normale Leben: Michel Foucaults Theorie der Normalisierungsmacht', diss. phil., Marburg.

Reichardt, R. (1985 ff.) *Handbuch politisch-sozialer Grundbegriffe in Frankreich 1680–1820*, Munich.

Reinke-Köberer, E. (1979), 'Schwierigkeiten mit Foucault', *Psyche*, 33, pp. 364–76.

Rüb, M. (1988) 'Von der Macht zur Lebenskunst: Foucaults letzte Werke und ihre Interpretation in der Sekundärliteratur', *Leviathan*, 16, pp. 97–107.

Rüsen, J. (1988) 'Vernunftpotentiale der Geschichtskultur' in J. Rüsen, E. Lämmert and P. Glotz (eds), *Die Zukunft der Aufklärung*, Frankfurt a. M., pp. 105–14.

Sachße, C. and F. Tennstedt (eds) (1986) *Soziale Sicherheit und soziale Disziplinierung*, Frankfurt a. M.

Sander, S. (1989) *Handwerkschirurgen: Sozialgeschichte einer verdrängten Berufsgruppe*, Göttingen.

Saurer, E. (1978) '(Review of) Michel Foucault, *Überwachen und Strafen*', *Zeitschrift der Savigny-Stiftung für Rechtsgeschichte, Germanistische Abteilung*, 95, pp. 350–4.

Schmid, W. (ed.) (1991) *Denken und Existenz bei Michel Foucault*, Frankfurt a. M.

Schmidt, F. (1985) *Die Entwicklung der Irrenpflege in den Niederlanden: Vom Tollhaus bis zur gesetzlich anerkannten Irrenanstalt*, Herzogenrath.

Schmitt, R. and A. Bühler (1983) 'Über Michel Foucaults Methodologie der Ideengeschichte', *Saeculum*, 34, pp. 212–24.

Schneider, U. (1988) 'Eine Philosophie der Kritik', *Zeitschrift für philosophische Forschung*, 42, pp. 311–17.

Schrenk, M. (1973) *Über den Umgang mit Geisteskranken: Die Entwicklung der psychiatrischen Therapie vom 'moralischen Regime' in England und Frankreich zu den 'psychischen Curmethoden' in Deutschland*, Berlin.

Schütz, E. (1989) 'Die These vom Ende des Menschen, oder: wer spricht bei Foucault?', *Vierteljahresschrift für wissenschaftliche Pädagogik*, 65, p. 378.

Schulze, W. (1987) 'G. Oestreichs Begriff "Sozialdisziplinierung in der Frühen Neuzeit"', *Zeitschrift für historische Forschung*, 14, pp. 265–302.

Schwerhoff, G. (1991) *Köln im Kreuzverhör: Kriminalität, Herrschaft und Gesellschaft in einer frühneuzeitlichen Stadt*, Bonn.

Seidler, E. (1973) 'Die Geometrie des Todes: Michel Foucaults großes Werk, "Die Geburt der Klinik" endlich in deutscher Sprache', *Frankfurter Allgemeine Zeitung*, 9 October 1973, p. 21L.

Seitter, W. (1980) 'Ein Denken im Forschen: Zum Unternehmen einer Analytik bei Michel Foucault', *Philosophisches Jahrbuch der Görres-Gesellschaft*, 87, pp. 340–63.

Sloterdijk, P. (1972) 'Michel Foucaults strukturale Theorie der Geschichte', *Philosophisches Jahrbuch der Görres-Gesellschaft*, 79, pp. 161–84.

Steinert, H. (1978) 'Ist es aber auch wahr, Herr F.? *Überwachen und Strafen* unter der Fiktion gelesen, es handle sich dabei um eine sozialgeschichtliche Darstellung', *Kriminalsoziologische Bibliographie*, 5, pp. 30–45.

Stekl, H. (1978) *Österreichs Zucht- und Arbeitshäuser 1671–1920: Institutionen zwischen Fürsorge und Strafvollzug*, Vienna.

Stekl, H. (1986) ' "Labore et fame": Sozialdisziplinierung in Zucht- und Arbeitshäusern des 17. und 18. Jahrhunderts' in C. Sachße and F. Tennstedt (eds), *Soziale Sicherheit und soziale Disziplinierung*, Frankfurt a. M.

Stolberg, M. (1985) 'Heilkinde zwischen Staat und Bevölkerung: Angebot und Annahme medizinscher Versorgung in Oberfranken im frühen 19. Jahrhundert', diss. med., Technische Universität München, Munich.

Thom, A. (1972) Review of Michel Foucault, 'Wahnsinn und Gesellschaft: Eine Geschichte des Wahns im Zeitalter der Vernunft', *Deutsche Zeitschrift für Philosophie*, 20, pp. 1066–9.

Treiber, H. and H. Steinert (1980) *Die Fabrikation des zuverlässigen Menschen: Über die 'Wahlverwandtschaft' von Kloster- und Fabrikdisziplin*, Munich.

Walz, R. (1989) 'Die autopoietische Struktur der Hexenverfolgungen', *Sociologia internationalis*, 27, pp. 39–55.

Weber, M. (1980) *Wirtschaft und Gesellschaft: Grundriss der verstehenden Soziologie*, 5th edn, Tübingen.

Weber, M. (1978ff.) *Gesammelte Aufsätze zur Religionssoziologie*, 3 vols., Tübingen.

Weinert, F. (1982) 'Die Arbeit der Geschichte: Ein Vergleich der Analysemodelle von Kuhn und Foucault', *Zeitschrift für allgemeine Wissenschaftstheorie*, 13, pp. 336–59.

White, H. (1986) 'Foucault decodiert: Notizen aus dem Untergrund' in H. White, *Auch Klio dichtet oder die Fiktion des Faktischen: Studien zur Tropologie des historischen Diskurses*, Stuttgart.

Wischhöfer, B. (1991) *Krankheit, Gesundheit und Gesellschaft in der Aufklärung: Das Beispiel Lippe 1750–1830*, Frankfurt a. M.

SELECT BIBLIOGRAPHY

The following list is divided into two parts. The first, *Texts by Foucault*, a bibliography of Foucault's key writings, lists, in alphabetical order by title, his major works and then some of his manifold other writings, such as essays, interviews, etc., which form an important complement to his main projects. We have concentrated here mainly on the works – happily in the majority – currently available in English translation.

In the second part, *Works on Foucault*, we provide a bibliography of some of the more important evaluations of Foucault's work that have appeared in English. We make no pretence at all to completeness. Helpful in this respect – though now out of date – is M. Clark, *Michel Foucault: An Annotated Bibliography, Toolkit for a New Age*, New York, Garland, 1982. It is not the aim of this volume to survey Foucault comprehensively, but rather to show how and where his writings are relevant to historians.

TEXTS BY FOUCAULT

Major works

The Archaeology of Knowledge, tr. A. M. S. Smith, London, Routledge, 1990 (orig. *L'archéologie du savoir*, Paris, Gallimard, 1969).

The Birth of the Clinic: An Archaeology of Medical Perception, tr. A. M. S. Smith, London, Routledge, 1990 (orig. *Naissance de la clinique: Une archéologie du regard médical*, Paris, PUF, 1963).

Le désordre des familles: Lettres de cachet des archives de la Bastille au XVIIIe siècle, co-edited with Arlette Farge, Paris, Juillard, 1982.

Discipline and Punish: The Birth of the Prison, tr. A. Sheridan, Harmondsworth, Penguin, 1991 (orig. *Surveiller et punir: Naissance de la prison*, Paris, Gallimard, 1975).

The History of Sexuality 1: An Introduction, tr. R. Hurley, Harmondsworth, Penguin, 1990 (orig. *L'histoire de la sexualité 1: La volonté de savoir*, Paris Gallimard, 1976).

The History of Sexuality 2: The Use of Pleasure, Harmondsworth, Penguin, 1988 (orig. *L'histoire de la sexualité 2: L'usage des plaisirs*, Paris, Gallimard, 1984).

The History of Sexuality 3: The Care of the Self, Harmondsworth, Penguin, 1990 (orig. *L'histoire de la sexualité 3: Le souci de soi*, Paris, Gallimard, 1984).

Les machines à guérir: Aux origines de l'hôpital moderne, in collaboration with B. Barret-Kriegel, A. Thalamy, F. Béguin and B. Fortier, Brussels, Pierre Mardaga, 1976.

I, Pierre Riviere, Having Slaughtered My Mother, My Sister and My Brother: A Case of Parricide in the 19th Century, Harmondsworth, Penguin, 1978 (orig. *Moi, Pierre Riviere . . .*, Paris, Gallimard, 1973).

Madness and Civilization: A History of Insanity in the Age of Reason, tr. R. Howard, London, Routledge, 1990 (orig. *Folie et déraison: Histoire de la folie à l'âge classique*, Paris, Gallimard, 1961; 2nd enlarged edn: Paris, Gallimard, 1972).

Mental Illness and Psychology, New York, Harper & Row, 1976 (orig. *Maladie mentale et personnalité*, Paris, PUF, 1954).

The Order of Things: An Archaeology of the Human Sciences, London, Routledge, 1990 (orig. *Les mots et les choses: Une archéologie des sciences humaines*, Paris, Gallimard, 1966).

Select essays, interviews and other pieces

Foucault: A Critical Reader, ed. D. Hoy, Oxford, Blackwell, 1986.

The Foucault Effect: Studies in Governmentality, ed. G. Burchell, C. Gordon and P. Miller, London, Harvester, 1991.

Foucault Live: Interviews 1966–1984, ed. S. Lotringer, tr. J. Johnston, New York, Semiotext(e), 1989.

A Foucault Reader, ed. P. Rabinow, Harmondsworth, Penguin, 1986.

Language, Counter-Memory, Practice, ed. D. Bouchard, Ithaca, Cornell University Press, 1977.

Politics, Philosophy, Culture: Interviews and Other Writings, ed. L. Kritzman, London, Routledge, 1990.

Power/Knowledge: Selected Interviews and Other Writings, 1972–1977, ed. C. Gordon, Brighton, Harvester, 1981.

WORKS ON FOUCAULT

L. Arac (ed.), *After Foucault: Humanistic Knowledge, Post Modern Challenges*, New York, Rutgers University Press, 1988.

S. J. Ball (ed.), *Foucault and Education: Disciplines and Knowledge*, London, Routledge, 1990.

Vikki Bell, *Interrogating Incest: Feminism, Foucault and the Law*, London, Routledge, 1993.

J. W. Bernauer, *Michel Foucault's Force of Flight: Towards an Ethic for Thought*, Atlantic Highlands, N.J., Humanities Press International, 1990.

J. Bernauer and D. Rasmussen (eds), *The Final Foucault*, Cambridge, Mass., MIT Press, 1987–8.

M. Blanchot, *Michel Foucault tel que je l'imagine*, Montpellier, Fata Morgana, 1986.

R. Boyne, *Foucault and Derrida: The Other Side of Reason*, London, Unwin Hyman, 1990.

P. Burke (ed.), *Critical Essays on Michel Foucault*, Aldershot, Scolar Press, 1992.

John D. Caputo and Mark Yount (eds), *Foucault and the Critique of Institutions*, University Park, Pennsylvania State University Press, 1993.

D. Carroll, *Paraesthetics: Foucault, Lyotard, Derrida*, New York, Methuen, 1987.

R. Cooper, *Michel Foucault: An Introduction to the Study of his Thought*, New York, Edwin Mellen Press, 1981.

M. Cousins and A. Hussein, *Michel Foucault*, London, Macmillan, 1984.

Nick Crossley, *The Politics of Subjectivity: Between Foucault and Merleau-Ponty*, Aldershot, Avebury, 1994.

Mitchell Dean, *Critical and Effective Histories: Foucault's Methods and Historical Sociology*, London, Routledge, 1994.

G. Deleuze, *Foucault*, London, Athlone Press, 1988.

I. Diamond and L. Quinby (eds), *Feminism and Foucault: Reflections on Resistance*, Boston, Mass., Northeastern University Press, 1988.

J. Dollimore, *Sexual Dissidence: Augustine to Wilde, Freud to Foucault*, Oxford, Clarendon Press, 1991.

H. Dreyfus and P. Rabinow (eds), *Michel Foucault: Beyond Structuralism and Hermeneutics*, 2nd edn, Chicago, Chicago University Press, 1983.

Thomas Dumm, *Michel Foucault and the Politics of Freedom*, London, Sage, 1996.

D. Eribon, *Michel Foucault (1926–84)*, London, Faber, 1992.

F. Ewald (ed.), *Michel Foucault Philosopher*, tr. T. J. Armstrong, London, Harvester, 1992.

N. Fraser, 'Foucault's body language: a post-humanistic political rhetoric', *Salmagundi*, 61, 1983, pp. 55–70.

M. Gane (ed.), *Towards a Critique of Foucault*, London, Routledge, 1986.

M. Gane and T. Johnson (eds), *Foucault's New Domains*, London, Routlege, 1993.

J. Goldstein, 'Foucault among the sociologists: the disciplines and the history of the professions', *History and Theory*, 23, 1984, pp. 170–92.

Jan D. Goldstein, *Foucault and the Writing of History*, Oxford, Blackwell, 1994.

J. E. Grumley, *History and Totality: Radical Historicism from Hegel to Foucault*, London, Routledge, 1989.

G. Gutting, *Michel Foucault's Archaeology of Scientific Reason*, Cambridge, Cambridge University Press, 1989.

G. Gutting, *The Cambridge Companion to Foucault*, Cambridge, Cambridge University Press, 1994.

David Halperin, *Saint Foucault: Towards a Gay Hagiography*, New York/Oxford, Oxford University Press, 1995.

M. Hewitt, *Social Policy and the Politics of Life: Foucault's Account of Welfare*, Hatfield, Hatfield Polytechnic School of Social Sciences, 1982.

Alan Hunt and Gary Wickham, *Foucault and the Law: Towards a Sociology of Law and Governance*, London, Pluto Press, 1994.

Michael Kelly, *Critique and Power: Recasting the Foucault/Habermas Debate*, Cambridge, Mass./London, MIT Press, 1994.

M. Kusch, *Foucault's Strata and Fields: An Investigation into Archaeological and Genealogical Science Studies*, Dordrecht, Kluwer, 1991.

D. Lecourt, *Marxism and Epistemology: Bachelard, Canguilhem and Foucault*, London, New Left Books, 1975.

215

C. Lemert and G. Gillan, *Michel Foucault: Social Theory as Transgression*, New York, Columbia University Press, 1982.

F. Lentricchia, *Ariel and the Police: Michel Foucault, William James, Wallace Stevens*, Brighton, Harvester, 1988.

Moya Lloyd and Andrew Thacker (eds), *The Impact of Michel Foucault on the Social Sciences and the Humanities*, Basingstoke, Macmillan, 1997.

David Macy, *The Lives of Michel Foucault*, London, Vintage, 1993, London, Hutchinson, 1994.

P. Major-Poetzl, *Michel Foucault's Archaeology of Western Culture: Towards a New Science of History*, Brighton, Harvester, 1983.

Todd May, *Between Genealogy and Epistemology: Psychology, Politics and Knowledge in the Thought of Michel Foucault*, University Park, Pennsylvania State Press, 1994.

Todd May, *The Moral Theory of Poststructuralism*, University Park, Pennsylvania State University Press, 1995.

A. W. McHoul, *A Foucault Primer: Discourse, Power and the Subject*, London, UCL Press, 1995.

Lois McNay, *Foucault and Feminism: Power, Gender and the Self*, Cambridge, Polity Press, 1992.

Lois McNay, *Foucault: A Critical Introduction*, Cambridge, Polity Press, 1994.

A. Megill, *Prophets of Extremity: Nietzsche, Heidegger, Foucault, Derrida*, Berkeley, Calif., University of California Press, 1985.

J. Q. Merquior, *Foucault*, Berkeley, Calif., University of California Press, 1987.

Ricardo Miguel-Alfonso and Silvia Caporale-Bizzini, *Reconstructing Foucault: Essays in the Wake of the 80s*, Amsterdam, Rodopi, 1994.

James Miller, *The Passion of Michel Foucault*, New York, Simon and Schuster, 1992.

Toby Miller, *The Well-Tempered Self: Citizenship, Culture and the Postmodern Subject*, Baltimore/London, Johns Hopkins University Press, 1993.

J. Minson, *Genealogies of Morals: Nietzsche, Foucault, Donzelot and the Eccentricity of Ethics*, Basingstoke, Macmillan, 1985.

M. Morris and P. Patton (eds), *Michel Foucault: Power, Truth, Strategy*, Sydney, Feral, 1979.

P. O'Brien, 'Michel Foucault's history of culture' in L. Hunt (ed.), *The New Cultural History*, Berkeley, Calif., 1989.

C. O'Farrell, *Foucault: Historian or Philosopher*, Basingstoke, Macmillan, 1989.

David Owen, *Maturity and Modernity: Nietzsche, Weber, Foucault, and the Ambivalence of Reason*, London, Routledge, 1994.

M. Perrot (ed.), *L'impossible prison: Recherches sur le système pénitentiaire au XIXe siècle*, Paris, Seuil, 1980.

M. Poster, *Foucault, Marxism and History*, Cambridge, Polity Press, 1984.

Walter Privitera, *Problems of Style: Michel Foucault's Epistemology*, Albany, State University of New York Press, 1995.

K. Racevskis, *Michel Foucault and the Subversion of the Intellect*, Ithaca, Cornell University Press, 1983.

J. Rajchman, *Michel Foucault: The Freedom of Philosophy*, New York, Columbia University Press, 1985.

SELECT BIBLIOGRAPHY

Caroline Ramazanoglu, *Up Against Foucault: Explorations of Some Tensions between Foucault and Feminism*, London, Routledge, 1993.

G. S. Rousseau, 'Foucault and Enlightenment' in *Enlightenment Crossings: Pre- and Post-Modern Discourses: Anthropological*, Manchester, Manchester University Press, 1991, pp. 40–60.

J. Sawicki, *Disciplining Foucault: Feminism, Power and the Body*, New York, Routledge, 1991.

C. E. Scott, *The Question of Ethics: Nietzsche, Foucault, Heidegger*, Bloomington, Indiana University Press, 1990.

A. Sheridan, *Michel Foucault: The Will to Truth*, London, Tavistock, 1980.

D. R. Shumway, *Michel Foucault*, Boston, Mass., Twayne, 1989.

Jon Simons, *Foucault and the Political*, London, Routledge, 1995.

B. Smart, *Michel Foucault, Marxism and Critique*, London, Tavistock, 1985.

Barry Smart (ed.), *Foucault: Critical Assessments*, London, Routledge, 1994–5.

A. Still and I. Velody (eds), *Rewriting the History of Madness: Studies in Foucault's 'Histoire de la folie'*, London, Routledge, 1992.

B. S. Turner, *Regulating Bodies: Essays in Medical Sociology*, London, Routledge, 1992.

R. Wuthnow et al., *Cultural Analysis: The Work of Peter L. Berger, Mary Douglas, Michel Foucault and Jurgen Habermas*, Boston, Routledge & Kegan Paul, 1984.

INDEX

abolition of slavery 12, 103–10
Abolition Society 105–6, 107
Ackerknecht, E. 18, 19
Adorno, Theodor W. 187, 202
Althusser, Louis 7
altruism *see* humanitarianism
Altwegg, J. 185
Annales school 7–9, 181
anti-medicine 12, 28–44
anti-realism: Foucault's discourse
  theory *see under* reality, creation
  of
anti-slavery movement 12, 103–10
archaeologies, archaeology of
  knowledge 3, 10, 48, 91, 154–76
Archaeology of Knowledge, The 5, 6,
  10, 34, 91, 115, 118, 152; critical
  assessment of 154–77; quoted
  42, 156, 157, 158, 160, 162–3,
  167, 168, 169–70, 171, 173
*Archaeology of the Human Sciences see
  Order of Things, The*
architecture, institutional 189, 194;
  moral powers of 120–1
architecture, urban 55, 64–5
Argument, Das 190
Ariès, Philippe 8
Armstrong, David 11, 12, 17, 29,
  30, 34
asylums 188, 189, 193, 194, 197,
  199–200
Austin 172
author: Foucault's demolition of
  notion of 3, 152

autonomous individual *see* liberty

Bachelard, Gaston 7, 181
Barthel, Christian 191, 197
beliefs 171; *see also* ideas and
  intentions
Bell, Thomas 75
benevolence *see* humanitarianism
Bentham, Jeremy 20, 119, 122
Bernard, Claude 28
Bichat, Xavier 32, 34–5, 36, 37,
  61, 68
Birth of the Clinic 5, 12, 17, 20, 28,
  48, 59, 61, 68, 115, 132, 181,
  182; critical assessment of 31–44;
  quoted 31, 37, 38, 39, 40, 41,
  43, 68–9, 89n34
Blake, Robert 75
Blasius, D. 184, 186, 192–3,
  206n29
Bloch, Marc 7, 8
Blumenberg, Hans 202
body 17–26, 73; doctor/patient
  relationship 18–20; knowledge of
  23–6; linked to medicine 53; and
  power 11, 20–1, 23, 116; and
  social constructivism 22–3;
  techniques of 20–2, 48
Boyd, M. F. 80
Braudel, Fernand 7–8, 181
Bright, R. 32
Brougham, Henry 125
Broussais, François-Joseph-Victor
  32, 34

218